Wine
Tourism UK

The ultimate guide to the wine estates of England & Wales

DANIEL SATCHELL
NICK SATCHELL
STEVE MOSS

All the English and Welsh wine regions | The best wine regional maps
Events | Festivals | Selected tourist attractions & destinations

❄ Foreword

It's time to put the English and Welsh wine industry firmly on the tourist map.

The wine industry in the UK has been steadily growing in terms of quality and stature, with UK wine achieving international recognition and winning many international awards along the way. The fact that there are over 400 wine estates/vineyards in the UK comes as a surprise to many, including myself when we started this venture.

Despite a considerable increase in levels of wine production in the last ten years, demand frequently outstrips supply, so wine producers have to look elsewhere for additional income to support further business growth. The development of wine tours, tastings and the like are not only beneficial to the wine producers but a great alternative to traditional tourist attractions. Visitors leave with an improved knowledge and appreciation of the quality and standard that UK wine has achieved, which in turn will help the wine industry grow.

There are books on wine and books on tourism but this book is unique in that it brings together wine production, wine and food festivals, major tourist attractions and places of note.

The vast majority of wine estates and vineyards are included; a good selection of wine and food fairs, and selected tourist attractions, this provides a good basis for general tourism in the eight wine regions. This first edition, in what will be an annual publication, is just the start of the journey, as it develops over the coming years; we hope it will be a journey that many will enjoy.

Nick Satchell

wine
Tourism UK

Published by:
LS Productions UK Ltd

Telephone: 01444 257789
Fax: 01444 257790
Email: info@winetourismuk.co.uk
Address: Wine Tourism UK LTD,
54 Bolney Grange Business Park,
Stairbridge Lane, Bolney,
West Sussex, RH17 5PB

Publisher: Nick Satchell
Art director: Daniel Satchell
Editor: Steve Moss
Marketing/Research: Alix Satchell
Map design: Konrad Cissowski
www.customdigitalmaps.com

Photography: Bordeaux &
Beyond Ltd, Chapel Down Winery,
Christchurch Food Fest,
Dales Festival of Food and Drink,
Exeter Food and Drink Festival,
Hampshire Fare, Kay Adkins -
Tetbury Food Festival 2009,
Kim Millon - Pebblebed Vineyard,
Ludlow Food Festival, New Lodge
Vineyard, Polgoon Vineyard &
Orchard, Real Food Harvest
Festival, Renishaw Hall, Rosemary
Vineyard & The Vineleaf Coffee
Shop, Stone Food and Drink
Festival, The Wine Show, Toast
Festival, www.dreamstime.com

Printed by: One Digital
www.one-digital.com

Copyright © 2010
Wine Tourism UK Ltd
ISBN: 978-0-9567257-0-7

❧ **Contents**winetourismuk

❧ Introduction
04.......How to use the handbook
06.......General tourism Info

❧ Chapter one
09.......The UK wine story

❧ Chapter two
13.......The art of wine
14.......Winemaking
16.......Glossary
18.......Understanding the label
20.......Wine styles
24.......Sparkling wines
26.......Rosé
28.......Brandy

❧ Chapter three
31.......Environmental issues

❧ Chapter four
35.......The UK wine regions
         introduction
36.......UK regional map
38.......Wine regions

❧ Chapter five
41.......The UK wine regions
43.......South West & Channel Isles
69.......South East & London
107.....East
125.....West Midlands
141.....East Midlands

155.....Yorkshire & The Humber
167.....North West
179.....Wales

❧ Chapter six
193.....Events and festivals
194.....Introduction
196.....Festival dates

❧ Chapter seven
201.....Buying and storing wine

❧ Index
204.....Index

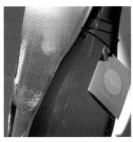

❧ How to use the handbook

All you need in order to participate in the regional wine experiences of England and Wales is an appreciation of all the good things in life, passion, curiosity and the Wine Tourism UK Guide!

T his book has seven chapters covering all aspects of wine tourism in the United Kingdom. We've provided a glossary of common wine terms, information on some of the most popular varietal and tips for getting the best out of your wine tourism experience.

Wine regions

We have grouped various counties into wine regions **(fig.1)**. We have attempted to include all wine estates in these regions along with contact details, opening hours and map grid reference **(fig.2)**. You will find additional information on the majority of wine estates, where we have been able to gather this information. These include full contact details, a little on the history of the producer, as well as other amenities they offer **(fig.3)**. We have also included a distance indicator of all the major cities in the UK. **(fig.4)**.

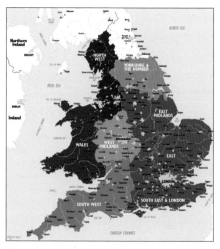

(fig.1)

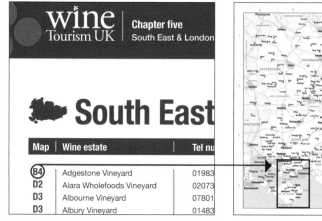

Map	Wine estate	Tel nu
B4	Adgestone Vineyard	01983
D2	Alara Wholefoods Vineyard	02073
D3	Albourne Vineyard	07801
D3	Albury Vineyard	01483

wine Tourism UK | **Chapter five**
South East & London

🐗 South East

(fig.2)

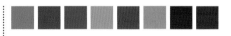

Isle of Wight

Adgestone Vineyard

We produce high quality award winning wines and in 1994 our wine was chosen for the dinner for H.M. Queen to celebrate the Anniversary of the D-Day Landings. Offering bed and breakfast.

a: Upper Road, Adgestone, Sandown, Isle of Wight, PO36 0ES | t: 01983 402503
www.adgestonevineyard.co.uk

(fig.3)

We hope you'll be so enchanted by the local wines that you'll be inspired to stock up. Therefore we have included some hints on how to buy and store wine and where you can buy it (see chapter seven).

Opening times
It's best you check the opening times of the wine estates beforehand to avoid disappointment.

Activities & destinations
We have listed some key attractions and destinations in each wine growing region.

Food and wine festivals
All major annual food and wine festivals are listed within each region as well as on our food and wine calendar. (see chapter six)

Colour-coding reference key

Each region has been allocated a colour.

These colours are maintained throughout the book to make cross referencing easy for you.

wine
Tourism UK
The ultimate guide to the wine estates of England & Wales

DANIEL SATCHELL
NICK SATCHELL
STEVE MOSS

2011 EDITION

NEW WINE REGION MAPS

All the English and Welsh wine regions | The best wine regional maps
Events | Festivals | Selected tourist attractions & destinations

---

United Kingdom distance chart

Distances given are in miles

(fig.4)

	ABERDEEN	ABERYSTWYTH	BIRMINGHAM	BRISTOL	CARDIFF	DERBY	DOVER	EDINBURGH	EXETER	GLASGOW	INVERNESS	LEEDS	LIVERPOOL	LONDON	MANCHESTER	NEWCASTLE	NORWICH	NOTTINGHAM	OXFORD	PORTSMOUTH	SHEFFIELD	SOUTHAMPTON	YORK
ABERDEEN	-	440	411	490	493	384	563	121	565	141	107	314	335	492	333	228	480	379	473	552	347	538	307
ABERYSTWYTH	440	-	115	124	110	140	285	320	199	321	477	171	105	212	131	259	271	156	157	218	156	198	195
BIRMINGHAM	411	116	-	88	102	40	185	290	164	292	448	110	90	111	81	204	161	49	63	141	76	128	129
BRISTOL	490	124	88	-	44	127	189	369	75	371	527	196	161	114	162	289	209	137	70	94	164	74	217
CARDIFF	493	110	102	44	-	142	228	373	120	374	530	206	165	150	173	301	235	151	104	138	178	118	231
DERBY	384	140	40	127	142	-	196	263	203	270	419	70	81	123	59	161	136	16	90	175	37	154	88
DOVER	563	285	185	189	228	196	-	442	244	466	600	257	270	74	257	343	156	196	129	131	229	143	264
EDINBURGH	121	320	290	369	373	263	442	-	444	45	158	193	214	372	213	107	360	359	353	431	227	418	186
EXETER	565	199	164	75	120	203	244	444	-	446	602	271	237	170	238	364	282	213	141	124	240	107	292
GLASGOW	141	321	292	371	374	270	466	45	446	-	167	211	216	389	214	145	383	279	354	432	241	419	210
INVERNESS	107	477	448	527	530	419	600	158	602	167	-	351	372	529	371	265	517	416	511	589	385	575	344
LEEDS	314	171	110	196	206	70	257	193	271	211	351	-	73	191	41	94	174	70	164	242	34	229	25
LIVERPOOL	335	105	90	161	165	81	270	214	237	216	372	73	-	198	34	155	217	99	153	231	72	217	97
LONDON	492	212	111	114	150	123	74	372	170	389	529	191	198	-	184	274	112	123	56	71	160	77	194
MANCHESTER	333	131	81	162	173	59	257	213	238	214	371	41	34	184	-	131	185	71	144	222	38	208	65
NEWCASTLE	228	259	204	288	301	161	343	107	364	145	265	94	155	274	131	-	260	159	254	332	129	319	82
NORWICH	480	271	161	209	235	139	156	360	282	383	517	174	217	112	185	260	-	123	141	184	146	190	181
NOTTINGHAM	379	156	49	137	151	16	196	359	213	279	416	70	99	123	71	159	123	-	95	173	38	160	80
OXFORD	473	157	63	70	104	90	129	353	141	354	511	164	153	56	144	254	141	95	-	78	130	65	174
PORTSMOUTH	552	218	141	94	138	175	131	431	124	432	589	242	231	71	222	332	184	173	78	-	208	17	252
SHEFFIELD	347	156	76	164	178	37	229	227	240	241	385	34	72	160	38	129	146	38	130	208	-	195	53
SOUTHAMPTON	538	198	128	74	118	154	143	418	107	419	575	229	217	77	208	319	190	160	65	17	195	-	239
YORK	307	195	129	217	231	88	264	186	292	210	344	25	97	194	55	82	181	80	174	252	53	239	-

🇬🇧 General tourist info

The UK is made up of Great Britain (England, Scotland and Wales) and Northern Ireland, and is one of the 27 member states of the European Union (EU).

- **Capital cities**
- **London – England**
- **Edinburgh – Scotland**
- **Cardiff – Wales**
- **Belfast – Northern Ireland**

- **Area**

Land and water: 152,033 square miles

- **Population**

The UK – approximately 60.6 million
(England 50,714,000; Wales 2,977,000;
Scotland 5,108,000; Northern Ireland 1,733,000).

- **Languages**

The two official languages in Britain are English and Welsh, English being the most widely spoken. Scottish Gaelic is also spoken in some parts of Scotland.

- **People**

The majority of the population is English, Scottish, Welsh and Irish. However, Britain is an extremely diverse nation with a strong culture of racial integration and unity.

- **Religion**

Most people are Christian (71%), although all other religions including Buddhism, Hinduism, Judaism, Islam and Sikhism are freely practised. About 23% of Britain follows no particular religion.

- **Government**

The UK is a constitutional monarchy that is a representative democracy, where Queen Elizabeth II is recognised as the head of state, and the Prime Minister – David Cameron – is the head of a coalition government.

- **Economic profile**

The UK is a leading trading power and a financial centre. Agriculture is an important industry and highly efficient. Primary energy, such as coal and oil, are major contributors to the economy, but services such as banking and insurance are the greatest contributors.

- **Currency**

Pounds Sterling (£)
The United Kingdom is not part of the Euro zone but some stores do accept it, and there is a large number of banks and bureau de change outlets where you can cash travellers cheques and change currency.
Cash points (ATMs) are widely available. You can ask for 'Cashback' when making purchases with a debit card at supermarkets. Visa and Access (Mastercard) are widely accepted, other cards are often accepted. Banking hours officially 09:30-15:30, but most banks open usually until about 17:00.

- **Time:**

Greenwich, in London, is where you will find the Prime Meridian - the line that divides the Earth into East and West and from which the world's time is set. Greenwich Mean Time (GMT) is the term used for the current time on this line, and clocks and watches all the world over are set in relation to this. Britain and Ireland in theory follow GMT, but in the summer months everything is confused by what is called Daylight-saving time. From late March to late October, Britain and Ireland are actually one hour ahead of GMT.

- **Weights & measures**

Historically Britain used the Imperial System, but new regulations make use of the Metric System compulsory with the exception of a few items, for example distance and speed are measured in miles and miles per hour.

- **Electricity**

Voltage is 240 volts AC at 50HZ. Appliances generally use standard 3-pin square plugs and sockets.

- **Posting a Letter**

Post offices are open Mon-Fri 9-5:30, Sat 9-1. A

first class letter posted by 18:00, should arrive the next morning within the UK - check the 'last posting times' on the red postboxes. Stamps can be bought individually at post offices or in books of four or ten at newsagents, off-licences and grocers.

• Telephoning
Traditional red phone boxes are now rare; instead kiosks come in a wide variety of designs and colours. Coin-operated phones accept 10p, 20p, 50p & £1 coins, but card-operated phones are more common. British Telecom phone cards are available in most newsagents or grocers. Calls from hotels are expensive. The UK international dialling code is +44

• Emergency services
To contact the police, fire brigade or ambulance service in an emergency, you can dial 999 free of charge from any public or private phone. In case of accident, most major hospitals have 24 hour accident and emergency departments.
UK operator: 100
International operator: 155

• Manners
The British have a reputation for being reserved in manners, dress and speech. We are famous for our politeness, self-discipline and especially for our sense of humour.

• Tipping
Tipping is discretionary. In restaurants a service charge is sometimes included; if not, a gratuity of 15% is the norm, unless the service was unsatisfactory.

Taxi drivers also expect a tip of 10%-15%. It's less common to tip minibus drivers. A standard tip for hotel service such as porters or door attendants is £1 or £2. Tipping is not customary when ordering drinks from the bar in a pub, but if you order food from a table and it is brought to you, then a tip might be appropriate. Bargaining is practically unheard of except occasionally at markets.

• Tax
Value-added tax (VAT) is 20% sales tax levied on goods and services. Non-EU and EU residents who will leave the EU/UK within three months of purchasing goods may claim a VAT refund. However, EU residents must be due to stay outside the EU for more than a year to claim. Shops will advertise "Tax-Free Shopping" in their window if they participate in the VAT refund scheme. The minimum purchase is around £75. You must show ID and ask for the VAT refund form, part of which must be completed by the retailer. When you leave the UK, allow at least an hour to claim your refund at the airport. You must show your receipts, the form and the goods to customs.

• Britain's countryside
Britain offers some of the most stunning natural beauty in the world. In fact, we are proud to have 49 designated Areas of Outstanding Natural Beauty, 40 National Scenic Areas, 14 National Parks and an amazing 27 World Heritage Sites, 5 of which have World Heritage status due to their outstanding natural features. Britain is crisscrossed with national trails and countryside walks that you're free to enjoy at your leisure. In order to protect our precious natural

heritage and allow visitors to continue enjoying it, it's important to take note of the Countryside Code, designed to help us all to respect, protect and enjoy our countryside. Occasionally trails and paths may be closed in order to preserve the natural heritage or for public safety. These will always be indicated so care should be taken to follow any signs.

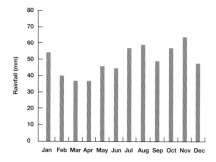

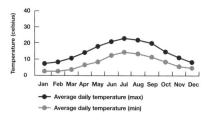

— Average daily temperature (max)
— Average daily temperature (min)

• Climate

Britain has a fairly temperate climate. We enjoy long summer evenings due to our northerly latitude and periods of fine weather can happen in all seasons. The weather can vary greatly from day to day, but generally summer (June-August) is a warm 14 - 25°C, and winter (December-February) is a cool 1 - 4°C. There is quite a difference in temperature between Scotland and Southern England. Generally, the further south, the warmer it is likely to be.

• Seasonal variation & what to wear

Whatever the season, the British weather is liable to change from day to day, so if you are wondering what to pack, it is a good idea to bring a selection of items

including some light clothes, items you can layer, at least one warm pullover and a waterproof coat or umbrella.

Spring (March - May)

In spring, we offer wonderful sunny weather, but it can also be cool or wet. Temperatures fluctuate from around 6 - 11 °C. May can have very warm days - up to about 18 °C.

Summer (June - August)

Most days in summer are warm to hot, but evenings can be cool. Temperatures average around 14 - 30 °C, although it can be up to around 35 °C on some days.

Autumn (September - November)

In autumn there can be very warm days, but equally there can be cool ones too. Temperatures fluctuate around the 7 - 18 °C mark, but are likely to be much warmer in September than November.

Winter (December - early March)

Winter sees Britain's shortest and coolest days (about 7-8 hours of daylight) but these can be crisp and bright. Temperatures fluctuate from around 1 - 5 °C

❧ Chapter one

The UK wine story

09.......The UK wine story

The UK wine story

Traditionally seen as struggling with an unhelpfully cold climate, the English and Welsh wine industry has been helped by the warmer British summers over recent years and it is speculated that climate change may encourage major growth in the future.

The United Kingdom is a major consumer, but only a very minor producer of wine, with English and Welsh wine sales combined accounting for just 1% of the domestic market.

In recent years, English sparkling wine has started to emerge as the UK wine style receiving the most attention. Theale Vineyard Sparkling Chardonnay 2003 beat off stiff competition from fine Champagnes and top sparkling wines to make it into the world's Top Ten Sparkling Wine at the world's only dedicated sparkling wine competition, French-based Effervescents du Monde (sparkling wines of the world) 2007.

Ridgeview who won Best Sparkling Wine in the World - Decanter 2010. They triumphed over prestigious Champagnes and sparkling wines at one of the most respected wine competitions, the Decanter World Wine Awards 2010.

Roman to 19th century
The Romans introduced winemaking to the United Kingdom, but the British climate was too cold and too wet to grow grapes for making wine. Winemaking continued at least down to the time

of the Normans with over 40 vineyards in England mentioned in the Domesday Book, although much of what was being produced was communion wine for the Eucharist.

From the Middle Ages, the English market was the main customer of clarets from Bordeaux, France, helped by the Plantagenet kingdom, which included England and large provinces in France. In the 18th century, the Methuen Treaty of 1703 imposed high duties on French wine. This led to the English becoming a main consumer of sweet fortified wines like sherry, port wine, and Madeira wine from Spain and Portugal. Fortified wine became popular because, unlike regular wine, it did not spoil after the long journey from Portugal to England.

Later in the 19th century, many upper and upper-middle class people started to drink wines from many parts of Europe such as France, Spain, Italy and Germany.

20th century
Viticulture was revived in the 1970s onwards, possibly helped by a rising local temperature due to global

warming, making many parts of Hampshire, Sussex, Kent, Essex, Suffolk, Berkshire and Cambridgeshire, dry and hot enough to grow grapes of high quality. The first English wines were influenced by the sweet German wines like Liebfraumilch and Hock that were popular in the 1970s, and were blended white and red sweet wines, called cream wine (creams). The largest vineyard in England is Denbies Wine Estate in Surrey, which has 265 acres (1.07 km2) under vines, and a visitors' centre that is open all year round.

The growth of English wine accelerated in the late 1990s, helped by popularity of wine from the new world, especially Australia, Chile, Argentina, New Zealand and South Africa which made consumers in the British Isles more accepting of wines that were not from the traditional wine growing regions of Europe. They were made popular by their single vintages, brand labels, and general non-fussiness of the wine. This influenced the English wine industry to copy what happened in the new world and produce good-quality wines with grapes such as Chardonnay and Pinot Noir. In 2004 a panel judging European sparkling wines awarded most of the top ten positions to English wines - the remaining positions going to French Champagnes.

> 'Significant plantings have been happening across the south of the country with a number of farmers contract growing vines for some of the major English producers.'

Winemaking has spread to the south-west, including Wiltshire, Dorset, Devon, Somerset, Cornwall and the Isle of Wight, and also to the Midlands and the north of England, with Yorkshire, Shropshire, Derbyshire, Leicestershire and Lancashire boasting at least one vineyard each as of 2007.

21st century
Significant plantings have been happening across the south of the country with a number of farmers contract growing vines for some of the major English

producers. Farmers are looking at the potential benefits of growing vines as the return per tonne for grapes over more traditional crops are not to be ignored. A field of wheat might yield 3 tonnes per acre at around £120 per tonne. Growing grapes could yield 3 to 4 tonnes per acre at around £950 to £1100 per tonne. It is a significant difference but growers will need to invest money for no initial return, as crops

> 'Ridgeview who won Best Sparkling Wine in the World - Decanter 2010.'

tend to come in the 3rd or 4th year.
Another explanation for the growth in viticulture in the UK is the local food movement, and the desire by consumers to cut the amount of food miles connected with the produce that they buy, including locally produced wine.

❧ Chapter two

The art of wine

14.......Winemaking
16.......Glossary
18.......Understanding the label
20.......Winemaking styles
24.......Sparkling wines
26.......Rosé
28.......Brandy

Winemaking

Winemaking or vinification is the production of wine, starting with selection of the grapes or other produce and ending with bottling the finished wine.

Although most wine is made from grapes, it may also be made from other fruit or non-toxic plant material. Mead is a wine that is made with honey being the primary ingredient after water.

In England and Wales, the viticultural year starts in April, flowering usually takes place in June and in July the young grapes begin to swell and grow and the grape bunches begin to develop. August is generally the warmest month and this is when the early grape varieties begin to ripen. The bulk of the harvest takes place in October.

The quality of the grapes is absolutely key, as they are the deciding factor on the final product. The process of making wine comprises a series of simple operations. The first is crushing, where the essential sugars in the juice are released for fermentation – the second stage – where the sugars react with yeast. There are other steps in the process, but the order in which they occur depends on the type of wine being made.

After the harvest, the grapes are taken into a winery and prepared for primary ferment, at this stage red wine making diverges from white wine making. Red wine is made from the must (pulp) of red or black grapes that undergo fermentation together with the grape skins. White wine is made by fermenting juice which is made by pressing crushed grapes to extract a juice; the skins are removed and play no further role.

Occasionally white wine is made from red grapes; this is done by extracting their juice with minimal contact with the grapes' skins. Rosé wines are made from red grapes where the juice is allowed to stay in contact with the dark skins long enough to pick up a pinkish color, but little of the tannins contained in the skins.

The most common species of wine grape is Vitis Vinifera, which includes nearly all varieties of European origin.

White wines

The extracted juice is pumped into settling tanks, allowed to settle and any extraneous material is removed. The remaining juice is adjusted for acid and is ready for fermentation. In some cases, such as Sauvignon Blanc, the juice can be kept in contact with the skins for additional flavour. Otherwise, white wine

'The science of wine and winemaking is known as oenology'

is always fermented off the skins.
The real work begins as the yeast cells in the juice work on the sugar, creating alcohol. Cultured yeasts are normally used as they can be more closely controlled and are chosen with specific results in mind. Once fermentation is complete, the wine is allowed to settle, filtered again and final chemical adjustments made. Almost all English wines are filtered and only a limited number are aged in oak. It is then put back into maturation tanks or in some cases barrels, until the wine is ready for bottling. Blending for consistency will be done just before bottling.

Red wines

The key difference between red and white wine is the colour which comes from the skins of the grapes. They also contain trace flavour elements and tannins which are vital to the longevity of red wines.

After the crushing process, the mash is cooled and then macerated – this is the process of extracting compounds from the skins. Fermentation is done in the same way as white wine with the introduction of yeast cultures. During this process, the fruit pulp separates from the skins and the whole mixture is agitated to keep the skins in contact with the juice. Once the wine is fermented, it is run through the press and put into a holding tank. Filtering follows to remove any sediment, it is adjusted with sulphur dioxide and left to settle.

'It takes about 1.13 kilograms of grapes to make the average bottle of wine'

If the wine is meant to age for a couple of years it would most likely go into barrels. Interaction between the wine and the wooden barrel further shapes it in terms of flavour, colour and softening the tannins. The depth of oakiness will change depending on the type of barrel. Some English wineries use oak staves in stainless steel tanks to pick up a little oak character.

Rosé wines

Rosé is very similar to white vinification with the exception of being given a period of skin contact to pick up colour and fruity flavour but very little tannin.

Glossary

There are loads of terms used by the wine connoisseurs that leave the rest of us in the dark. Here are some of the most common.

ACID: The components of wine that give it its fresh, tart taste. Most drinks that are refreshing have acids in them.

ALCOHOL: Ethanol is produced as a by-product of fermentation. The alcoholic strength of a wine is a measure of its concentration of Ethanol.

BALANCE: A tasting term. A wine is balanced when all of its characteristics work together in harmony, with no single element – fruit, TANNIN, ACIDITY, ALCOHOL - overpowering anything other.

BÂTONNAGE: French term for stirring of the LEES.

BODY: Tasting term for the weight and texture of a wine on the PALATE – the "mouthfeel" of the wine. A combination of ALCOHOL, EXTRACT and glycerol.

BOTRYTIS: A fungus to which grapes are prone. Often it is bad news in the vineyard where it destroys grapes, but in a few places conditions allow it to develop beneficially as "Noble Rot". Botrytis draws the water content from the grape and leaves concentrated sugary juice that makes luscious sweet wine.

BREATHING: The practice of opening a bottle of wine prior to pouring to allow characteristics to develop.

BOUQUET: A posh term for the aroma of the wine.

CAP: The bubbling mass of skins and pips that floats to the surface during FERMENTATION of red wine. It must be submerged regularly.

CARBON DIOXIDE: Another by-product of FERMENTATION, winemakers take great pains to make sure none is left in the wine before bottling, unless they are making a sparkling wine.

CHAPTALIZATION: Named after its "inventor" Jean-Antoine Chaptal who suggested adding sugar to under-ripe juice before FERMENTATION so that more ALCOHOL could be produced.

CORKED: A "Corked" wine suffers from a specific fault where a mouldy cork (or faulty processing of the cork) has caused a chemical called trichloranisole to form, imparting a dirty aroma and flavour to the wine.

DOSAGE: French term for the small amount of top-up liquid added to Champagne just before bottling, sweetened to desired level.

EISWEIN: German term (Icewine in English). Grapes are left on the vine until they freeze. Temperatures of -7C are required. The water content is removed as ice, and the resulting wine is sweet, concentrated and luscious.

EXTRACT: The substances, mostly derived from grape skins and just under the skin's surface, that contribute TANNIN, colour, glycerol and flavour to a wine. Some wines can be "over-extracted" meaning too much of these elements have been extracted making the wine inky and bitter.

FINISH: Synonymous with "length": the amount of time a flavour lingers on the PALATE after the wine is swallowed. More is good.

FILTRATION: A process used to clarify wine. Some claim it can also strip flavour so many producers filter very lightly or not at all.

FINING: Another clarifying process where some gelatinous agent (for example, whisked egg whites) is added to the barrel and sinks through the wine trapping even minute solids.

FLOR: Protective YEAST that is encouraged to grow on certain maturing wines, particularly Sherry. Stops OXIDISATION and adds flavour.

FORWARD: Tasting term indicating a young wine that is maturing quickly or is made to be drunk young.

HYBRID: Any vine crossing where one or both "parents" is not from the wine vine, VITIS VINIFERA.

LATE HARVEST: Designation appearing on bottles (in French, Vendange Tardive) where grapes were allowed to hang on the vine beyond physiological maturity. This over-ripens grapes, usually producing wines that are high in ALCOHOL and off-dry to sweet.

LAYING DOWN: Describes the long-term storage of wine in the belief that it will improve with age. Not many wines are suitable for laying down.

LEES: The solids left behind after FERMENTATION is complete: dead YEAST cells and grape matter. White wines matured in contact with the lees (in French, Sur Lie) can develop creamy, nutty flavours.

MATURE: A wine that has aged sufficiently.

METHODE CHAMPENOISE: The traditional and best way of making a sparkling wine. The EU has banned the term from bottles not produced in Champagne, so look out for "Methode Traditionelle" or "Fermented in this Bottle" instead.

NOSE: Tasting term. Wine is assessed by taste (the PALATE) but also by smell (the nose).

OENOLOGY: The science of winemaking. Spelled Enology in the USA.

OXIDATION/OXIDISED: What happens to the surface of a cut apple when exposed to air. Grapes and grape juice oxidise if not handled carefully. Bottled wine will also oxidise if the seal is not airtight.

PALATE: Tasting term. Wine is assessed by smell (the NOSE) and by taste (the palate). The palate confirms flavours detected on the nose, but adds BODY, ACIDITY, TANNINS, FINISH, etc. to the picture.

PHYLLOXERA: A louse that eats vine roots. Devastated Europe in the late nineteenth century until it was discovered that American rootstock was resistant. Since then, most European vines are grafted onto American rootstock.

QUINTA: Portuguese term for a wine estate. "Single Quinta" Port comes from a single vintage and farm.

RACKING: Labour intensive process of siphoning wine from one barrel to another in order to leave some sediment behind and gradually clarify the wine.

RECIOTO: Italian wine made made from grapes that have been dried on mats after harvest. This raisins the grapes, making them very sweet. Amarone is made from Recioto grapes, but fermented out fully to be dry and concentrated.

REMUAGE: French term for the process by which the dead YEAST cells in maturing Champagne and other quality sparkling wines are gradually moved into the neck of the bottle before being removed. Traditionally done by hand, more often nowadays by machine.

SHORT: A tasting term for little or no aftertaste.

SMOOTH: A non-precise term for a pleasant mouthfeel.

SOFT: A tasting term for low tannins.

SOLERA: A system of fractional blending that gives Sherry its character. A complex process by which several vintages are blended together over many years in a building known as a Solera, before bottling.

STRUCTURE: Tasting term. To describe a wine as "well-structured" is very complimentary. It means it has an "architecture" of fruit, ACIDITY, ALCOHOL and TANNINS, that should allow it to age and stop it from being bland or wishy-washy.

TANNIN: A naturally occurring chemical that helps to preserve red wine and adds a savoury edge to the flavour. Tannins are present in grape stems, pips and skins. Tannin also comes from oak ageing of wine. As the grape ripens on the vine so do tannins, making them less astringent. Bottle age also lessens tannins, which will eventually precipitate as sediment.

VITIS VINIFERA: The wine vine. Almost all important wines are made from this species.

YEAST: A single-cell organism that is naturally present on the surface of grapes. In commercial winemaking is more likely to be laboratory-grown. It devours grape sugar, converting it into Ethanol (ALCOHOL).

Understanding the label

All but UK Table Wine have to go through a testing and tasting procedure before they can be labelled.

There are several official categories of wine in the UK. For still wines (i.e. not sparkling) there are United Kingdom Table Wine, English Regional Wine, English Quality Wine, Welsh Regional Wine and Welsh Quality Wine. For sparkling wines the categories are English Sparkling Wine and English Quality Sparkling Wine with Welsh equivalents. These wines do not have to be tested or tasted before being so labelled.

> 'Over 90% of English wine is white wine. This is mainly from Germanic vines.'

Quality Wine Status

You may have noticed that some English wines are labelled "English Table Wines" while some are labelled as "English Quality Wine p.s.r.". Recently more regional wines have been named by the county where the grapes originate, and you might occasionally see a wine labelled as "UK Table Wine". So what is the difference and what does it all mean?

English Table Wine is the equivalent of the French Vin de Table, and basically means that it is wine from grapes grown in England (the Welsh have their own version). There is no quality assurance - the wine may be very good, but it could be disappointing. This description is now illegal, and producers have to use the words "UK Table Wine" instead. Any wine labelled in this way is not allowed to state a grape variety, vintage or geographical description on the label (apart from UK). It is basically designed to be the bottom level of wine produced in the UK.

English Quality Wine p.s.r. is the equivalent of the French Appellation Controlée, and means that the wine has:
• been through a detailed independent chemical analysis to ensure it is sound and in good condition (and likely to remain that way),
• a professional tasting panel has assessed the wine's quality and agreed that it meets the standard.
• the wine department of DEFRA have checked the winemaker's records to ensure it complies with the European winemaking regulations.

In short it is a guarantee that the wine is of a reasonable quality (or better). An increasing percentage of English wines carry this label, and they are worth looking out for. p.s.r. stand for "produced in a specified region" which means Made in England (and from English-grown grapes). Some grape varieties are not allowed to have the Quality wine label, because European law will not allow hybrid grape varieties into this scheme. Silly really, but that's European law for you. All dry wines will have passed the Quality Wine Scheme, and have therefore been assessed by professional tasters and accepted as Quality products.

The regional wine scheme caters for producers who grow varieties such as Seyval Blanc, which are banned from the Quality Wine Scheme. The producer can submit his own chemical analysis of the wine, rather than getting one from an independent laboratory. The wine is tasted by a professional panel but the pass mark is slightly lower than for the Quality Wine Scheme. There is also no need for winemaking records to be checked by the Wine Standards Board. These wines would be labelled "Sussex Regional Wine" or equivalent from other counties.

Sparkling wines can be labelled as English Quality Sparkling Wines if they are made by the Traditional method (i.e. bottle fermented and aged on lees for over 9 months). These wines have no requirement to pass the rigorous assessment mentioned above, and therefore the term English Quality Sparkling Wine is not any assurance of Quality, but rather a guide to the production method. A better guide to sparkling wine quality is by looking for wines that have won awards in competitions. Most competitions have extremely competent judges, and they don't give away the prizes easily.

What's on the label

There are four different categories of still English Wine. You can identify which one of the categories a wine belongs to by reading the label on the bottle.

English Vineyards Quality Wine – made from one of the approved varieties and has passed the Quality Wine Scheme. Roughly a third of wine is classified as Quality Wine.

English Counties Regional Wine – essentially a table wine (like the French Vin de Pays), but has passed the Regional Wine Scheme and does not have to bear the 'Table Wine' label.

English Table Wine – made from one of the approved varieties but is not a Regional Wine or a Quality Wine.

UK Table Wine - made from UK grown grapes where the grape variety used is not an approved one.

Success of English sparkling wine

English sparkling wine, most of it made by the proper Champagne method, has a very good reputation. One theory is that this is because much of southern England is in the same chalk basin as Champagne. The soil and climate are similar and, increasingly good winemakers, English Sparkling Wine can give Champagne a very good run for its money.

Some English wines have actually beaten great French champagnes in blind tastings!

Regulations governing Wine Labels
• Compulsory
• Country of Origin
• Appellation of Origin
• Quality Standard
• Name & Address of Producer/Brand Owner
• Bottle Content
• Alcohol Content

Wine styles

The style of a wine is dependent upon a significant number of factors spanning the natural contributors and the human element.

The style of winemaking depends very much on the type and quality of grape and several other factors including; the climate and soil conditions in the region of production and the method of vinification. The various styles include; sparkling wine, fortified wines and brandy production.

In addition, wines can be dry, off-dry, semi-sweet or sweet and can be light, medium or full-bodied, oaked or unoaked and have differing alcohol contents.

The majority of wines can be categorised into the following classes:

Fresh, Unoaked White Wines
Light, crisp, refreshing whites with fairly subdued aromas and flavours, such as Muscadets, inexpensive white Bordeaux wines, Pinot Grigios and various other European whites.

Earthy Whites
Unoaked or gently-oaked wines with broad, earthy flavours, such as Rhône whites, Mâcons, Vouvrays and similar wines.

Aromatic Whites
Flavourful, unoaked whites from aromatic grapes, such as Rieslings, Grüner Veltliners, Gewürztraminers, Viogniers, Albariños, some Pinot Gris wine and some Sauvignon Blancs.

Rich, Oaky Whites
Full-bodied, flavourful whites with oaky character, such as most New World Chardonnays, oaked Sauvignon Blancs, elite white Bordeaux wines and other wines.

Soft and Fruity Reds
Uncomplicated, youthful reds, such as most Beaujolais, many Southern Rhône wines, some Southern Italian reds, some Pinot Noirs from the New World, some U.S. Merlots and inexpensive American and Australian reds.

Fresh, Spicy Reds
Savoury, firm reds with lots of personality, such as Dolcettos, Barberas, some Zinfandels, Cru Beaujolais wines, Argentine Malbecs, Chilean Carmenères and other wines

Powerful Reds
Full-bodied, intense red wines, such as elite California

Cabernets and Merlots, elite red Bordeaux wines, Barolos, Brunello di Montalcinos, most Northern Rhône reds and similar wines

Two Rosé Wines in Two Styles
Blush wines and dry rosés

Sparkling Wines in Two Styles
Fruity, bubbly wines such as Prosecco and serious, complex sparklers such as Champagne.

The main grape varieties growing in the UK (as described by English Wine Producers)

White varieties:

Auxerrois
Valued for its low acidity and for producing exciting and long lasting wines if yields are kept low. It adds 'body' to blended wines. Also grown in Alsace, where it is usually blended into 'Edelzwicker', and found in Luxembourg, Burgundy, Canada, New Zealand and USA. As a neutral Pinot Blanc/Chardonnay style variety it is also useful for barrel ageing or as a sparkling wine base.

Bacchus
(Silvaner x Riesling) x Muller Thurgau
Its grapes have a strong and distinctive aromatic flavour, with high sugar content. It is regularly made into a single varietal wine and, although common in Germany, it is also very successful in this country. Some wines produced from this grape develop good New World Sauvignon Blanc characters.

Chardonnay
Grown largely as a fundamental ingredient of the finest sparkling wines, with plantings on the increase, along with Pinot Noir and Pinot Meunier for production of sparkling wine.

Faberrebe
Pinot Blanc x Müller-Thurgau
Not extensively planted in this country but seems to blend well with Müller-Thurgau. It develops good must weight and, in Germany, can qualify for spätlese status. Produces wines that are very fruity with crisp acidity.

Huxelrebe
Chasselas x Courtillier Musqué
Bred in 1927 in Germany. Has a somewhat Muscat style and is a good cropper with good sugar levels. It has a high natural acidity and strong aromas of elderflowers, producing very fruity wines that age well.

Kerner
Trollinger (Black Hamburg) x Riesling
Bred in 1929 in Germany, this is a very successful grape that ripens reliably and produces excellent fruit. It has a style similar to Riesling and is popular in Germany.

Madeleine Angevine (MA)
(or Madeleine x Angevine 7672)
Designed for northern planting, it flowers late and is an early, reliable cropper. On its own it produces wines that are light and fruity with a pronounced muscatty bouquet.

Müller-Thurgau (MT)
(also known as Rivaner)
Uncertain parentage, though now generally thought to be Riesling x Riesling Bred in 1882. The main grape in Liebfraumilch, this grape was among the first planted in the U.K when grape growing resumed and was the single most widely grown variety for many years.

Optima
(Silvaner x Riesling) x Müller-Thurgau
First registered in the early 1970's. An early ripening variety that achieves high must weights, and therefore suitable for 'late harvest' wines.

Orion

Hybrid. Optima x Seyve Villard 12-375 (Villard Blanc)
Crossing in Germany first registered in 1984. One of a new generation of hybrid varieties bred both for wine quality and disease resistance.

Ortega

Müller-Thurgau x Siegerrebe
First introduced to the UK in 1971. This vine suits our climate, although is prone to disease, and is planted widely. It produces very full flavours and high natural sugars and has been used for late harvest wines.

Phoenix

Hybrid. Bacchus x Seyve Villard 12-375 (Villard Blanc)
A recent cross and one of a new generation of hybrid varieties bred for quality and disease resistance. Wines from Phoenix are also quite Bacchus-like, sometimes Sauvignon Blanc in character.

Pinot Blanc

This is a mutation of Pinot Gris. There are various strains of this grape. The wine has a strong nose and, where planted, seems to ripen its fruit well and produces wine with good and full fruit flavours and crisp acidity.

Pinot Gris

Widely grown in France, where its main home is Alsace and known there as Tokay Pinot Gris. It is also grown in Germany, Italy and Switzerland and known by various names including Rülander, Malvoisie and Pinot Beurot. It is not widely planted in the UK, and does not produce such exceptional flavours as found in other countries.

Reichensteiner

Müller-Thurgau x (Madeleine Angevine x Calabreser Fröhlich)
A popular variety in the UK – currently the second most widely grown variety after Seyval Blanc (2002). It ripens early and performs reliably, and is capable of producing large crops of relatively neutral grapes, high in natural sugars.

Regner

Luglienca Bianca x Early Gamay
Has Proved itself capable of good yields, ripens early with good sugars and relatively low acids – in short an ideal candidate for the UK climate! Wine quality can be excellent.

Schönburger

Pinot Noir x (Chasselas Rosé x Muscat Hamburg)
This grape is very successful in the UK, producing white wines with low acidity but high sugar levels and good Muscat tones (some resembling a less powerful version of Gewürztraminer). When fully ripe it has a pink tinge.

Seyval Blanc

Seibel 5656 x Seibel 4986
Developed in the 1920's in France, now the most widely grown variety in the UK (2002). It crops heavily in this country, even producing good crops in cooler years, and has effective disease resistance. It is a good 'all rounder' - often used for blending, and is well suited to oak aging and used for still or sparkling wines.

Siegerrebe

A small berried and intensely aromatic variety. One of its parents was the famously spicy Gewürztraminer grape. It ripens sometimes to excessive levels and has a very dominating flavour.

Würzer

Müller-Thurgau x Gewürztraminer
This crossing was developed in 1932. It is not widely planted. An early ripening variety that does not carry a heavy crop and produces quite strong, spicy flavours.

Sparkling wines

Affectionately called Bubbly, England and Wales produce a range of excellent sparkling wines at different prices.

The highest quality ones are made in the traditional Champagne method which is referred to in England & Wales as Methode Traditionelle.

Sparkling wine is a wine with significant levels of carbon dioxide in it making it fizzy. The carbon dioxide may result from natural fermentation, either in a bottle, as with the méthode champenoise, in a large tank designed to withstand the pressures involved (as in the Charmat process) or as a result of carbon dioxide injection.

Sparkling wine is usually white or rosé but there are many examples of red sparkling wines such as Italian Brachetto and Australian sparkling Shiraz. The sweetness of sparkling wine can range from very dry "brut" styles to sweeter "doux" varieties.

The classic example of a sparkling wine is Champagne, but many other examples are produced in other countries and regions, such as Espumante in Portugal, Cava in Spain, Franciacorta, Trento and Asti in Italy (the generic Italian term for sparkling wine being Spumante) and Cap Classique in South Africa.

In some parts of the world, the words "champagne" or "spumante" are used as a synonym for sparkling wine, although laws in Europe and other countries reserve the word Champagne for a specific type from the Champagne region of France. The French terms "Mousseux" or "Crémant" are used to refer to sparkling wine not made in the Champagne region.

> 'The average bottle of Champagne contains enough carbon dioxide to potentially produce 49 million bubbles.'

German and Austrian sparkling wines are called Sekt. The United States is a significant producer of sparkling wine: California in particular has seen French Champagne houses open wineries in the state to make American sparkling wine according to the Champagne method. Recently the United Kingdom, which produced some of the earliest examples of sparkling wine, has started producing Champagne-style wines again.

An initial burst of effervescence occurs when the Champagne contacts the dry glass on pouring. These bubbles may form on imperfections in the glass that facilitate nucleation or on cellulose fibres left over from the wiping/drying process. Nucleations are needed to stimulate the formation of bubbles because carbon dioxide has to first diffuse from the wine solution before it can rise out of the glass and into the air. A poured glass of sparkling wine will lose its bubbliness and carbon dioxide gas much more quickly than an open bottle alone would. The frothiness or "mousse" of the sparkler, along with the average size and consistency of the bubbles, can vary depending on the quality of the sparkler and the type of glass used.

The average bottle of Champagne contains enough carbon dioxide to potentially produce 49 million bubbles. The bubbles initially form at 20 micrometers in diameter and expand as they gain buoyancy and rise to the surface. When they reach the surface they are approximately 1 millimeter in size. It is speculated that the bubbles in sparkling wine may speed up alcohol intoxication by helping the alcohol to reach the bloodstream faster. A study conducted at the University of Surrey gave subjects equal amounts of flat and sparkling Champagne which contained the same levels of alcohol. After 5 minutes following consumption, the group that had the sparkling Champagne had 54 milligrams of alcohol in their blood while the group that had the same Champagne, only flat, had 39 milligrams.

'Sparkling wine is usually white or rosé but there are many examples of red sparkling wines such as Italian Brachetto and Australian sparkling Shiraz. The sweetness of sparkling wine can range from very dry "brut" styles to sweeter "doux" varieties.'

Rosé

Rosé wine originally came from Bordeaux in France. It first became popular just after WW2 when there was a demand for medium sweet rosés for mass-market consumption.

The classic examples are Mateus Rosé and the American "blush" wines in the 1970s.

The pendulum now seems to be swinging back towards a drier, 'bigger' style. These wines are made from Rhone grapes like Syrah, Grenache and Carignan in hotter regions such as Provence, the Languedoc and Australia. In France, rosé has now exceeded white wines in sales. In the United States a record 2005 California crop has resulted in an increased production and proliferation of varietals used for rosés, as winemakers chose to make rosé rather than leave their reds unsold.

Blush wine

In the early 1970s, demand for white wine exceeded the availability of white wine grapes, so many California producers made "white" wine from red grapes, in a form of saignée production with minimal skin contact, the "whiter" the better. In 1975 Sutter Home's "White Zinfandel" wine experienced a stuck fermentation, a problem in which the yeast dies off before all the sugar is turned to alcohol. Winemaker Bob Trinchero put it aside for two weeks, and then upon tasting it he decided to sell this pinker, sweeter wine.

In 1976, wine writer Jerry D. Mead visited Mill Creek Vineyards in Sonoma County, California. Charlie Kreck had been one of the first to plant Cabernet Sauvignon vines in California, and offered Mead, a wine made from Cabernet that was a pale pink and as yet un-named.

'In France, rosé has now exceeded white wines in sales. In the United States a record 2005 California crop has resulted in an increased production and proliferation of varietals used for rosés, as winemakers chose to make rosé rather than leave their reds unsold.'

Kreck would not call it "White Cabernet" as it was much darker in colour than red grape "white" wines of the time, yet it was not as dark as the rosés he had known. Mead jokingly suggested the name "Cabernet

Blush", then that evening phoned Kreck to say that he no longer thought the name a joke. In 1978 Kreck trademarked the word "Blush". The name caught on as a marketing name for the semi-sweet wines from producers such as Sutter Home and Beringer, although Mill Creek no longer produces any rosé wine.

The term "blush" is generally restricted to wines sold in North America, although it is sometimes used in Australia and by Italian Primitivo wines hoping to cash in on the recently discovered genetic links between Primitivo and Zinfandel. Although "blush" originally referred to a colour (pale pink), it now tends to indicate a relatively sweet pink wine, typically with 2.5% residual sugar; in North America dry pink wines are usually marketed as rosé but sometimes as blush. In Europe almost all pink wines are referred to as rosé regardless of sugar levels, even semi-sweet ones from California.

There are three major ways to produce rosé wine.

Skin contact
Rosé wine is made in a range of colours, from a pale orange to a vivid near-purple, depending on the grapes, additives and wine making techniques. The first is used when rosé wine is the primary product. Red-skinned grapes are crushed and the skins are allowed to remain in contact with the juice for a short period, typically two or three days. The grapes are then pressed, and the skins are discarded rather than left in contact throughout fermentation (as with red wine making). The skins contain much of the strongly flavoured tannin and other compounds, thereby leaving the taste more similar to a white wine. The longer that the skins are left in contact with the juice, the more intense the colour of the final wine.

Saignée
Rosé wine can be produced as a by-product of red wine fermentation using a technique known as Saignée, or bleeding the vats. When a winemaker desires to impart more tannin and colour to a red wine, some of the pink juice from the must can be removed at an early stage. The red wine remaining in the vats is intensified as a result of the bleeding, because the volume of juice in the must is reduced, and the must involved in the maceration is concentrated. The pink juice that is removed can be fermented separately to produce rosé.

Blending
Blending, the simple mixing of red wine to a white to impart colour is uncommon. This method is discouraged in most wine growing regions except for Champagne. Even in Champagne, several high-end producers do not use this method but prefer the saignée method.

Brandy

Brandy is unique as it is the only alcoholic drink made from another alcohol – wine.

The word brandy comes from the Dutch word brandewijn meaning burnt wine. It was originally a way of preserving wine for long sea journeys.

Brandy is a spirit produced by distilling wine, the wine having first been produced by fermenting grapes. Brandy generally contains 35%–60% alcohol by volume and is typically taken as an after-dinner drink. While some brandies are aged in wooden casks, most are coloured with caramel colouring to imitate the effect of such ageing.

> 'Brandy has more pleasant aromas and flavours at a lower temperature, e.g., 16 °C (61 °F). In most homes, this would imply that brandy should be cooled rather than heated for maximum enjoyment. '

The European Union legally enforces Cognac as the exclusive name for brandy produced and distilled in the Cognac area of France, and Armagnac from the Gascony area of France, using traditional techniques. Since these are considered PDO (Protected Designation of Origin), they refer not just to styles of brandy but brandies from a specific region, i.e. a brandy made in California in a manner identical to the method used to make cognac, and which tastes similar to cognac, cannot be so called in Europe as it is not from the Cognac region of France.

Grape brandy is traditionally drunk in western countries at room temperature from a tulip-shaped glass or a snifter, while in the Orient it is usually over ice. When drunk at room temperature, it is often slightly warmed by holding the glass cupped in the palm or by gently heating it. However, heating brandy may cause the alcohol vapor to become too strong, so that the aromas are overpowered.

Brandy has more pleasant aromas and flavors at a lower temperature, e.g., 16 °C (61 °F). In most homes, this would imply that brandy should be cooled rather than heated for maximum enjoyment. Furthermore, alcohol (which makes up 40% of a typical brandy) becomes thin as it is heated and more viscous when cooled. Thus, cool brandy produces a fuller and smoother mouthfeel and less of a "burning" sensation.

Brandy has a rating system to describe its quality and condition; these indicators can usually be found near the brand name on the label:
• A.C.: aged two years in wood.
• V.S.: "Very Special" or 3-Star, aged at least three years in wood.
• V.S.O.P.: "Very Superior Old Pale" or 5-Star, aged at least five years in wood.
• X.O.: "Extra Old", Napoleon or Vieille Reserve, aged at least six years, Napoleon at least four years.
• Vintage: Stored in the cask until the time it is bottled with the label showing the vintage date.
• Hors d'age: These are too old to determine the age,

although ten years plus is typical, and are usually of great quality.

In the case of Brandy de Jerez Regulatory Council classifies it according to:
• Brandy de Jerez Solera – one year old.
• Brandy de Jerez Solera Reserva – three years old.
• Brandy de Jerez Solera Gran Reserva – ten years old.

'Grape brandy is traditionally drunk in western countries at room temperature from a tulip-shaped glass or a snifter, while in the Orient it is usually over ice.'

   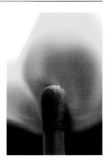

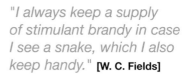

"*I always keep a supply of stimulant brandy in case I see a snake, which I also keep handy.*" **[W. C. Fields]**

❊ Chapter three

Environmental issues

31.......Environmental issues

Environmental issues

The most widely accepted definition of Organic wine is wine made from grapes grown in accordance with principles of organic farming, which typically excludes the use of artificial chemical fertilizers, pesticides, fungicides and herbicides.

O rganic wine is generally consumed for its perceived health benefits and reduced environmental impact. The consumption of organic wine grew at a rate of almost 4 percent over the year ending September 2009, out-pacing growth in the consumption of non-organic wine which grew 2% during a similar period. An estimated 1500-2000 organic wine producers globally, including negociant labels, with more than 885 of these organic domaines in France alone. The legal definition of Organic Wine is a complex issue and varies from country to country. The primary difference in the way that organic wine is defined relates to the use (or non use) of preservatives during the wine-making process.

In conventional agriculture, chemical fertilisers are used to promote larger yields and protect against disease. These same chemicals are absorbed through the roots into the vine's sap and are then passed through the leaves and stems into the fruit. As a result, residues of these chemicals find their way into the finished wine. In addition to the effects of direct consumption, conventional 'chemical based' farming has a significant impact on soil and water quality. Wine growers farming with chemicals have to wear 'hazmat'

style clothing and breathing apparatus to protect themselves while crop spraying.

Proponents of natural wine believe that chemical farming destroys the uniqueness of the land, and the unique flavor that this 'terroir' imparts to the wine.

'There are an estimated 1500-2000 organic wine producers globally.'

In the USA strict rules govern the winemaking process at all stages of production including harvesting, the types of yeasts that can be used during fermentation, as well as storage conditions. These rules are applied for all imported and domestic wines that acquire USDA certification.

Whilst in the USA organic wine certification prohibits the addition of sulphur dioxide, it is important to remember that sulfites are a natural byproduct of the fermentation process and that it is impossible for any wine to be completely free of sulfites. Organic wines may have naturally occurring sulfites, but the total sulfite level must be less than 20 parts per million in order to receive organic certification.

Natural Wines

For many consumers organic wine is synonymous with natural wine. However, it's important to note the distinction. In terms of legal and practical definitions, organic wine refers only to the absence of chemicals in the growth and production process. It doesn't prohibit other forms of intervention (popularly referred to as spoofulation) in the winemaking process such as micro oxygenation, reverse osmosis, excessive filtration, or flavour additives (such as oak chips).

Natural winemakers are usually also organic or biodynamic farmers who abstain from these practices and take a non-interventionist approach. They often use wild yeast that occurs naturally on the grapes and in the winery, and use minimal or no sulphur dioxide.

Sustainable Wines

Some farmers take additional steps beyond standard organic winemaking to apply sustainable farming practices. Examples include the use of composting and the cultivation of plants that attract insects that are beneficial to the health of the vines. Sustainable practices in these vineyards also extend to actions

that have seemingly little or nothing to do with the production of grapes, such as providing areas for wildlife to flourish near vineyard sites (this provides vegetation for the animals, which keeps them from eating the grapes) and allowing weeds and wildflowers to grow between the vines (this stresses the vines and forces them to produce fewer bunches of grapes with

> 'The consumption
> of organic wine grew
> at a rate of almost
> 4 percent over the year
> ending September, 2009.'

a greater concentration of flavor). Sustainable farmers are increasingly using bio-diesel for tractors in the vineyard (which reduces harmful emissions among the vines) or ploughing with horses. Another popular practice is to offset the carbon emissions of glass production and transportation through other offsets such as planting trees or sponsoring other initiatives.

❧ Chapter four

The UK wine regions introduction

36.......UK regional map
38.......Wine regions

UK regional map

The rolling moors of Yorkshire, the relaxing atmosphere of the Lake District, the ancient forests of Nottinghamshire, the stunning beaches of Wales, the slow paced lifestyle of Devon and Cornwall, the UK has something to offer everyone!

Each UK wine growing region, as illustrated on the opposite page, has been indivually coloured to co-ordinate with the regional chapter colours used throughout the book. Below is a list of all eight wine growing regions and the counties within them.

South West & Channel Isles
- Cornwall
- Devon
- Dorset
- Gloucestershire
- Somerset
- Isles of Scilly
- Wiltshire
- Jersey

South East & London
- Berkshire
- Buckinghamshire
- East Sussex
- Hampshire
- Isle of Wight
- Kent
- London
- Oxfordshire
- Surrey
- West Sussex

East
- Essex
- Hertfordshire
- Bedfordshire
- Cambridgeshire
- Norfolk
- Suffolk

West Midlands
- Herefordshire
- Shropshire
- Staffordshire
- Warwickshire
- West Midlands
- Worcestershire

East Midlands
- Derbyshire
- Leicestershire
- Rutland
- Northamptonshire
- Nottinghamshire
- Lincolnshire

Yorkshire & the Humber
- Northern Lincolnshire
- Yorkshire

North West
- Cumbria
- Lancashire
- Greater Manchester
- Merseyside
- Cheshire

Wales
- Blaenau Gwent
- Bridgend
- Caerphilly
- Cardiff
- Carmarthenshire
- Ceredigion
- Conwy
- Denbighshire
- Flintshire
- Gwynedd
- Isle of Anglesey
- Merthyr Tydfil
- Monmouthshire
- Newport
- Neath Port Talbot
- Pembrokeshire
- Powys
- Rhondda Cynon Taff
- Swansea
- Torfaen
- Vale of Glamorgan
- Wrexham

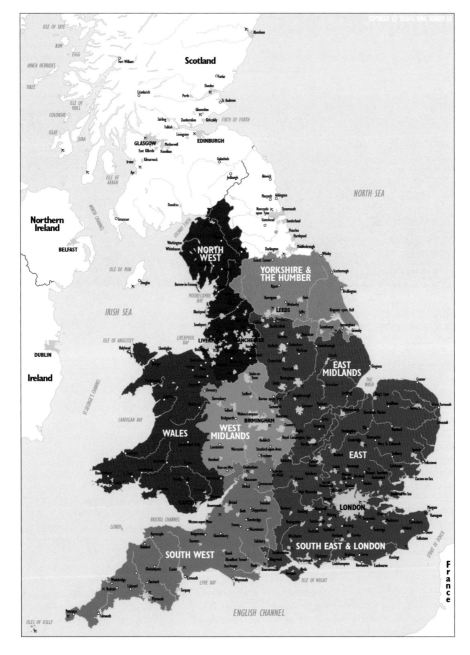

Wine regions

The vineyards of England are spread throughout seven major regions. For the purposes of this guide, we have treated Wales as a separate region; making eight county clusters in all.

Of the approximate 400 vineyards in England & Wales, some 44% are based in the South East and 25% are in the South West; this is due to the slightly more temperate climate in these regions and the similarity of the soil, climate and conditions (or terroir, to use the correct term) to that of Northern France. The most successful counties being Cornwall, Kent and Sussex.

The wine related landscape of England & Wales is changing rapidly with winemakers not only producing their own very high quality wines, but also winning international accolades and competitions.

Sparkling wines in the Champagne style have been the most successful of these. A number of vineyards from the South and East have won trophies, medals and awards, for their sparkling wines in particular, and have beaten long established names such as Bollinger in blind tastings at competitions.

The first important point to make when talking about wine-making in England and Wales is that we are not talking about British wine! British wine is the name given to wine made in the UK but not from grapes

grown in the UK. It can be made from imported grapes or grape juice or a mixture, and is likely to be of low quality. On the other hand, English and Welsh wines are made from grapes grown in those countries, and are recognised and come under the governance of the European Union Wine Regime.

> 'Each county has its own unique personality and characteristics rich in diversity and variety.'

A Brief Early History

Wine drinking was certainly introduced by the Romans but experts think it unlikely that vines were grown here, and almost definitely not in the quantity that would have been required. Over the next 1,000 years, the number of vineyards increased. The Domesday Book records at least 42 vine-growing areas in the South of England, and by the time of King Henry VIII, that had increased to 139 throughout England and Wales.

From the early 16th century until the latter part of the 19th century, the number of vineyards declined.

From 1875 to 1914, the only commercially produced wine came from Castell Coch in South Wales. No-one appears to satisfactorily explain this decline, or why, for about 25 years following the First World War, commercial production of wine in England and Wales stopped completely.

A Brief Modern History
After the Second World War, three men could be said to be responsible for re-establishing the English wine industry:

Ray Barrington Brock
A research chemist, began to evaluate which grape varieties were best suited to the English climate and soil.

Edward Hymans:
A gardening writer, planted a vineyard to facilitate the research of a book.

Sir Guy Salisbury-Jones
Planted a small vineyard in 1951 from which commercially produced wine was sold from 1955.

> 'The wine related landscape of England & Wales is changing rapidly with winemakers not only producing their own very high quality wines, but also winning international accolades and competitions.'

From the 1950s onwards the number of vineyards increased due to those who wanted to prove that producing really good English wine was not impossible. There are approximately 400 registered vineyards in England and Wales, producing approximately 4 million bottles of mainly white wine.

Against the odds
The British Isles lie further north than is usually the case for a wine-growing country. It is the effect of the Gulf Stream bringing a warmer, more temperate climate to our shores that has enabled the production of wine at all. However, we do have our fair share of rain meaning that only 2 years out of every 10 are likely to be very good for wine in England.

The high quality of a number of the wines made from grapes grown in England and Wales is due in no small part to the dedication and expertise of the wine-makers and what can be achieved by choosing the right location and deftly managing a vineyard.

Wines in England and Wales
The grape varieties most usually grown in England and Wales are: Seyval Blanc, Chardonnay, Pinot Noir, Reichensteiner and Bacchus. Only 1% of wine bought and consumed in England and Wales originates here. A Quality Wine Scheme for testing and tasting exists in the UK. Wines that pass the test are permitted to have on their label "English or Welsh Vineyards Quality Wine psr" psr meaning: Produced in Specific Regions.

Each county has its own unique personality and characteristics rich in diversity and variety.
From the rolling moors in Yorkshire, to the relaxing atmosphere of the Lake District, to the ancient forests of Nottinghamshire, to the stunning beaches of Wales and the slow paced lifestyle of Devon and Cornwall, the UK has something to offer everyone.

❊ Chapter five

The UK wine regions

43.......South West & Channel Isles
69.......South East & London
107.....East
125.....West Midlands
141.....East Midlands
155.....Yorkshire & the Humber
167.....North West
179.....Wales

☐ Notes:

....
....
....
....
....
....
....
....
....
....
....
....
....
....
....
....
....
....
....

JERSEY

La Mare Wine Estate

Introduction:

La Mare Wine Estate in Jersey, is a working 25 acre estate of vineyards, orchards and beautiful grounds. Established in 1972, La Mare is committed to creating the very best wines, ciders, spirits and liqueurs including our Apple Brandy made in the "Cognac Style" distillery. We also produce speciality foods and chocolates.

Address: La Route de Hogue Mauger, St Mary, Jersey, JE3 3BA
Tel: 01534 481178 | **Fax:** 01534 485210
Email: tim@lamarewineestate.com
www.lamarewineestate.com

South West & Channel Isles

✚ England ✕ Jersey

**Cornwall, Devon, Dorset, Gloucestershire,
Somerset, Isles of Scilly, Wiltshire & Jersey**

South West

The South West covers Cornwall, Devon, Dorset, Gloucestershire, Somerset, the Isles of Scilly, Wiltshire and Jersey.

The South West has just over 100 vineyards and wine estates and is the 2nd largest wine growing region in the UK. The South West coast has some of the best beaches in the country with the Jurassic Coast World Heritage Site in Dorset being a must for fossil hunters and the wild seas of Cornwall being a paradise for surfers. The Isles of Scilly is an island archipelago, 20 minutes from Cornwall with over 100 islands including St Mary's, Tresco, St Martin's, St Agnes and Bryher. Somerset is famous for cider and as you move into Wiltshire you'll find the iconic Stonehenge. Gloucestershire is home to the Forest of Dean and the Cotswolds.

Majestic cathedrals grace cities like Salisbury, Gloucester, Wells, Truro and Exeter, while Bath boasts famous Roman remains and Georgian splendour. Maritime history features strongly in Plymouth from where the Pilgrim Fathers and Sir Francis Drake sailed. For contemporary arts, Bristol, the largest city in the South West, is home to the wonderful Arnolfini.

Wherever you go you're guaranteed spectacular scenery, wonderful countryside and a stunning coastline. Walk the coastal paths, discover sandy beaches, dramatic cliffs, secluded coves and picturesque fishing villages. Inland, visit prehistoric sites quaint villages with thatched roofs, cob cottages and riverside pubs, stately homes with landscaped gardens or the wide open spaces of the outstanding National Parks, Exmoor and Dartmoor.

Selected vineyards
Camel Valley Vineyard (Cornwall)
La Mare Wine Estate (Jersey)
Old Walls Vineyard (Devon)
Three Choirs Vineyard (Gloucestershire)

Camel Valley
At Camel Valley, they've been producing award winning, world-class wines in a beautiful corner of Cornwall for twenty years. What is it that makes their wines so good? It's really quite simple - an idyllic setting on sun-drenched slopes near the famous Camel River; excellent grapes that perfectly suit the soil and climate; a respect for traditional vineyard practices combined with a modern approach to wine making and, most importantly, a passion for creating wines that provide pure pleasure.

La Mare Wine Estate

A working 25 acre estate of vineyards, orchards and beautiful grounds. Established in 1972, La Mare is committed to creating the very best wines, ciders, spirits and liqueurs including their Apple Brandy made in the "Cognac Style" distillery. They also produce speciality foods and chocolates.

Old Walls Vineyard

There is evidence of a vineyard on the site over 2000 years ago. The Romans took advantage of the south facing slopes and well drained soil just like Old Walls is doing once more. The vineyard is now in the caring hands of the Dawe family whose family have farmed the surrounding land for over 90 years.

Three Choirs: A friendly way to discover how healthy vines and classic wines have once again taken root in England after an absence of nearly 900 years.

They invite you to stroll among 70 acres of carefully cultivated vines, where they nurture well-chosen modern varieties alongside world-renowned grapes such as Pinot Noir.

Cultivation systems from around the world give an international flavour to the vineyard, where they mingle new techniques with traditional skills.
A vineyard isn't a place of hustle and bustle, but that doesn't mean that there is little to see or do at Three Choirs. Their visitor centre includes an exhibition and video that reveals the mysteries of winemaking and the life of Three Choirs throughout the changing seasons. Every current estate wine - white, red, rosé and sparkling - is available in their well stocked shop along with a range of gifts for wine and food lovers.

Selected destinations:

Bath: Nourished by natural hot springs, Bath offers a unique experience with stunning architecture, great shopping and iconic attractions. An outstanding Georgian spa city, boasting the Royal Crescent, Roman Baths and Thermae Bath Spa. Founded by the Romans and now a World Heritage Site.

Bournemouth: With seven miles of golden sands and sparkling sea, Bournemouth is the perfect family-friendly holiday and short break destination. Renowned for its golden beaches, beautiful parks, gardens and cosmopolitan ambience.

Bristol: This unique city boasts a history rich in nautical exploration, adventure and industry; a heritage that has helped transform Bristol into the exciting, cultural place that it is today.

Truro: The only city in Cornwall, the skyline dominated by the 250 foot towers of the cathedral. This market town and port dates back 800 years, booming during the tin mining era. The port is now mainly used for pleasure cruises along the tributaries of the river Fal to Falmouth and St Mawes.

> 'The South West coast has some of the best beaches in the country with the Jurassic Coast World Heritage Site in Dorset being a must for fossil hunters and the wild seas of Cornwall being a paradise for surfers.'

Torquay: The heart of the English Riviera, with its palm tree lined elegant seafront, but alas no Basil Fawlty. There are pavement cafés, pubs and restaurants, grand seafront hotels and beautiful beaches. The clifftop coastal paths offer spectacular views.

Lyme Regis An historic, unspoiled seaside resort and fishing port on the world famous Cobb harbour, the setting for the 1981 film, The French Lieutenant's Woman. Surrounded by beautiful coastline and countryside, the area has now been awarded World Heritage Site Status; famous for its geology and fossil finds.

 South West

Map	Wine estate	Tel number	Opening times
H2	a'Beckett's Vineyard	01380 816669	Thur-Sat inc bank holidays 10.30-17.30
D3	Alder Farm Vineyard	01566 783480	Not open to the public
G2	Aldwick Venue and Vineyard	01934 862305	Not currently open to the public but building a visitor centre and winery. Ready for end of 2010
F2	Aller Hill Vineyard	01458 259075	Not open to the public
E3	Ashwell Vineyard	01626 830031	Not open to the public
G2	Avalon Vineyard	01749 860393	Open to the public
G2	Avonleigh Organic Vineyard	07503 999906	Open May-Oct
G3	Avonwood Vineyard	07779 085420	Not open to the public
E4	Beenleigh Manor Vineyard	01803 732395	Mar-Dec, Mon-Sat 10.00-17.00, May-Sep inc Sun/bank holidays
F3	Blackdown Hills Vineyard	01404 47442	Seasonal 10.00-18.00, By appointment only
F3	Borough Hill Farm Vineyard	01404 811006	Not open to the public
C4	Bosue Vineyard	01726 843159	Open to the public
H1	Bow-in-the-Cloud Vineyard	01666 823040	By appointment only
E3	Brick House Vineyard	07802 246270	Not open to the public
G3	Bride Valley Vineyard	01308 482367	Not open to the public
C3	Camel Valley Vineyard	01208 77959	Easter-Oct
F3	Carpenters Vineyard	01935 881255	Not open to the public
F3	Castlewood Vineyard	01297 552068	By appointment only
G3	Charlton Barrow Vineyard	01929 480387	Not open to the public
D3	Clawford Vineyard	01409 254177	Not open to the public
D4	Cobland Mill Estate	01503 230656	Open to the public
G1	Compton Green Vineyard	01989 720465	Not open to the public
C4	Cornish Garden Nurseries	01872 888412	Mon-Sat 9.00-17.30, Sun 10.30-17.00
H1	Cowley Estate Vineyard	01285 640974	Not open to the public
G2	Coxley Vineyard	01749 670285	Open to the public
G3	Crawthorne Vineyard	01258 839239	Not open to the public
G3	Doles Ash Farm Vineyard	08452 681553	Not open to the public
E2	Dunkery Vineyard - Exmoor	01643 841505	By appointment only
F2	Dunleavy Vineyards	01179 245415	Not open to public
D3	Eastcott Vineyard	01837 811012	Wed-Sun inc Bank Holidays 10.30-17.00
G3	English Oak Vineyard	01258 858205	Not open to the public
G2	Fonthill Glebe Vineyard	01722 716770	Open to the public
F3	Furleigh Estate	01308 488991	By appointment only
G2	Head of the Vale Vineyard	01963 33316	Not open to the public
E2	Higher Bumsley Vineyard	01598 763325	By appointment only
G3	Higher Sandford Vineyard	01930 220275	Not open to the public
E3	Huxbear Vineyard	07846 407713	Opening early 2011
E3	Kenton Vineyard	01626 891091	Open to the public
G1	Kents Green Vineyard	01452 790171	Open day once a year, otherwise not open to the public

Map	Wine estate	Tel number	Opening times
G1	Kilcott Valley Vineyard	01454 238007	Not open to the public
E3	Knightshayes Vineyard	01884 253264	Open to the public
H4	La Mare (Jersey)	01534 482762	Easter-Oct, Mon-Sun 10.00-19.00, Nov-Dec Mon-Fri 10.00-16.00
C4	Lambourne Vineyard	01872 501212	Open to the public
G2	Leigh Park Hotel Vineyard	01225 864885	By appointment only
F3	Lily Farm Vineyard	01395 443877	Thur-Sat 10.30-15.30
G1	Little Foxes Vineyard	01453 828930	Not open to public
G3	Littlebredy Vineyard	01305 898055	Not open to public
F3	Lopen Vineyard	01460 249119	By appointment only
F3	Lyme Bay Winery	01297 551355	Mon-Fri 9.00-17.00, Sat 10.00-16.00, Sun 11.00-15.00
E3	Manstree Vineyard	01392 832218	Tues-Sun 10.00-17.00 inc bank holidays
G3	Melbury Vale Vineyard	07730 955593	By appointment only
G2	Mumfords Vineyard	01225 858367	By appointment only
H2	New Mill Vineyard	01672 562402	By appointment only
G1	Newtown Nurseries	01531 821847	Not open to the public
E3	Oakford Vineyard	01398 351486	By appointment only
F2	Oatley Vineyard	01278 671340	By appointment only
E3	Old Walls Vineyard	01626 770877	May-Sept, Wed-Sun 11.00-16.00, Thur-Sun 11.00-15.30 inc bank holidays
F3	Otter Farm Vineyard	01404 548927	Not open to the public
G3	Parhams Vineyard	01747 853122	By appointment only
H1	Pear Tree at Purton Vineyard	01793 772100	Open to public - people should go to hotel reception
E3	Pebblebed Vineyard - (Ebford, Clyst St. George, West Hill)	07814 788348	Topsham wine cellar open Wed-Sat 9.30-17.30, Sat 11.00-14.00
B4	Penberth Valley Vineyard	01736 810714	Not open to the public
B4	Polgoon Vineyard	01736 333946	Wine tours Wed-Fri 14.00, Shop Mon-Sat 10.00-16.00
C4	Pollaughan Vineyard	01752 812178	Not open to the public
C4	Polmassick Vineyard	01726 842239	By appointment only
G3	Portesham Vineyard	01305 871444	Open selected dates each year
H3	Purbeck Vineyard	01929 481525	Open to the public
F2	Quantock Hills Vineyard	01278 663775	Not open to the public
G2	Quoins Organic Vineyard	01225 862334	Open to the public
E3	Redyeates Wedge Vineyard	01823 256741	Not open to the public except in English Wine Week
E3	Rock Moors Vineyard	01647 24743/4	Not open to the public
G1	Saint Anne's Vineyard	01989 720313	Open to the public
G1	Saint Augustine's Vineyard	01454 632236	By appointment only
A4	Saint Martin's Isles of Scilly Vineyard	01720 423418	Tue-Thur 10.30-16.00, other times by appointment only
A4	Saint Mary's Vineyard	01720 422317	Not open to the public
E3	Sandridge Barton Vineyard	01179 452631	Not open to the public

South West

Map	Wine estate	Tel number	Opening times
F2	Secret Valley Vineyard	01278 671945	Open to the public
E3	Sharpham Vineyard	01803 732203	Apr-Sep, Mon-Sun inc bank holidays
G3	Sherborne Castle Vineyard	01935 813182	Open to the public
F3	Southcote Vineyard	01297 551355	See Lyme Bay Winery for opening times
H2	Southcott Vineyard	01672 569190	Not open to public
F3	Southwood Vineyard	01884 277945	Not open to the public
G3	Stalbridge Weston Vineyard	01963 362281	Not open to the public
F2	Staplecombe Vineyard	01823 451217	Not open to the public
G1	Strawberry Hill Vineyard	01531 822669	By appointment only
F3	Struddicks Farm Vineyard	01752 812178	Not open to the public
E2	Summermoor Vineyard	01769 520776	Apr-Sep, Tues-Thur & Sat 12.00-17.00
F3	The Somerset Distillery	01460 240782	Not open to the public
G1	Thornbury Castle Vineyard	01454 281182	By appointment only
G1	Three Choirs Vineyard	01531 890223	Open to public only
G3	Timber Lane Vineyard	01305 880069	Not open to the public
D3	Torview Wines	01409 895773	Not open to the public
C3	Trevibban Mill Vineyard	01841 532186	Not open to the public
H2	Tytherley Vineyard	01794 340644	Not open to the public
F3	Watchcombe Vineyard	01297 551355	See Lyme Bay Winery for opening times
F3	Wayford Vineyard	01460 74321	Not open to the public
D3	Weir Quay Vineyard	01822 840480	Not open to the public
F3	Willhayne Vineyard	01297 553463	By appointment only
G1	Winner Hill Vineyard	01453 844237	By appointment only
F3	Wodetone Vineyard	01297 561364	Not open to the public
G2	Wootton Vineyard	01749 831146	Not open to the public
G2	Wraxall Vineyard	01749 860331	By appointment only
G2	Wylye Valley Vineyard	01985 846767	Open to the public Mon-Sat 10.00-17.30
E3	Yearlstone Vineyard	01884 855700	Wed-Sun 11.00-16.00

Wiltshire
a'Beckett's Vineyard
Situated half way between Avebury and Stonehenge in the village of Littleton Panell. 9 acres down to vines and 6 acres of orchards. We are developing a range of English wines, cider and apple juice.

a: High Street, Littleton Panell, Devizes, Wiltshire, SN10 4EN
t: 01380 816669
ww.abecketts.co.uk

Devon
Alder Farm Vineyard
In 2009, 650 grape vines were planted followed by a further planting of 2500 in 2010. The grape variety used is MA. The vineyard is only in it's second year and a new venture for Sarah and Michael Hodgetts.

a: Lewdown, Oakhampton, Devon, EX20 4PJ
t: 01566 783480

Somerset
Aldwick Venue and Vineyard
The Aldwick Venue and Vineyard is due to be completed in December 2010 and the vines have already been planted at the farm in readiness for next summer.

a: Redhill, Bristol, North Somerset, BS40 5RF
t: 01934 862305

Somerset
Aller Hill Vineyard
In May 2008 we planted Chardonnay, Pinot Noir and Pinot Meunier vines to make sparkling wine. In 2009 we planted an additional 500 Pinot Meunier and Bachus. First harvest will be in 2010. First wines 2012.

a: Aller Road, Langport, Somerset, TA10 0QL
t: 01458 259075
www.allerhill.blogspot.com

Devon
Ashwell Vineyard
At Ashwell Vineyard, Bill and Diane Riddell bring a scientific approach to vine growing in their small but delightful walled cottage garden.

a: East Street, Bovey Tracey, Devon, TQ13 9EJ
t: 01626 830031

Somerset
Avalon Vineyard
Explore our range of organic wines, fruit wines, mead and cider. Free of chemical residues, these products are grown and created in harmony with wildlife and the environment, deep in the Somerset countryside.

a: The Drove, East Pennard, Shepton Mallet, Somerset, BA4 6UA | t: 01749 860393
www.pennardorganicwines.co.uk

Wiltshire
Avonleigh Organic Vineyard
The vineyard was planted in 2006 by two old school friends, Di Francis & Ingrid Lindskog, and was certified as organic by the Soil Association. We produce high quality wine and grow fruit in the traditional way.

a: 14 Otago Terrace, St Saviours Road, Bath, Avon, BA1 6SX
t: 07503 999906
www.avonleighorganics.co.uk

Somerset
Avonwood Vineyard
Every year the half-acre private vineyard produces 1,000 bottles of Avonwood crisp white wine - named after the house - for quaffing by family and friends.

a: Seawalls Road, Sneyd Park, Bristol, Avon, BS9 1PH
t: 07779 085420

Devon
Beenleigh Manor Vineyard
The vineyard is part of an agricultural partnership based around Sharpham house. The winery makes the highly acclaimed Beenleigh Red, a blend of Cabernet Sauvignon & Merlot.

a: Owls Roost, Beenleigh, Harbertonford, Totnes, Devon, TQ9 7EF
t: 01803 732395

Devon
Blackdown Hills Vineyard
Blackdown Hills Vineyard and Winery in Monkton, near Honiton, East Devon offers tours of the vineyard followed by a tasting of selected Blackdown Hills Wines.

a: Oaklands Farm, Monkton, Honiton, Devon, EX14 9QH
t: 01404 47442
www.blackdownhills-vineyard.co.uk

Devon

Borough Hill Farm Vineyard

Not open to the public and do not wish to be contacted as the vineyard is in it's early stages. Currently growing nine varieties of vines on 4 hectares of land. First harvest expected in 2012.

a: Wiggaton, Ottery St. Mary, Devon, EX11 1PZ
t: 01404 811006

Cornwall

Bosue Vineyard

The first vines planted in 1996, followed by more extensive plantings from 1997-1999. More planting followed in 2004-2005, We now have over 3500 vines producing red, white,rosé and sparkling wine.

a: St Ewe, St Austell, Cornwall, PL26 6EU
t: 01726 843159
www.cornwallwines.co.uk

Wiltshire

Bow-in-the-Cloud Vineyard

The vineyard was planted in 1992 and 1993 and has been producing wine for corporate customers and local trade since 1995. one acre of Bacchus, one of Seyval Blanc and one of Schonburger.

a: Noahs Ark, Garsdon, Malmesbury, Wiltshire, SN16 9NS
t: 01666 823040
www.bowinthecloud.co.uk

Devon

Brick House Vineyard

Planted in 2008 and expecting their first harvest in 2011, Brick House vineyard is just over half a hectare in size. Currently growing nine varieties. The wine will eventually be on sale at Kenton Vineyard.

a: Mamhead, Exeter, Devon, EX6 8HP
t: 07802 246270

Dorset

Bride Valley Vineyard

Planted in 2009 and currently 3 hectares in size. Grape varieties: Chardonnay, Pinot Noir, Pinot Meunier. Plans to increase to 8 hectares in the not too distant future. First release expected in 2014.

a: The Court House, Litton Cheney, Dorchester, Dorset, DT2 9AW
t: 01308 482367

Cornwall

Camel Valley Vineyard

We've been producing award-winning, world-class wines for twenty years. The sun-drenched slopes near the Camel River produce grapes that perfectly suit the soil and climate.

a: Nanstallon, Bodmin, Cornwall, PL30 5LG
t: 01208 77959
www.camelvalley.com

Somerset

Carpenters Vineyard

Grape varieties: Siegerrebe, MA Seyval blanc, Bacchus.

a: High Street, Norton-Sub-Hamdon, Somerset, TA14 6SN
t: 01935 881255

Dorset

Castlewood Vineyard

A working dairy farm with selfcatering accommodation. Grape varieties: Pinot Noir, Chardonnay, Pinot Meunier, MA, Reichensteiner, Rondo. Producing sparkling wine, available soon to buy locally.

a: Castlewood Farm, Musbury, Axminster, Dorset, EX13 8SS
t: 01297 552068
www.castlewoodcottages.co.uk

Dorset

Charlton Barrow Vineyard

Grape varieties: Bacchus, Orion, Phoenix, Seyval Blanc, MT, Sylvaner. Also have bed and breakfast and guest house accommodation.

a: Charlton Marshall, Blandford Forum, Dorset, DT11 9DD
t: 01929 480387

Devon

Clawford Vineyard

A private 78 acre estate, situated in the peaceful & tranquil setting of the Claw Valley in the rolling hills of the glorious Devon countryside. Superb views of the vineyards, orchards, woods and lakes.

a: Clawton, Holsworthy, Devon, EX22 6PN
t: 01409 254177
www.clawford.co.uk

Cornwall

Cobland Mill Estate

Located in a hidden valley, metres from the coastal path on the Rame Peninsula in South East Cornwall. Currently produces 'Cobland Mill White' and it is hoped to produce the first red wines in 2010.

a: Eglarooze, Torpoint, Cornwall, PL11 3DY
t: 01503 230656
www.coblandmill.co.uk

Cornwall

Cornish Garden Nurseries

The garden nursery does have a vineyard which is 0.5 hectares in size, which last produced wine around 4 years ago. The vineyard is still in place but not fully operational.

a: Barras Moor Farm, Perran-ar-worthal, Truro, Cornwall, TR3 7PE | t: 01872 888412
www.cornishgardennurseries.net

Somerset

Coxley Vineyard Hotel

Popular venue for weddings, functions and conferences with views across the Mendip Hills. We are situated in the village of Coxley, just two miles from the historic City of Wells.

a: Coxley, Somerset, BA5 1RQ
t: 01749 670285
www.coxleyvineyard.com

Dorset

Doles Ash Farm Vineyard

Lying in the picturesque Piddle Valley are the twelve acres of gorgeous rolling countryside in which these holiday cottages are set. Doles Ash Farm now has an established vineyard producing English wines.

a: Doles Ash Farm, Piddletrenthide, Dorset, DT2 7RE
t: 08452 681553

Somerset

Dunleavy Vineyards

Planted in 2008 with Pinot Noir Précoce and Seyval Blanc. The first harvest is due in 2011. Hoping to release and sell a róse and a sparkling white wine within Bristol area and on the website.

a: c/o 18 Wolseley Road, Bishopston, Bristol, Somerset, BS7 8EN. Location of vineyard: BS40 5RS | t: 01179 245415
www.dunleavyvineyards.com

Gloucestershire

Compton Green Vineyard

Situated over 60 metres above sea level, facing south towards the Severn Valley, this vineyard is ideally situated for wine growing. Compton Greens wines are made nearby at Three Choirs Vineyard.

a: c/o Maxstoke, Aston Ingham, Ross-on-Wye, Herefordshire, HR9 7LS. Vineyard location between Newent & Redmarley
t: 01989 720465

Gloucestershire

Cowley Estate Vineyard

A small experimental vineyard in the village of South Cerney. It has been set up to gain experience in vineyard management/winemaking. If successful we hope to move on to bigger things eventually.

a: 14 Bowly Cresent, Siddington, Cirencester, Gloucestershire
t: 01285 640974
w: www.cowley-estate.com

Dorset

Crawthorne Vineyard

First planted in 2009 on 10 hectares of land. Grape varieties: Chardonnay, Pinot Noir and Pinot Meunier. Hoping to produce a sparkling wine which will be ready for release in 2012.

a: Dewlish, Dorchester, Dorset, DT2 7NG
t: 01258 839239

Somerset

Dunkery Vineyard - Exmoor

We have one of the best equipped wineries in England. All our wines are made entirely from the grapes we grow in the vineyard. We make/bottle the wines in the winery. Our speciality is dark red wine.

a: Wotton Courtenay, Minehead, Somerset, TA24 8RD
t: 01643 841505
www.exmoor-excellence.com

Devon

Eastcott Vineyard

Our grape varieties have been carefully chosen to suit the English climate and for the production of high quality sparkling wine, as well as a range of white, rosé and red wines.

a: Lower Eastcott, Northlew, Okehampton, Devon, EX20 3PT
t: 01837 811012
www.eastcottvineyard.co.uk

Dorset
English Oak Vineyard
English Oak Vineyard is dedicated to the production of quality English Sparkling Wine, from classic Champagne grape varieties, prepared faithfully by méthode traditionnelle.

a: Flowers Drove, Lytchett Matravers, Poole, Dorset, BH16 6BX | t: 01258 858205
www.englishoakvineyard.co.uk

Wiltshire
Fonthill Glebe Vineyard
The winery is situated in the picturesque village of Teffont Evias, which is approx 8 miles west of Salisbury. The wine is made, bottled and marketed from this licenced, customs & excise bonded winery.

a: The Winery, Teffont Evias, Salisbury, Wiltshire, SP3 5RG
t: 01722 716770
www.fonthillglebewines.co.uk

Dorset
Furleigh Estate
Dedicated to the production of fine wine made from grapes grown in the English countryside. Where once apple trees were common, grape vines now flourish. Alongside them a purpose-built winery.

a: Salway Ash, Bridport, Dorset, DT6 5JF
t: 01308 488991
www.furleighestate.co.uk

Somerset
Head of the Vale Vineyard
Grape varieties: Rondo, Regent

a: Mitchells Farm, Stoke Trister, Wincanton, Somerset, BA9 9PH
t: 01963 33316

Devon
Higher Bumsley Vineyard
Grape varieties: MA

a: Parracombe, Devon, EX31 4PT
t: 01598 763325

Dorset
Higher Sandford Vineyard
Grape varieties: Reichensteiner, Bacchus

a: Higher Sandford House, Sandford Orcas, Sherborne, Dorset, DT9 4RP
t: 01930 220275

Devon
Huxbear Vineyard
2010 represents the first year that we intend to take a crop from our vineyard (planted in 2007) as we plan our first vintage.

a: Chudleigh, Newton Abbot, Devon, TQ13 OEH
t: 07846 407713
www.huxbear.co.uk

Devon
Kenton Vineyard
Planted in 2003 on an old farm, the south facing slopes and sandy soil together with the mild and sunny climate are ideal for growing vines and ripening grapes for wine production.

a: Helwell Barton, Kenton, Devon, EX6 8NW
t: 01626 891091
www.kentonvineyard.co.uk

Gloucestershire
Kents Green Vineyard
We are a family run vineyard growing grapes to make stilll and sparkling wine in the heart of the Gloucestershire countryside.

a: Kents Green House, Kents Green, Tibberton, GL19 3AJ
t: 01452 790171
www.kentsgreenwine.co.uk

Gloucestershire
Kilcott Valley Vineyard
Grape Varieties: Seyval Blanc

a: Bank Cottage, Lower Kilcott, Wotton-under-Edge, Gloucestershire, GL12 7RL
t: 01454 238007

Devon
Knightshayes Vineyard
A quarter of an acre in size with 400 red / 40 white grape vines. In 2007 they produced 300 bottles of róse, 50 bottles of white wine. The Harvest of 2010 is looking great! Wine is sold in the shop and resturant.

a: c/o Knighshayes Court , Bolham, Tiverton, Devon, EX16 7RQ. Location of Vineyard: EX16 7RD
t: 01884 253264 | www.nationaltrust.org.uk

Cornwall
Lambourne Vineyard
Lambourne Vineyard is on the Roseland Peninsula. Producer of a limited quantity of quality Cornish red and white wines.

a: Ruanhighlanes, Truro, Cornwall, TR2 5NL
t: 01872 501212
www.lambournevineyard.co.uk

Devon
Lily Farm Vineyard
Situated at Knowle in its own vale surrounded by beautiful East Devon countryside. Within easy walking distance is the town of Budleigh Salterton which is part of the historic Jurassic Coast.

a: Moormead, Budleigh Salterton, Devon, EX9 6QA. Location of vinyard: EX9 7AH
t: 01395 443877 | www.lilyfarmvineyard.com

Wiltshire
Littlebredy
This is a small test grapevine plantation which is part of the Littlebredy Walled Gardens and is a member of the Wessex Vineyards Association.Visitors to the gardens are welcome to include it in their stroll.

a: Littlebredy Walled Gardens, Littlebredy, Dorchester, Wiltshire, DT2 9HL | t: 01305 898055
www.wgw.org.uk/littlebredy.com/index2.html

Devon
Lyme Bay Winery
Producing sparkling and country wines, ciders, ales, brandy, cordial & vinegar, preserves and so much more! We have a winery and shop which offers our complete range of products.

a: Lyme Bay Winery, Shute, Axminster, Devon, EX13 7PW
t: 01297 551355
www.lymebaywinery.co.uk

Jersey
La Mare (Jersey)
Set in the peaceful grounds of a traditional 18th century granite farmhouse, La Mare Wine Estate is a working 25 acre domain, committed to creating the very best wines, ciders and spirits.

a: St Mary, Jersey, JE3 3BA, Channel Isles
t: 01534 482762
www.lamarewineestate.com

Wiltshire
Leigh Park Hotel Vineyard
Sample a bottle of the Hotel's own medium-dry white wine, produced from grapes grown in its own vineyard, which is exclusively available to the Best Western Leigh Park Hotel.

a: Leigh Road West, Bradford-on-Avon, Wiltshire, BA15 2RA
t: 01225 864885
www.latonahotels.co.uk/best-western-leigh-park.html

Gloucestershire
Little Foxes Vineyard
Grape Varieties: Auxerrois

a: 111 Gloucester Road, Stonehouse, Gloucestershire, GL10 2HB
t: 01453 828930

Somerset
Lopen Vineyard
Planted in 2003. We grow Pinot Noir, Pinot Meunier and Pinot Gris vines, with the intention to produce sparkling wine (white and rosé), red wine, white wine, rosé and a late harvest dessert wine.

a: Lopen Lane, Lopen, Somerset, TA13 5LW
t: 01460 249119

Devon
Manstree Vineyard
Our 31 year old MA and Seyval Blanc vines are the oldest commercially productive vines in Devon which produce a consistently high yielding crop of top quality grapes.

a: New Barn Farm, Manstree Road, Shillingford St. George, Exeter, EX2 9QR | t: 01392 832218
www.boyces-manstree.co.uk

Dorset

Melbury Vale Vineyard

Planted in may 2006 on 2 acres of land. The vineyard has 2,000 vines and four grape varieties, two red and two white. A full crop was harvested in 2009, samples made for visitors to taste and comment on!

a: 9a Lambourn Road, Speen, Newbury, Berkshire, RG20 8AA
Location of vineyard: Barfoot Farm, SP7 0DB
t: 07730 955593 | www.melburyvaleco.co.uk/vineyard.html

Somerset

Mumfords Vineyard

A family run business dedicated to producing the finest quality English wines. We produce several varieties of white wine, an award winning rosé, and an outstanding English red wine.

a: Shockerwick Lane, Bannerdown, BA1 7LQ
t: 01225 858367
www.mumfordsvineyard.co.uk

Wiltshire

New Mill Vineyard

Planted in 2007 with Pinot Noir Prècoce, Seyval Blanc and Phoenix. Produced 1600 bottles of wine in 2009 which will be sold locally in 2011. Aiming to produce 4000 bottles in the 2010 harvest.

a: Totteridge Farm, Littleworth, Milton Lilbourne, Pewsey, Wiltshire, SN9 5LF
t: 01672 562402

Gloucestershire

Newton Nurseries

Grape varieties: Phoenix, Schönburger, Seyval Blanc

a: Strawberry Hill, Newent, Gloucestershire, GL18 1LH
t: 01531 821847

Devon

Oakford Vineyard

Visitors welcome, French, Spanish and German spoken. Wine sales (please ring first), Accommodation (non-smoking). Wines produced Dry and Medium dry white wines, red, róse.

a: The Old Rectory, Holme Place, Oakfrod, nr Tiverton, EX16 9EW | t: 01398 351486
www.ukvines.co.uk/vineyards/oakford.htm

Somerset

Oatley Vineyard

Established in 1986 on England's famous west-country red soil, producing natural, usually fully-dry white wines that reflect the year, the varieties and the "terroir". We produce two dry white wines a year.

a: Cannington, Bridgwater, Somerset, TA5 2NL
t: 01278 671340
www.oatleyvineyard.co.uk

Devon

Old Walls Vineyard

Evidence of a vineyard on the site over 2000 years ago. Now in the caring hands of the Dawe family. Tea rooms and a shop on site.

a: Old Walls Road, Bishopsteignton, Teignmouth, TQ14 9PQ
t: 01626 770877
www.oldwallsvineyard.co.uk

Devon

Otter Farm Vineyard

Otter Farm lies on the sunny banks of the River Otter in Devon and is home to some of the finest food you can grow. Peaches, apricots, olives, pecans, mulberries, medlars, quinces and wine grapes.

a: Weston, Honiton, Devon, EX14 3PAt: 01345 678900
t: 01404 548927
www.otterfarm.co.uk

Dorset

Parhams Vineyard

Roy Phillips planted 0.40 hectares of Reichensteiner in 1993 on a south facing slope, overlooking the River Sturkle. These vines are now producing elegant dry wines. Possibility of a sparkling wine to follow.

a: Melbury Abbas, Shaftesbury, Dorset, SP7 0DE
t: 0174 7853122
www.ukvines.co.uk/vineyards/parhams.htm

Wiltshire

Pear Tree at Purton Vineyard

A truly delightful historic, former Saxon Rectory, just outside the village of Purton. The 7 acres of grounds are idyllic for an evening stroll. Appreciate the newly cultivated vineyard.

a: Church End, Swindon, Wiltshire, SN5 4ED
t: 01793 772100
www.peartreepurton.co.uk

Devon
Pebblebed Vineyard
Our vineyards are certified organic and our wines regularly win awards in national/regional competitions. We have a tasting cellar which welcomes people to try Pebblebed wines and local tapas.

a: The Wine Cellar, 46a Fore Street, Topsham, Devon, EX3 0HY. Vineyard locations vary | t: 07814 788348
www.pebblebed.co.uk

Cornwall
Penberth Valley Vineyard
Grape varieties: Triomphe, Léon Millot, Rondo.

a: Penberth Valley, St Buryan, Penzance, Cornwall, TR19 6HH
t: 01736 810714

Cornwall
Polgoon Vineyard
Award winning winery in Penzance. Polgoon Vineyard has succeeded due to the determination and passion of its owners. The products are highly regarded not just in the South West but all over the UK.

a: Rosehill, Penzance, Cornwall, TR20 8TE
t: 01736 333946
www.polgoonvineyard.vpweb.co.uk

Cornwall
Pollaughan Vineyard
Grape varieties: Pinot Noir, Pinot Noir Précoce, Seyval Blanc, Bacchus, Riesling, Rondo, Dornfelder, Dunkelfelder, Chardonnay.

a: Deviock Wine Company, Looe Hill, St. Martin, Looe, Cornwall, PL13 1PA. Location of Vineyard: TR2 5EH
t: 01736 33394

Cornwall
Polmassick Vineyard
Barbara Musgrave welcomes visitors, By appointment only. Wine: White and red Cornish wines. Rudhya Rose Wine: A medium dry rosé table wine 14% ABV.

a: St Ewe, St Austell, Cornwall, PL26 6HA
t: 01726 842239

Dorset
Portesham Vineyard
Set 250 feet above sea level, a coastal vineyard with a complex "terroir" from the Jurassic period. We grow Phoenix, Seyval and Chardonnay for white wines and Pinot Noir and Regent for red wines and rosé.

a: East Portesham, Brookside, Waddon, Weymouth, Dorset, DT3 4ER | t: 01305 871444
www.porteshamvineyard.com

Dorset
Purbeck Vineyard
A four star boutique hotel set on a working English Vineyard in the heart of Purbeck offering luxury bed and breakfast accommodation and contemporary dining serving fresh fabulous food.

a: Valley Road, Harmans Cross, Wareham, Dorset, BH20 5HU
t: 01929 481525
www.vineyard.uk.com / www.purbeckvineyard.com

Somerset
Quantock Hills Vineyard
Fine English grape wines made from several varieties grown in our own vineyard - and striking apple wines made from traditional Somerset apples. The results are a unique range of new and surprising tastes.

a: Greenway barton, Rhode, Bridgwater, Somerset, TA5 2AD
t: 01278 663775
www.perceptivecreation.co.uk/bbsite/qvmain.htm

Wiltshire
Quoins Organic Vineyard
Planted in 2002 and the first crop of grapes was harvested in Oct 2005 with the first bottles of wine available being sold from Aug 2006. Developed under Soil Association organic certification.

a: Little Ashley, Bradford-on-Avon, Wiltshire, BA15 2PW
t: 01225 862334
www.quoinsvineyard.co.uk

Devon
Redyeates Wedge Vineyard
In English wine see the development of a young vineyard in its third year only! Take the tour and talk to the owner of this new organically grown vineyard.

a: Chapel Hill, Cherriton Fitzpaine, Devon, EX17 4HG
t: 01823 256741

Devon

Rock Moors Vineyard

Rock Moors vineyard has been making wine for the last 25 years and on average produces around 100-350 litres per year. Consumed only by friends and family. Red and white varietals.

a: Woodland Head, Yeoford, Crediton, Devon, EX17 5HE
t: 01647 24743/4

Gloucestershire

Saint Anne's Vineyard

The vineyard was initially planted in 1979, and came into commercial production in 1984. A wide variety of vine varieties are grown and can be purchased at the shop.

a: Wain House, Oxenhall, Newent, Gloucestershire, GL18 1RW | t: 01989 720313
www.stannesvineyard.com

Gloucestershire

Saint Augustines Vineyard

You wouldn't expect a vineyard near the Severn Bridge, but the neat vines outside this old village parsonage produce a couple of thousand bottles a year!

a: Passage Road, Aust, South Gloucestershire, BS35 4BG
t: 01454 632236
www.staugustinesvineyard.co.uk

Isles of Scilly

Saint Martin's Isles of Scilly Vineyard

Situated on gently sloping, southerly facing slopes we are the most South-Westerly vineyard in England. Val and Graham Thomas started the project in 1996 as a holiday hobby.

a: 4 Signal Row, St Martin's, Isles of Scilly, TR25 0QL
t: 01720 423418
www.stmartinsvineyard.co.uk

Isles of Scilly

Saint Mary's Vineyard

The unique flavour of this wine is influenced by the black granite soil, the pure sea air and above average annual hours of sunshine. This wine has a light, fresh and delicately fruity flavour.

a: Star Castle Hotel, St. Mary's, Isles of Scilly, TR21 0TA. Location of Vineyard: Holy Vale, Maypole, Silver Carn, Helvear | t: 01345 678900 | www.wineestate.co.uk

Devon

Sandridge Barton Vineyard

Grape varieties: Pinot Noir, Pinot Noir Précoce, Bacchus,

a: Sandridge barton, Stoke Gabriel, Totnes, Devon, TQ9 6RL / Knight Frank LLP, Crown House, 37-41 Prince Street, Bristol, BS1 4PS | t: 01179 452631

Somerset

Secret Valley Vineyard

At Cobbs Cross Farm there are real opportunities to study in close up, Nature, wildlife and aspects of a working farm. The 2008 Vineyard has four varieties of grapes.

a: Cobbs Cross Farm, Goathurst, Bridghurst, Somerset, TA5 2DN | t: 01278 671945
www.cobbscrossactivitycentre.co.uk

Devon

Sharpham Vineyard

A marriage of soil, climate & grape variety known as terroir has bestowed her gifts freely upon us. We use both New World and traditional techniques to best develop our unique regional characteristics.

a: Sharpham Estate, Ashprington, Totnes, Devon, TQ9 7UT
t: 01803 732203
www.sharpham.com

Dorset

Sherborne Castle Vineyard

The Sherborne Castle Estates Vineyard produces dry fruity wines which are sold through the Sherborne Castle gift shop, wine merchants, hotels and supermarkets.

a: Sherbourne Castle, Digby Estate Office, 9 Cheap Street, Sherborne, Dorset, DT9 3PY | t: 01935 813182
www.sherbornecastle.com

Devon

Southcote Vineyard

Owned by Lyme Bay Winery. See Lyme Bay Winery for more information. Southcote Vineyard was planted in April 2010 on 7 hectares of land. Grape varieties: Seyval Blanc, Pinot Noir and Bacchus.

a: c/o Lyme Bay Winery, Shute, Axminster, Devon, EX13 7PW. Location of vineyard: unknown | t: 01297 551355
www.lymebaywinery.co.uk

Wiltshire
Southcott Vineyard
In 2005-2006 around 2000 vines were planted on 0.6 hectares of land including the grape varieties of Chardonnay, Pinot Noir and Pinot Meunier.

a: Southcott, Pewsey, Wiltshire, SN9 5JF
t: 01672 569190

Devon
Southwood Vineyard
Grape varieties: Léon Millot, Dornfelder, Triomphe. Siegerrebe, Pinot gris, MA.

a: St Andrew's Wood, Dulford, Cullompton, Devon, EX15 2DF
t: 01884 277945

Dorset
Stalbridge Weston Vineyard
Grape varieties: MA, MT

a: Stalbridge Weston, Sturminster Newton, Dorset, DT10 2LA
t: 01963 362281

Somerset
Staplecombe Vineyard
Small vineyard, around 0.3 hectares, managed by Martin Cursham. Grapes are collected by Yearlstone Vineyard. Grape varieties: MA, Rondo, Huxelrebe, Reichensteiner.

a: Burlands Farm, Staplegrove, Somerset, TA2 6SN
t: 01823 451217

Gloucestershire
Strawberry Hill Vineyard
First vines planted outside in 1999, with extended planting each year after. in 2002 we planted an acre of vines in commercial glass houses. We currently produce: Chardonnay, Merlot, Cab Sav, Pinot Noir.

a: 47 Orchard Road, Newent, Gloucestershire, GL18 1DQ
t: 01531 822669
www.strawberryhillvineyard.co.uk

Cornwall
Struddicks Farm Vineyard
Grape varieties: Seyval Blanc, Auxerrois, Pinot Noir, Pinot Noir Précoce, Rondo, Chardonnay.

a: Deviock Wine Company, Looe Hill, St. Martin, Looe, Cornwall, PL13 1PA
t: 01752 812178

Devon
Summermoor Vineyard
Grape varieties: MA, Chardonnay, Siegerrebe, Rondo, Phoenix.

a: Marsh Cottage, Mill Lane, Burrington, Umberleigh, Devon, EX32 0QH. Location of vineyard: Hearson, Swimbridge, Barnstaple, Devon, EX32 0QH | t: 01769 520776

Somerset
The Somerset Distillery
Somerset's only apple distillery and traditional cider house. Copper stills, huge barrels & cider brandy and ciders to sample from the farm's own orchards. Visitors are welcome to sample all of the above.

a: Pass Vale Farm, Burrow Hill, Kingsbury Episcopi, Martock, Somerset, TA12 6BU
t: 01460 240782 | www.ciderbrandy.co.uk

Gloucestershire
Thornbury Castle Vineyard
Currently growing 0.2 hectares of Muller Thurgau vines. The wine is produced by Three Choirs Vineyard and sold in Thornbury Castle's restaurant. It is a medium-dry, white wine.

a: Castle Street, Thornbury, South Gloucestershire, BS35 1HH | t: 01454 281182
www.thornburycastle.co.uk

Gloucestershire
Three Choirs Vineyard
Three Choirs Vineyard is a friendly way to discover how classic wines have once again taken root in England after an absence of nearly 900 years. We invite you to stroll among 70 acres of vines.

a: Newent, Gloucestershire, GL18 1LS
t: 01531 890223
www.three-choirs-vineyards.co.uk

Dorset

Timber Lane Vineyard

Grape varieties: unknown.

a: 19 Barnes Way, Dorchester, Dorset, DT2 2DZ
Location of vineyard: Timber Lane, Dorchester, Dorset,
DT2 9DS | t: 01305 880069

Devon

Torview Wines

Planted in 2007 with the first significant harvest
in 2010. Produce around 2000 bottles of red wine.
Grape varieties: Dornfelder, Pinot Noir, Pinot Noir
Précoce, Acolon.

a: Beara Farm, Sheepwash, Beaworthy, Devon, EX21 5PB
t: 01409 895773
www.torviewwines.co.uk

Cornwall

Trevibban Mill Vineyard

Grape varieties: Seyval Blanc, Reichensteiner,
Dornfelder, Pinot Noir Précoce.

a: St. Issey, Wadebridge, Cornwall, PL27 7SE
t: 01841 532186

Wiltshire

Tytherley Vineyard

Wall enclosed vineyard immediately north of
the garden house. Grape varieties: Bacchus,
MT, Triomphe.

a: The Garden House, West Tytherley, Salisbury, Wiltshire,
SP5 1NL
t: 01794 340644

Devon

Watchcombe Vineyard

Owned by Lyme Bay Winery.
See Lyme Bay Winery for more information.
Watchcombe has the grape varieties of Seyval Blanc
and Pinot Noir. Planted 2009.

a: Lyme Bay Winery, Shute, Axminster, Devon, EX13 7PW
Location of vineyard: Watchcombe, Shute, Axminster, Devon,
EX13 7QN | t: 01297 551355 | www.lymebaywinery.co.uk

Somerset

Wayford Vineyard

Grape varieties: Pinot Noir

a: Wayfrod West Country Wines, Dunsham Lane, Wayford,
Crewkerne, Somerset, TA18 8QN
t: 01460 74321

Devon

Weir Quay Vineyard

Grape varieties: Kernling.

a: Cleave Farm, Weir Quay, Bere Alston, Devon, PL20 7BS
t: 01822 840480

Devon

Willhayne Vineyard

Award winning winemaker located in East Devon.
Received a highly commended award in the 2007
English & Welsh Wines of the Year Awards. The 2010
awards gave them a Silver for 'Dry White 2009'.

a: Willhayne Cottage, Colyton, Devon, EX24 6DT
t: 01297 553463

Gloucestershire

Winner Hill Vineyard

Planted in 2001 with the first significant harvest
in 2006. Producing around 2000 bottles a year for
friends and family. Grape varieties: Bacchus, Seyval
Blanc, Regent. In 2009 produced a sparkling wine.

a: Winner Hill Farm, Alderly, Gloucestershite, GL12 7QT
t: 01453 844237

Dorset

Wodetone Vineyard

Nigel & Mary Riddle run Wodetone vineyard. Planted
only a few years ago they are hoping to harvest the
first crop from their 10,000 vines this autumn, ready
to make English sparkling wine.

a: Spence Farm, Wootton Fitzpaine, Dorset, DT6 6DF
t: 01297 561364

Somerset

Wootton Vineyard

Well-drained soil and a south-facing slope prove ideal conditions for North Woottons vineyard located near Shepton Mallet. Owned by George Martin and his gang of grape-pickers.

a: Bagborough Winery, Pylle, Shepton Mallet, BA4 6SX.
Location of vineyard: North Wootton, Shepton Mallet,
Somerset, BA4 4AG | t: 01749 831146

Somerset

Wraxall Vineyard

Lying on a beautiful warm South-facing slopes between the Mendip and Quantock Hills. It is the perfect location for growing a variety of grapes that capture the very essence of English wine.

a: Wraxall, Nr Shepton Mallet, Somerset, BA4 6RQ
t: 01749 860331
www.wraxallvineyard.co.uk

Wiltshire

Wylye Valley Vineyard

Wylye Valley, planted in the early 90's, is already starting to gain a serious reputation. The attractive labels and wines, with names such as 'Teal & Green' and 'Watson's Fancy' follow a fly fishing theme.

a: Sutton End, Crockerton, Warminster, BA12 8BB
t: 01985 846767
www.ukvines.co.uk/vineyards/wylye.htm

Devon

Yearlstone Vineyard

Roger and Juliet have owned the vineyard since 1991 and have built: A private house, a vineyard shop, a complete winery to make the wine onsite, a café with outdoor terrace.

a: Bickleigh, Tiverton, Devon, EX16 8RL
t: 01884 855700
www.yearlstone.co.uk

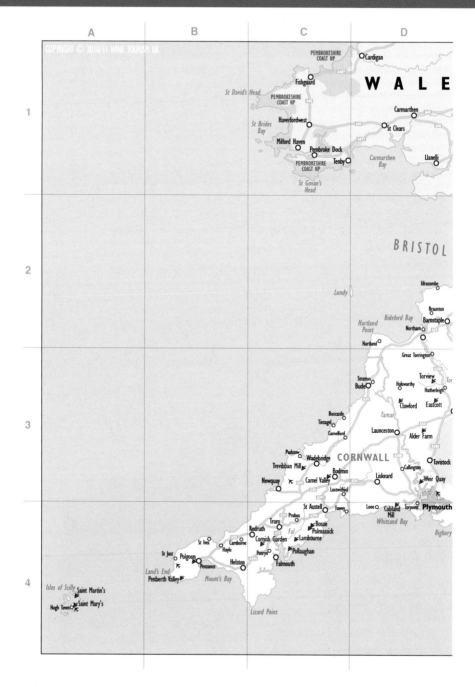

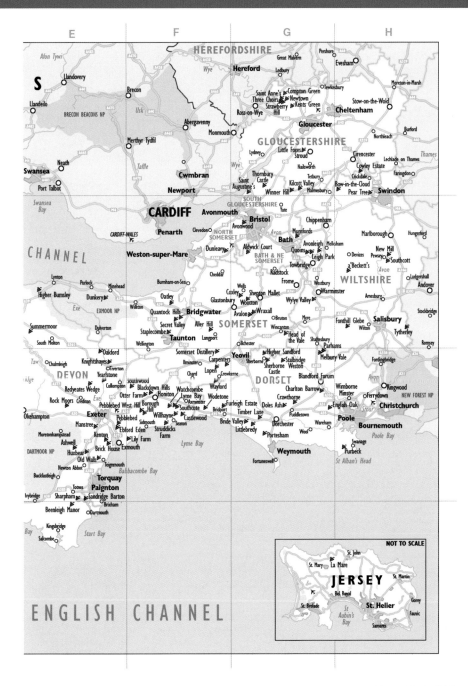

CORNWALL

Daphne Du Maurier's Smugglers at Jamaica Inn

Set in one of the most breathtaking locations in Cornwall. Built in 1750 as a coaching inn and used by travellers crossing Bodmin Moor some of which were smuggling brandy and tea into the UK!, It is also thought that the Inn did a considerable trade in rum, hence how it got its name. In 1778 the Inn was extended to include a coach house. Housing one of the finest and most extensive collections of smuggling artefacts in the UK.

a: Jamaica Inn Courtyard, Bolventor, Launceston, Cornwall, PL15 7TS
t: 01566 86250 | **www.jamaicainn.co.uk**

CORNWALL

Goonhilly Station

Goonhilly Station is a unique experience which attracts over 80,000 visitors every year and has over 60 Giant Satellite dishes. Set in the dramatic landscape of the Lizard Peninsula the giant dishes of Goonhilly Satellite Earth Station rise up from the heathland. Through the Visitor Centre and guided bus tour, explore the history of communication at the largest and oldest satellite station in the World. The attraction is popular with visitors of all ages.

a: The Visitor Centre, Goonhilly Downs, Helston,Cornwall, TR12 6LQ
t: 01872 325602 | **www.goonhilly.bt.com**

CORNWALL

Land's End

Land's End is the most South-Westerly point of the British Isles and one of Cornwall's most popular tourist attractions. Many generations have come to have their photo taken under the famous signpost and to look out to the amazing views stretching across to the Isles of Scilly and beyond. The breathtaking scenery is only the beginning of what there is to see and do, with 5 fantastic visitor attractions!

a: Lands End, Sennen, Penzance,Cornwall, TR19 7AA
t: 08717 200044 | **www.landsend-landmark.co.uk**

CORNWALL

The Eden Project

The Eden Project is an unforgettable experience in a breathtaking epic location. Eden is a gateway into the fascinating world of plants and people and a vibrant reminder of how we need each other for our mutual survival. Its home is a dramatic global garden the size of thirty football pitches, nestling like a lost world in a crater overlooking St Austell Bay. It is a place to tell a hundred plant stories from cocoa and coffee to bananas and rubber.

a: Bodelva, St Austell, Cornwall, PL24 2SG
t: 01726 811900 | **www.edenproject.com**

DEVON

Babbacombe Model Village

Babbacombe Model Village has captured the essence of England's past, present and future in thousands of miniature buildings, people and vehicles. Feel on top of the world when you take time out from the hustle and bustle of everyday life to visit this fascinating attraction. Visit during the day or evening with lots to see and do for all ages.

a: Hampton Avenue, Babbacombe, Torquay, Devon, TQ1 3LA
t: 01803 315315 | **www.babbacombemodelvillage.co.uk**

Exeter Cathedral

DEVON

One of England's most beautiful medieval cathedrals and one of the finest examples of decorated Gothic architecture in this country. Famous for its two Norman towers; impressive west front carvings and the longest unbroken stretch of Gothic vaulting in the world. Of note are the Minstrels' Gallery, the 15th Century Astronomical Clock, a complete set of Misercords and the highly decorated tombs, bosses and corbels. Exhibitions throughout the year.

a: The Cloisters, Exeter, Devon, EX1 1HS
t: 01392 285983 | www.exeter-cathedral.org.uk

Buckfast Abbey

DEVON

Buckfast Abbey is home to a Roman Catholic community of Benedictine monks. It is believed that there has been an abbey on the site since 1018 built by King Canute. The impressive grounds have immaculate lawns and fine old stone buildings.

a: Buckfastleigh, Devon, TQ11 0EE
t: 01364 65500 | www.buckfast.org

Golden Hind Museum Ship

DEVON

Sir Francis Drake was the first Captain to sail around the world. Step back in time and relive his incredible voyage 1577-1580 onboard this full sized replica of the Golden Hind. Permanently moored in the picturesque harbour and fishing village of Brixham. Explore below decks and experience the hardships of the 80 crew and wonder at the incredible treasure recovered and fascinating discoveries made. A great visit for all the family; superb value

a: The Quay, Brixham Harbour, Brixham, Devon, TQ5 8AW
t: 01803 856223 | www.goldenhind.co.uk

Avon Valley Railway

BRISTOL, SOMERSET

More than just a train ride, offering a whole new experience for some or a nostalgic memory for others. It´s a real treat for the whole family! Based at Bitton Station, midway between Bristol and Bath, this former Midland Railway station has been painstakingly restored from a derelict state to provide visitors with refreshment, a railway shop, a pleasant garden, and outdoor seating.

a: Bitton Station Bath Road, Bitton, Bristol, BS30 6HD
t: 01179 325538 | www.avonvalleyrailway.org

Bristol Zoo Gardens

BRISTOL, SOMERSET

A visit to Bristol Zoo Gardens is a trip to an amazing world of animals, all set within award winning 12 acre gardens. Meet over 450 species of exotic, endangered and just plain cute animals from the four corners of the globe. Visit the primates in Monkey Jungle, stroll through the lemur garden, come face to face with penguins/seals. Other favourites include Gorilla Island, Asiatic lions, Twilight World, an Aquarium, Reptile house, Bug World and Butterfly Forest.

a: Clifton, Bristol, BS8 3HA
t: 01179 738951 | www.bristolzoo.org.uk

BRISTOL, SOMERSET

SS Great Britain

Brunel's masterpiece of ship design and engineering, is housed in the original 'Great Western Dock' in which she was built in 1843. The ship is the world's first great ocean liner - before she was built, long distance sea voyages that were made on wooden sailing ships were dangerous and unpredictable. Sea travel took a great leap forward when famous Victorian engineer Isambard Kingdom Brunel applied his remarkable skill to the problem.

a: Great Western Dock, Gas Ferry Road, Bristol, BS1 6TY
t: 01179 260680 | **www.ssgreatbritain.org**

SOMERSET

Cheddar Caves and Gorge

Cheddar Gorge, with its 450ft high cliffs, is the most dramatic geological formation in Somerset. Created by ice age melt-waters, it was once an ancient river bed. Its karst limestone cliffs and beautiful caves are now home to Peregrine falcons and rare Horseshoe bats. Both Gough's Cave and Cox's Cave contain passages, festooned with stalactites and stalagmites. There is a Museum, a Lookout Tower, The Explorers Cafe-Bar and Cargo Cult Shop.

a: Cheddar, Somerset, BS27 3QF
t: 01934 742343 | **www.cheddarcaves.co.uk**

SOMERSET

Glastonbury Abbey

Step through time with our wide range of events. From May to October, immerse yourself in the sights, sounds and smells of medieval living, when the Abbey's fascinating 2000 year history is brought to life by knowledgeable living history guides. They will tell of Glastonbury's reputation as the richest monastery in England and reveal its fascinating connection with the legendary King Arthur. Explore the grounds, discover the wildlife and bring a picnic!

a: Abbey Gatehouse, Magdelene Street, Glastonbury, Somerset, BA6 9EL
t: 01458 832267 | **www.glastonburyabbey.com**

SOMERSET

Jane Austen Centre

Jane Austen is perhaps the best known and best loved of Bath's many famous residents and visitors. The Centre is a new permanent exhibition, which tells the story of Jane's Bath experience and has been created with the guidance of local members of the Jane Austen Society and authorities on Jane Austen. It aims to not only be informative, but exciting. With knowledgeable staff, it makes the perfect starting point to an exploration of Jane Austen's Bath.

a: 40 Gay Street, Bath, Bath & Northeast Somerset, BA1 2NT
t: 01225 443000 | **www.janeausten.co.uk**

SOMERSET

Roman Baths

Around Britain's only hot spring, the Romans built a magnificent temple and bathing complex that still flows with natural hot water. See the water's source, meet Roman costumed characters every day and hear the stories of those who lived and worked here 2,000 years ago. Audio guides in 8 languages, with a special one for children in English and French, are included in the admission price. Open until 10pm, last entry 9pm, during July and August.

a: Abbey Church Yard, Bath, Somerset, BA1 1LZF
t: 01225 477785 | **www.romanbaths.co.uk**

SOMERSET

Seaquarium

Located on the promenade sea front in Weston Super Mare - close encounters with our colourful creatures! Come along and see some of the weirdest, most fascinating and deadliest animals on the planet all in one incredible family visit. Walk under the waves, see sharks, eels, rays, Seahorse, Lionfish and many, many more creatures close up! Children can take part in the Discovery Trail Quiz and we have daily Touch & Talk Demonstrations!

a: Marine Parade, Weston-super-Mare, Somerset, BS23 1BE BL
t: 01934 613361 | www.seaquarium.co.uk

SOMERSET

Tower Tour at Bath Abbey

Bath Abbey is the last of the great medieval churches of England. The West Front is unique as it depicts the dream that inspired the Abbey's founder, Bishop Oliver King, to pull down the ruined Norman cathedral and raise the present building on its foundations. Worship has taken place on the site of today's Abbey for over one thousand years and continues to this day.

a: Abbey Churchyard, Bath, Somerset, BA1 1LY
t: 01225 422462 | www.bathabbey.org

SOMERSET

Wells Cathedral

One of England's most beautiful cathedrals. Nestling at the foot of the Mendip Hills in Somerset it is the centrepiece of the medieval city of Wells, the smallest city in England. Its West Front still carries almost three hundred medieval statues and the cathedral houses the second oldest mechanical working clock in the world where at every quarter hour four horsemen joust and the same one has had his head cut off for over six hundred years!

a: Cathedral Green, Wells, Somerset BA5 2UE
t: 01749 674483 | www.wellscathedral.org.uk

WILTSHIRE

Stonehenge

Stonehenge stands impressively as a prehistoric monument of unique importance, a World Heritage Site, surrounded by remains of ceremonial and domestic structures - some older than the monument itself. Many of these features - earthworks, burial mounds and other circular monuments - are accessible by road or public footpath. visit the superb gift shop and Cafe. Audio tour in ten languages; disabled access; hearing loop and Braille guide available.

a: Near Amesbury, Wiltshire, SP4 7DE
t: 08703 331181 | www.english-heritage.org.uk

WILTSHIRE

Wardour Castle

Set in the Wiltshire countryside beside a lake, Old Wardour Castle, was once one of the most daring and innovative homes in Britain. It was built in the 14th century as a lightly fortified luxury residence for comfortable living and lavish entertainment. Today the castle ruin provides a relaxed, romantic day out for couples and families. An audio tour is included in the price. Climb the turrets and experience the movie, Robin Hood Prince of Thieves, which was filmed here.

a: Near Tisbury, Wiltshire, SP3 6RR
t: 01747 870487 | www.english-heritage.org.uk

⚑ Food & Wine Festivals
South West & Channel Isles

BRISTOL SOMERSET

Bristol Wine and Food Fair | July
www.bristolwineandfood.co.uk
Address: Lloyds Amphitheatre & Waterfront Square, Bristol, BS1 5LL | **Tel:** 01173 169736

CORNWALL

Boscastle Food, Art and Crafts Festival | 1st October 2011 - 2nd October 2011
www.boscastlefestival.co.uk
Address: Boscastle, Cornwall | **Tel:** 01840 250010 | **email:** sales@castang-wines.co.uk

---

CORNWALL

Cornwall Food & Drink Festival | September
www.cornwallfoodanddrinkfestival.com
Address: Centre of Truro, Cornwall | **Tel:** 01840 250010 | **email:** info@cornwallfoodanddrinkfestival.com

---

CORNWALL

Falmouth Oyster Festival | 13th October 2011 - 16th October 2011
www.falmouthoysterfestival.co.uk
Address: Events Square, Falmouth, Cornwall | **Tel:** 01326 312300 | **email:** info@falmouthtic.co.uk

---

CORNWALL

Newquay Fish Festival | September/October
www.newquayfishfestival.co.uk
Address: Newquay Harbor, Cornwall

CORNWALL

Newlyn Fish Festival | August
www.newlynfishfestival.org.uk
Address: North Pier, Newlyn, Cornwall, TR18 5JB | **Tel:** 07518 603955 | **email:** info@newlynfishfestival.org.uk

---

CORNWALL

St Ives Food and Drink Festival | 18th June 2011 - 19th June 2011
www.stivesfoodanddrinkfestival.co.uk
Address: St Ives Town Centre, Cornwall | **Tel:** 08456 038456 | **email:** info@mercury-pr.co.uk

---

DEVON

Exeter Food and Drink Festival | 29th April 2011 - 1st May 2011
www.exeterfoodanddrinkfestival.co.uk
Address: Regal courtyard of Exeter Castle and the surrounding Northernhay Gardens, Devon | **Tel:** 01392 278801

DORSET

Christchurch Food Fest | 6th May 2011 - 13 May 2011
www.christchurchfoodfest.co.uk
Address: Christchurch, Dorset | **Tel:** 01202 471780 | **email:** enquiries@christchurchtourism.info

---

DORSET

Feast of Dorset | 17th September 2011 - 18th September 2011
www.feastofdorset.com
Address: Deans Court, Wimborne, Dorset | **Tel:** 01202 880515 | **email:** info@feastofdorset.co.uk

---

GLOUCESTERSHIRE

Tetbury Food Festival | September
www.tetburyfooddrinkfestival.com
Address: Tetbury, Gloucestershire | **Tel:** 08712 30559

WILTSHIRE

Salisbury Food and Drink Festival | 2nd/3rd weekend in September 2011
www.salisburyfestival.co.uk
Address: Salisbury city centre, Wiltshire | **Tel:** 01722 332241

☐ Notes:

....
....
....
....
....
....
....
....
....
....
....
....
....
....
....
....
....
....
....

wine
Tourism UK

South East & London

✚ England

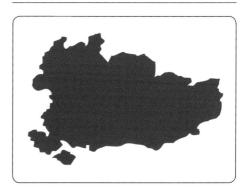

Berkshire, Buckinghamshire, East Sussex, Hampshire, Isle of Wight, Kent, London, Oxfordshire, Surrey, West Sussex

South East & London

The South East of England covers Berkshire, Buckinghamshire, East Sussex, Hampshire, Isle of Wight, Kent, Oxfordshire, Surrey, West Sussex and London.

With nearly 200 wine estates the south east and London is the largest wine growing region in the country. The South East has played an important role in the military history of Britain from great naval battles to world wars and there are sites across the South East that pay tribute to this past. Strong royal connections, royal residences, stately homes, castles, fortresses and momentous events mean the region has a wealth of places to visit.

Relax in the tranquil settings of some of the most beautiful gardens and parks, stroll through the streets, villages, towns and cities and experience the architectural heritage on offer.

Selected vineyards
Chiltern Valley Vineyard (Oxford shire)
Bookers (West Sussex)
Chapel Down (Kent)

Chiltern Valley Vineyard
Set in an area of outstanding natural beauty, Old Luxters is home to 'Chiltern Valley Wines', its vineyard, winery, brewery and cellar shop. Their first vines were planted in 1982 on the slopes of the Chiltern Hills,

surrounded by beech woodland and overlooking the beautiful Hambleden Valley near Henley-on-Thames, Oxfordshire, UK.

Their modern production, bottling and labelling facilities, cellar shop and wine vats are all housed in traditional farm buildings.

Since their first harvest in 1984, they have produced an increasing range of fine, award-winning English wines to delight the eye and excite the palate. With over 70 trophies, awards and commendations they have gained an enviable reputation for quality both here and abroad.

Bookers
Take the opportunity to see what they do and try one of their various Tours and Tastings. Visit an English Vineyard in Bolney, mid-way between Gatwick and Brighton, taste their fabulous sparkling, red and white wines.

In the heart of rural Sussex, one of Britain's most beautiful southern counties, lays Bolney Wine Estate, a vineyard which carries on a tradition brought to

Britain by the Romans nearly 2,000 years ago. Located in the village, Bolney Wine Estate, the vision of Janet and Rodney Pratt, is situated on a hill which was part of the Butting Hill One Hundred, listed in the Domesday Book. Village tradition has it that the Prince Regent was a frequent visitor to Bolney when travelling to Brighton, staying at Bolney Lodge of which Bolney Wine Estate formed a part in the 19th Century.

Chapel Down
Named Best Leisure and Tourism Business 2010 at the annual Kent Excellence in Business Awards which took place on the 1st July 2010.

They don't tend to talk about the generalities of English wine; they talk about Chapel Down; because they are different. It's not just the gold medals and awards that makes their jobs such a pleasure, but the real excitement they get from winning friends and converts. If you have never visited the winery and vineyard in Tenterden, then give it a try. No matter what your experience of wine has been, you're guaranteed to be surprised and delighted.

Selected destinations:
Brighton: One of England's favourite seaside cities, with a wonderful, cosmopolitan vibe, you're sure to see and meet all walks of life. If you're lucky enough to be in town at the beginning of March then take in, the one night a year only, 'Brighton the Musical' at the Dome. Brighton is historic, elegant and offbeat and the perfect place for a break.

Canterbury: Historic cathedral city, 'Pilgrims' are welcomed to this walled city for its shopping, restaurants and wealth of visitor attractions. The Cathedral, St Augustine's Abbey and St Martin's Church form the World Heritage Site, but there are many other attractions in the city too; river tours, walking tours, museums and much, much more.

Dover: Famous for its white cliffs and known as the gateway to Europe this channel port welcomes millions of visitors from all over the globe every year. White Cliffs Country is brimming with things to see and do. It has a unique place in history and you could spend weeks exploring castles, museums and beautiful gardens.

Isle of Wight: Steeped in history with 60 miles of stunning unspoilt scenery and a wealth of attractions, the Isle of Wight has something for everyone. From historic sites to natural delights, music festivals and major national events, it is a unique holiday destination.

> 'Strong royal connections, royal residences, stately homes, castles, fortresses and momentous events means the region has a wealth of places to go and places to see.'

The New Forest: There is something for everyone in The New Forest, whether you're looking to relax, explore or just enjoy, The New Forest is the ideal location. Created by William the Conqueror in 1079, the New Forest is a place of wilderness heathland, dappled woodland and thatched hamlets.

Oxford: The City of Dreaming Spires and Inspector Morse, Oxford is famous the world over for its University and its place in history. For over 800 years it has been a home to royalty and scholars. This ancient University City is both timeless and modern, its dreaming tranquil college quadrangles coexisting with lively arts venues, bustling shops and fashionable restaurants.

Windsor: Windsor is a town full of history and charm, dominated by Windsor Castle which is over 900 years old and the largest inhabited castle in the world. The town boasts fine shopping and dining, sports, leisure activities and events.

Add: Hawkhurst Rd, Cripps Corner, Robertsbridge, East Sussex, TN32 5SA
Tel: 01580 830715
Email: enquiries@englishorganicwine.co.uk
www.englishorganicwine.co.uk

Postcode (GPS): TN32 5SA
Map Reference: F3

Sedlescombe Organic Vineyard

Introduction:

England's first organic wine producers Roy and Irma cook, of Sedlescombe Vineyard, in East Sussex, have set themselves a new challenge...Biodynamic cultivation.

The Cooks, who planted the first organic English vineyard in 1979, started using Demeter standards set by the Biodynamic Association in 2010. Released Easter 2011, these wines are be the first in England to be Demeter certified. With this move Sedlescombe is joining a worldwide grouping of prestigious Biodynamic vineyards known as 'Return to Terroir' who are attempting to emphasise the individuality of style and flavour of their wines. By meeting the additional demands that mark Biodynamic out from organic, the Cooks expect to give their wines an extra edge of quality. They are convinced that even better Sedlescombe wines will be the result.

Roy chooses organic techniques for their benefit to the environment and wild-life habitats on his farm as well as for the higher quality of the end product, the latter evident from some of the awards attained for his wines.
Their wines range from Sparkling (both white and rosé), oak-matured Red, and whites of all styles from dry to dessert. Also, Fruit wines, Fruit Juices, Liqueurs and Cider are all made organically on-site.

Opening times:

Mon-Sun, 10.30-17.30, Easter to Christmas.
Mon-Fri, Jan-Mar, noon to dusk.

TOP THREE WINES

2009 OLD VINE (ORGANIC)

Made exclusively from our 30+ year old Reichensteiner vines planted in 1979. A special edition Old Vine (Vieille Vigne) wine celebrating our 30th anniversary! An elegant, light wine reminiscent of ripe bramley apples and limes, with exotic grassy flavours. **11.5% vol. Price: £12.95**

2009 REGENT (ORGANIC)

Matured in barrique oak. Juicy, fruit driven, ripe red colour with damson, plum and morello cherry on the nose. Medium bodied flavour of black cherries and raspberries, soft supple tannins, enhanced with oak complexity.
11.5% vol. Price: £16.95

CUVÉE BODIAM BRUT SPARKLING

Our White Fizz is produced from classic 'whole bunch pressed' Seyval Blanc grapes from our Bodiam Castle vineyard. Heady bouquet of apples and limes with a rich palate of tropical fruit.
12.5% vol. Price: £25.00

ATTRACTIONS

A visit to this beautifully located vineyard, in the heart of '1066 Country' is a rich experience of all things organic/biodynamic. You can follow the Vineyard & Woodland Nature Trail, see the self-built Eco house, visit the Winery, see the huge antique cast iron and oak grape press in the shop, and taste remarkable wines full of character and style - just as Nature intended!

Add: Twyford, Berkshire, RG10 0BN
Tel: 01189 340176 | **Fax:** 01189 320914
Email: info@stanlakepark.com
www.stanlakepark.com

Postcode (GPS): RG10 0BN
Map Reference: C2

Stanlake Park Wine Estate

TOP THREE WINES

KINGS FUMÉ

A big, bold, rich, dry wine, made in French oak. Sophisticated and complex, this wine has vanilla, oaky, buttery characteristics. Made with Ortega, Regner, Scheurebe.

PINOT BLUSH

Made from 3 different Pinots. this wine has a fruity, refreshing, off-dry, rose-petal taste. There are lush tones of wild strawberries and summer fruits.

STANLAKE BRUT

The flagship sparkling wine of the Estate, with a rich, sophisticated, complex bouquet, made with the traditional champagne grapes of Chardonnay, Pinot Noir and Pinot Meunier.

THE CELLAR SHOP

Introduction:

Stanlake Park Wine Estate lies in the heart of the Thames Valley in Berkshire, close to Twyford, Ruscombe and Hurst. It has a rich history going back to 1166 and the current Manor House, built by Nicholas Stanlake, dates from around 1590. The 150 acres Estate is home to a wide variety of vines including Bacchus, Pinot Noir, Chardonnay and Gewurztraminer. It was planted around 30 years ago and produces many of England's award-winning wines, such as Kings Fumé, Bacchus, Hinton Grove, Regatta, Pinot Blush, Ruscombe red, Heritage Brut and Stanlake Brut. The Estate also makes the only Kir Royale in England made entirely from fruit (grapes and blackcurrants) grown on the Estate.

Quite simply, we have a passion for wine at Stanlake. Our winemaker has the experience of 20 vintages. Our team is completely dedicated to producing the best wine. Twenty English wines, mostly from Stanlake, are available in our Shop. We also sell everything to do with wine – branded boxes, books and bags, coolers and closures, and all other wine accoutrements. We have tables to enjoy wine both inside and also in the Vineyard Gardens. The new Cellar Shop is open every day – see times below. We also have many special events – please check our website for details. We look forward to welcoming you at Stanlake!

Opening times:
Mon-Sat 10.00-17.00
Sun Noon-17.00

South East & London

Map	Wine estate	Tel number	Opening times
B4	Adgestone Vineyard	01983 402503	10-5.30 everyday from Easter-oct, winter hours vary
D2	Alara Wholefoods Vineyard	02073 879303	Not open to the public
D3	Albourne Vineyard	07801 665159	Not open to the public
D3	Albury Vineyard	01483 229159	Not open to the public
D3	Alexandra Road Allotments	01372 729601	Not open to the public
D3	Ashey Vineyard	01983 617007	Not open to the public
E3	Bad Boys Vineyard	----------------	Not open to the public
E3	Barnsgate Manor Vineyard	01825 713366	Open to the public
G3	Barnsole Vineyard	01304 812530	Apr-Oct everyday 10.30-17.0, Nov-Mar everyday 10.20-16.00pm, Closed 25th Dec-4th Jan
F3	Battle Wine Estate	01424 870449	Not open to the public
A4	Beaulieu Vineyard	01590 614621	By appointment only
B3	Beeches Hill Vineyard	01489 892356	Not open to the public
E3	Bewl Water Vineyard	01892 782045	Not open to the public
F3	Biddenden Vineyard	01580 291726	Mon-Sat 10.00-17.00, Sun & Bank Holidays 11.00-19.00, closed Sun During Jan & Feb
C2	Binfield Vineyard	01344 411322	Sat 10.00-16.00
A4	Birchenwood Vineyard	023 8081 2595	by appointment only
B3	Bishop's Waltham Vineyard	01489 896803	Not open to the public
D4	Black Dog Hill Vineyard	01273 844338	Not open to the public
E3	Bluebell Vineyard Estates	01825 790395	Not open to the public
F3	Bodiam Vineyard	----------------	Not open to the public
D3	Bookers Vineyard	01444 881575	9.00-16.30
B2	Bothy Vineyard	01865 390067	10.00-17.00 every Fri & Sat, and every first Sun of the month
F3	Bourne Farm Vineyard	01580 850296	Open to the public, visitors welcome to walk the vineyards and farm at any time
E4	Breaky Bottom Vineyard	01273 476427	Open by appointment only, with free wine tasting
A1	Bridewell Organic Gardens	01993 864530	Open only to Mental Health sufferers
B2	Brightwell Vineyard	01491 832354	Fri-Sun 12.00-18.00, other times by appointment
D3	Brinsbury College Vineyard	01903 814998	Not open to the public
G3	Broadway Green Farm Vineyard	01227 700058	Not open to the public
F3	Budds Farm Vineyard	01797 270245	Not open to the public
D3	Burnt House Wines	07980 306575	Not open to the public
E3	Burwash Weald Vineyard	01424 441979	By appointment only
F4	Carr Taylor Vineyard	01424 752501	Open 7 days a week 10.00-17.00, closed 25th Dec-1st Jan
A3	Chalk Vale Vineyard	01798 813989	Not open to the public
G3	Chalksole Estate Vineyard	01304 828881	By appointment only
D4	Chanctonbury Vineyard	01903 892721	Not open to the public
F3	Chapel Down Wines	01580 763033	Everyday 10.00-17.00

Map	Wine estate	Tel number	Opening times
F3	Charles Palmer Vineyard	01797 226216	Open to the public
A1	Childrey Manor Vineyard	01235 751244	Not open the public
C2	Chiltern Valley Vineyard	01491 638330	Shop open weekdays 9.30-18.00, Mon-Fri 11.00-18.00, Sat-Sun, 11.00-17.00, closed in winter
E3	Chingley Oast Vineyard	01580 879528	Not open to the public
C1	Claydon Vineyard	01296 730730	Not open to the public
D2	Clocktower Vineyard	----------------	Not open to the public
A3	Coach House Vineyard	01794 323345	By appointment only
A3	Cottonworth Vineyard	01264 860221	By appointment only
D4	Court Garden Vineyard	01273 844479	By appointment only
B3	Court Lane Vineyard	01962 773391	By appointment only
A3	Danebury Vineyard	01264 781851	By appointment only
E3	Davenport Vineyard	01892 852380	Not open to public
C2	Daws Hill Vineyard	01494 483358	By appointment only
B3	Deans Farm Vineyard	01730 269111	Not open to the public
D2	Decanter Magazine Vineyard	02031 485000	Not open to the public
D3	Denbies Wine Estate	01306 876616	Jan-Mar Mon-Fri 9.30-17.00, Sat 9.30-17.30, Sun 10.00-17.30, Apr-Dec Mon-Sat 9.30-17.30, Sun 10.00-17.30
D4	Ditchling Vineyard	----------------	See Plumpton College for contact details
C2	Dropmore Vineyard	01628 664376	By appointment only
B3	Dunley Vineyard	01256 892876	Not open to the public
B3	East Meon Vineyard	01730 823274	Not open to the public
F3	East Sutton Vine Garden	01622 844811	Open Thur-Sat, other times by appointment
C3	Ebernoe Vineyard	01428 707269	Not open to the public
G3	Elham Valley Vineyard	01227 832022	Tue-Fri 10.30-16.00, Sat-Sun 11-17.00
E4	English Wine Centre	01323 870164	Open 10.00-17.00
B3	Exton Park Estate Vineyard	01489 877834	By appointment only
C2	Fawley Vineyard	01491 577998	By appointment only
C3	Fernhurst Vineyard	01428 654120	By appointment only
A1	Floreys Vineyard	01476 550191	By appointment only
F3	Forstal Farm Vineyard	02073 036321	Not open to the public
D2	Forty Hall Vineyard	02088 001358	Community vineyard
F3	Friday Street Vineyard	01622 842162	Open by appointment
D3	Godstone Vineyard	01883 744590	Vineyard & Shop open all year round
D2	Goose Green Vineyard	02086 881797	Not open to the public
A1	Grange Farm Vineyard	01608 737313	By appointment only
C3	Greyfriars Vineyard	01483 813712	Set open weekends during summer months
E3	Groombridge Place Vineyard	01892 861444	Open to the public
F3	Gusbourne Estate Vineyard	01233 758666	By appointment only
C2	Hale Valley Vineyard	01296 623730	By appointment only

South East & London

Map	Wine estate	Tel number	Opening times
C4	Halnaker Vineyard	01903 730140	Not open to the public
B4	Hambledon Vineyard	01239 2632066	By appointment only
F3	Harbourne Vineyard	01797 270420	Open to the public
E3	Harden Vineyard	01892 870221	Not open to the public
B3	Hattingley Valley Vineyard	01256 389188	Not open to the public
B2	Hendred Vineyard	01235 820081	Selected dates throughout the year for wine tasting
E4	Henners Vineyard	01323 831746	By appointment only
E3	Herons Ghyll Estate	07956 388272	By appointment only
E3	Hidden Spring Vineyard	01435 812640	By appointment only
D3	High Clandon Vineyard	01483 225660	Not open to the public
D4	Highdown Vineyard	01903 500663	Open to the public Tue-Sun 10.00-17.30
E3	Hobdens Vineyards	----------------	Not open to the public
E3	Horsmonden Vineyard	----------------	By appointment only
F3	Hush Heath Estate Vineyard	02074 799500	Not open to the public
D3	Iron Railway Vineyard	01737 551829	By appointment only
A3	Jays Farm Vineyard	01794 511314	By appointment only
C3	Jenkyn Place Vineyard	02077 363102	By appointment only
G3	Kempes Hall Vineyard	01233 812217	Not open to the public
F3	Kit's Coty Vineyard	----------------	Not open to the public
E3	Lamberhurst Vineyard	01892 890412	Open to the public
B3	Laverstoke Park Vineyard	01256 772659	Open to the public
A3	Leckford Estate Vineyard	01264 810585	Open to the public
B2	Linch Hill Vineyard	07775 583737	By appointment only
F3	Little Knoxbridge Vineyard	01580 893643	By appointment only
B4	Little West End Farm Vineyard	+33 (0)326 577704	By appointment only
C3	Lurgashall Winery	01428 707292	Not open to the public
C2	Magpie Lane Vineyard	01476 550191	Not open to the public
C1	Manor Fields Vineyard	01296 641178	Open to the public
F3	Marden Organic Vineyard	07956 163519	By appointment only
A4	Marlings Vineyard	01590 681606	By appointment only
F3	Mayshaves Vineyard	01233 820286	Not open the public
A2	Meadowgrove Vineyard	01235 767913	By appointment only
E2	Meopham Valley Vineyard	01474 812727	Open Fri-Sun 11.00-Dusk
F3	Methersham Vineyard	01797 260491	Not open to the public
D2	Mill Hill Village Vineyard	02089 592214	Not open to the public
E4	Mount Harry Vines	01273 474456	By appointment only
E3	Mount Vineyard	01959 524008	By appointment only
G3	Mystole Members Vineyard	01227 738348	By appointment only
G3	National Fruit Collection - Brogdale	01795 536250	Open to the public
D3	Netherland Vineyard	01798 813989	Not open to the public

Map	Wine estate	Tel number	Opening times
F4	New House Farm Vineyard	01424 752501	Not open to the public
D2	North Court Farm Vineyard	02089 796556	Not open to the public
B3	Northbrook Springs	01489 892659	Not open to the public
D3	Nutbourne Lane Vineyard	01798 813989	Not open to the public
D3	Nutbourne Vineyards	02076 273800	May-Oct Mon-Fri 14.00-17.00, Weekends & Bank Holidays 11.00-17.00
D3	Nyetimber Vineyard	01798 813989	Not open to the public
E2	Olding Manor Vineyard	02076 523151	Not open to the public
D3	Painshill Park Vineyard	01932 868113	Open to the public
C2	Pheasants Ridge Vineyard	01491 576087	Open to the public
D4	Plumpton College Vineyard	01273 890454	Not open to the public
G3	Port Lympne	01303 264647	Open to the public
C3	Primrose Hill Vineyard	01428 643360	Not open to the public
C3	Priors Dean Vineyard	01730 894147	By appointment only
D3	Redfold Farm Vineyard	01798 817202	Not open to the public
D3	RidgeView Wine Estate	01444 241441	Mon-Sat 11.00-16.00
D3	River Walk Vineyard	01798 813989	Not open to the public
D4	Rock Lodge Vineyard	01273 890454	Not open to the public.
D3	Roman Villa Vineyard	01798 813989	Not open to the public.
E3	Rosemary Farm Vineyard	07710 111800	Not open to the public
B4	Rosemary Vineyard	01983 811084	Not open to the public
C2	Rossi Regatta Vineyard	----------------	Not open to the public
A4	Rossiters Vineyard	01983 761616	Apr-Oct Tue-Fri 10.00-16.00, Sat-Sun 10.00-16.00
C3	Rother Valley Vineyard	01730 816888	Not open to the public
D2	Saint Andrew's Vineyard	02089 613029	Not open to the public
F3	Sandhurst Vineyard	01580 850296	Open to the public
F3	Sculdown Vineyard	01424 883127	Open to the public
F3	Sedlescombe Organic Vineyard	01580 830715	Easter-Xmas Mon-Sun 10.30-18.00, Jan-Mar weekends only noon-dusk
A4	Setley Ridge Vineyard	01590 622246	Mon-Sun 10.00-17.00
C2	Shardeloes Vineyard	01494 433333	Not open to the public
E3	Sheffield Park Vineyard	01825 790775	Open daily to the public
D3	Shere Vineyard	01483 203491	By appointment only
A3	Somborne Valley Vineyard	01794 388547	Not open the public
A3	Sour Grapes Vineyard	01794 367300	By appointment only
D4	Southlands Valley Vineyard	01903 892203	Not open to the public
F3	Sedlescombe Vineyard	01580 830715	Open to the public
B2	Springfield Vineyard	01491 612095	Not open to the public
E3	Springfields Vineyard	01825 713421	Not open the public
E3	Squerryes Court Vineyard	01959 562345	Not open to public
E3	Standen Vineyard	01342 328835	By appointment only

South East & London

Map	Wine estate	Tel number	Opening times
F3	Stanford Bridge Vineyard	----------------	Not open to public
C2	Stanlake Park Wine Estate	01189 340176	Mon-Sat 10.00-17.00, Sun Noon-17.00
D3	Stopham Vineyard	01273 566826	By appointment only
D4	Storrington Priory Vineyard	01903 742150	By appointment only
F3	Surrenden Vineyard	01233 840214	Not open to the public
F3	Syndale Valley Vineyards	01795 890693	By appointment only
F3	Tenterden Vineyard		See Chapel Down Wines for contact information
		01580 766111	Open to the public
G3	Terlingham Vineyard	01303 892743	Daily Jun-Aug 14.00-16.00, Apr-May / Sep-Dec 14.00-16.00 weekends only, by appointment only all other times
B2	Theale Vineyard	01189 030903	By appointment only
D3	Thorncroft Vineyard	01642 791792	Not open to the public
F3	Throwley Vineyard	01795 890276	Open to the public
E3	Ticehurst Vineyard	01424 441979	Not open to the public
C4	Tinwood Vineyard	01243 788478	Not open to the public
B4	Titchfield Vineyard	01489 895773	By appointment only
D3	Tullens Vineyard	01798 872108	By appointment only
C1	Tyringham Hall Vineyard	02072 350422	Not open to the public
C3	Upperton Vineyard	01798 343958	Not open to the public
D3	Upperton Vineyard (Nyetimber)	01798 813989	Not open to the public
C2	Virginia Water Vineyard	01189 030903	Open to the public
--	Waitrose Estate	----------------	Not open to the public
D3	Warnham Vale Vineyard	01306 627603	Not open to the public
C3	Warren Farm Vineyard	02031 162959	Not open the public
B4	Webb's Land Vineyard	01329 833633	By appointment only
B3	Westward House Vineyard	01256 851599	Not open to the public
F3	Westwell Wines	01622 862102	Not open to the public
G3	White Horse Vineyard	01303 892743	Daily Jun-Aug 14.00-16.00, Apr-May / Sep-Dec 2-16.00 weekends only, by appointment only all other times
B4	Wickham Vineyards	01329 834042	Mon-Sun 10.30-17.30
B3	Winchester Vineyard	01962 863492	Not open to the public
D3	Wisley Vineyard at the RHS Garden	01483 224234	Open to the public
D4	Wiston Estate Winery	01903 877845	By appointment only
B3	Wooldings Vineyard	01256 771461	Not open to the public
G3	Wootton Park Vineyard	01303 844334	Not open to the public
F2	Wrangling Lane Vineyard	07967 585632	Not open to the public
D4	Wychwood House Vineyard	01403 710328	Not open to the public
B2	Wyfold Vineyard	01491 680495	Not open to the public

Isle of Wight

Adgestone Vineyard

We produce high quality award winning wines and in 1994 our wine was chosen for the dinner for H.M. Queen to celebrate the Anniversary of the D-Day Landings. Offering bed and breakfast.

a: Upper Road, Adgestone, Sandown, Isle of Wight, PO36 0ES | t: 01983 402503
www.adgestonevineyard.co.uk

East Sussex

Albourne Vineyard

Planted in 2005. The first harvest was in 2007 and produced 800 bottles of spakling wine, made by RidgeView. The wine is currently distrubuted between friends and family. Future plans to go commercial!

a: Yew Tree Farm House, Church Lane, Ditchling, East Sussex, BN6 9BX
t: 07801 665159

Surrey

Alexandra Road Allotments

An informal group of plotholders with the aim of helping everyone at the Alexandra Road allotment site in Epsom to get the best from their plots and enjoy the allotment together as much as possible.

a: Copse End Road, Epsom, Surry, KT17 4EQ
t: 01372 729601
www.alexallotment.co.uk

East Sussex

Bad Boys Vineyard

Planted in 2007 with Chardonnay, Pinot Meunier and Pinot Noir. The 2009 harvest produced 1700 bottles of sparkling pink. The 2010 harvest is expected to produce 7,000 bottles, ready for sale in 2012.

a: Tickerage Lane, Blackboys, Uckfield, East Sussex, TN22 5LT
e: abvineyards@btinternet.com

East Sussex

Barnsole Vineyard

Visitors are most welcome to this family run vineyard which currently extends over 3 acres. Planted in 1993. Full guided vineyard tours are also available by prior arrangement.

a: Herons Ghyll, Uckfield, East Sussex, TN22 4DB
t: 01304 812530
www.barnsole.co.uk

London

Alara Wholefoods Vineyard

From ground up, we are very involved in local food production. Our factory is in Kings Cross in London and yet we have an orchard here, a vineyard here and a permaculture forest and community gardens.

a: 110-112 Camley Str, London, N1C 4PF
t: 02073 879303
www.alara.co.uk

Surrey

Albury Vineyard

At Albury Organic Vineyard we aim to produce the finest quality organic sparkling and rosé wines from vines grown exclusively in the Surrey Hills, namely Albury Organic Sparkling and Albury Organic Rosé.

a: Weston Lodge, Albury, Guildford, GU5 9AE. Location of vineyard: Behind Silent Pool car park, GU5 9BW
t: 01483 229159 | www.alburyvineyard.com

Isle of Wight

Ashey Vineyard

Grape varieties: Unknown.

a: Ashey Road, Ryde, Isle of Wight, PO33 4BB
t: 01983 617007

East Sussex

Barnsgate Manor Vineyard

Situated in the heart of the Sussex countryside. The ideal venue for your wedding ceremony or reception. On a nice day you can enjoy a walk around the vineyard and say hello to donkeys and llamas.

a: Leeford Vineyards, Whatlington, Battle, East Sussex, TN33 0ND | t: 01825 713366
www.barnsgate.co.uk

Kent

Battle Wine Estate

Established in 1983, we pride ourselves on producing consistently high quality wine. The Estate's wines are known as the 'Saxon' range of wines. Now producing a range of delicious fruit liqueurs and kir.

a: Fleming Road, Staple, Canterbury, Kent, CT3 1LG
t: 01424 870449
www.battlewineestate.com

Hampshire

Beaulieu Vineyard

Grapes have been grown at Beaulieu since medieval times and today white and sparkling white wine are produced from grapes grown on the Estate. Tour & tastings available.

a: John Montagu Building, Beaulieu, Brockenhurst, Hampshire, SO42 72N | t: 01590 614621
www.beaulieu.co.uk/beaulieu/groups

Hampshire

Beeches Hill Vineyard

Planted in 1998 and producing around 500 bottles annually for friends and family. Grape varieties: Schönburger and Seyval Blanc which produce a dry white wine.

a: 3 Margaret's Cottages, Beeches Hill, Bishops Waltham, Hampshire, SO32 1FE
t: 01489 892356

East Sussex

Bewl Water Vineyard

Boat cruises, beautiful waterside walks, cycle hire, picnic areas, woodland playground, restaurant and gift shop.

a: Little Butts Lane, Cousley Wood, Wadhurst, East Sussex, TN5 6EX | t: 01892 782045
www.bewlwater.co.uk

Kent

Biddenden Vineyard

Established by the Barnes family in 1969. The vineyards are set in 22 acres in a shallow sheltered valley. Ten varieties of grapes are grown to produce White, red, rosé and quality sparkling wines.

a: Gribble Bridge Lane, Biddenden, Ashford, Kent, TN27 8DF | t: 01580 291726
www.biddendenvineyards.com

Berkshire

Binfield Vineyard

We are dedicated to the promotion of English sparkling wine as a viable alternative to more traditional foreign varieties. Established in 1992 when 5 acres were planted entirely by hand.

a: Forest Road, Wokingham, Berkshire, RG40 5SE
t: 01344 411322
www.championwine.co.uk

Hampshire

Birchenwood Vineyard

Planted in 1999. Wine is grown and made on site. Sold at the gate. Grape varieties: Pinot Noir, Dornfelder, Triomphe, Bacchus and Reichensteiner which produce white and róse wines.

a: Brook, Kyndhurst, Hampshire, SO43 7JA
t: 023 8081 2595

Hampshire

Bishop's Waltham Vineyard

Established in 1982. The first crop was harvested in 1986. Wine is made on site.

a: Tangier Lane, Bishop's Waltham, Southampton, Hampshire, SO32 1BU
t: 01489 896803

East Sussex

Black Dog Hill Vineyard

Planted in 2008. The first harvest was in 2010. Grape varieties Chardonnay, Pinot Noir and Pinot Meunier to produce a sparkling wine. Big ideas and plans on the horizon. Wine to be sold locally.

a: Clayes, Underhill Lane, Westmeston, West Sussex, BN6 8XG
t: 01273 844338

East Sussex

Bluebell Vineyard Estates

Established for the production of high quality sparkling wine. We aim to build a community of vineyards and bring agriculture back into the spotlight of UK industry.

a: Glenmore Farm, Sliders Lane, Furners Green, East Sussex, TN22 3RU | t: 01825 790395
www.bluebellvineyard.co.uk

East Sussex

Bodiam Vineyard

Grape varieties: Auxerrois, Bacchus, Blaubuger, Faberrebe, Kerner, Optima, Ortega, Pinot Noir, Regner, Reichensteiner, Seyval Blanc. The vineyard is rented by Sedlescombe organic vineyard.

a: Court Lodge Farm, Bodiam, East Sussex, TN32 5UJ

West Sussex

Bookers Vineyard

We are proud to be fine English wine producers. Take the opportunity to see what we do and try one of our various Tour and Tastings. Taste our fabulous Sparkling, Red and White wines.

a: Foxhole Lane, Bolney, West Sussex, RH17 5NB
t: 01444 881575
www.bookersvineyard.co.uk

Oxfordshire

Bothy Vineyard

Our philosophy is to produce the highest quality wines from grapes cultivated in as environmentally friendly way as possible. Visit us to experience the freshness and character of English wine at its best.

a: Frilford Heath, Abington, Oxfordshire, OX13 6QW
t: 01865 390067
www.bothy-vineyard.co.uk

Kent

Bourne Farm Vineyard

Grape varieties: Chardonnay, Pinot Noir, Pinot Meunier. Vineyard under contract to Hush Heath Esate.

a: c/o Sandhirst Vineyards, Hoads Farm, Crouch Lane, Sandhurst, Cranbrook, Kent, TN18 5PA. Location of vineyard: TN18 5NT | t: 01580 850296 | www.sandhurstvineyards.co.uk

East Sussex

Breaky Bottom Vineyard

Breaky Bottom lies in a fold in the South Downs, about 5 miles from Lewes in East Sussex.
Visits are by appointment and can usually be made at short notice.

a: Rodmell, Lewes, East Sussex, BN7 3EX
t: 01273 476427
www.breakybottom.co.uk

Oxfordshire

Bridewell Organic Gardens

We are an award-winning charity based in a walled garden and five-acre vineyard. All the wines we produce have been still white however in 2007 we harvested a sparkling wine which was ready in 2010.

a: The Walled Garden, Wilcote, Oxfordshire, OX7 3EB
t: 01993 864530
www.bridewellorganicgardens.co.uk

Oxfordshire

Brightwell Vineyard

Producing award-winning, English wines which frequently win medals at National and International competitions. Our wines are available by mail order and are also sold in many reputable shops.

a: Rush Court, Shillingford, Wallingford, Oxfordshire, OX10 8LJ | t: 01491 832354
www.brightwellvineyard.co.uk

West Sussex

Brinsbury College Vineyard

Grape varieties: Bacchus, Rondo.

a: East Clayton Farm Trust, Penlands Vale, Steyning, West Sussex, BN44 3PL. Location of vineyard: RH20 1DL
t: 01903 814998

Kent

Broadway Green Farm Vineyard

Grape varieties: Pinot Noir, Chardonnay.
Hope to produce a sparkling róse from the first harvest in 2010. Just under one hectare in size. Plans to build a winery on the horizon.

a: The broadway, Petham, Canterbury, Kent, CT4 5RX
t: 01227 700058

Kent

Budds Farm Vineyard

Set in peaceful, rural surroundings. Budds Farm Vineyard outsource to Chapel Down Vineyard.

a: Budds Lane, Wittersham, Tenterden, Kent, TN30 7EL
t: 01797 270245

Surrey

Burnt House Wines

Planted in 2009, with the plan to produce still wines. Grape varieties: Chardonnay, Pinot Noir, Cabernet Sauvignon, Merlot, Sauvignon Blanc. Ken, the owner also has a vineyard in S.Africa called Devon Valley.

a: Lansdowne, Hound House Road, Shere, Surrey, GU5 9JJ
t: 07980 306575

East Sussex

Burwash Weald Vineyard

Grape varieties: Bacchus, Pinot Meunier, Huxelrebe.

a: Burnt House Farm, Burwash Weald, Etchingham,
East Sussex, TN19 7LA
t: 01424 441979

East Sussex

Carr Taylor Vineyard

The finest English wines from a vineyard deep in East Sussex. Offering visitors an enchanting vineyard and wine experience. Winning over 100 awards and medals since the vineyard was founded!

a: Wheel Lane, Westfield, Hastings, East Sussex,
TN35 4SG | t: 01424 752501
www.carr-taylor.co.uk

Hampshire

Chalk Vale Vineyard

Nyetimber's Chalk Vale vineyard was planted in May 2009. Grape varieties: Pinot Noir, Chardonnay, Pinot Meunier.

a: Nyetimber Vineyard, Gay Street, West Chiltington, West Sussex, RH20 2HH. Location of vineyard: SO20 6RE
t: 01798 813989 | www.nyetimber.com

Kent

Chalksole Estate Vineyard

Not open to the public. Do not wish to be contacted at the moment. Planted in 2008, first harvest due in 2011 to produce a sparkling róse. Grape varieties: Pinot Noir, Chardonnay, Pinot Meunier.

a: Chalksole Green Lane, Alkham, Folkestone, Kent,
CT15 7EE
t: 01304 828881

West Sussex

Chanctonbury Vineyard

Being replanted with red varieties.

a: North Lane, Ashington, Pulborough, West Sussex,
RH20 3DF
t: 01903 892721

Kent

Chapel Down Wines

Chapel Down boasts a state of the art winery and produces all wines on the estate, both still and sparkling. Chapel Down conducts guided tours of the winery and vineyards.

a: Tenterden Vineyard, Small Hythe, Tenterden, Kent,
TN30 7NG | t: 01580 763033
www.englishwinesgroup.com

East Sussex

Charles Palmer Vineyard

An historic property built in the 16th century and now owned by the National Trust. For the past 11 years it has been the family home of Sally and Mason Palmer and the centre of their 750 acre farm.

a: Wickham Manor, Wickham Roack Lane, Winchelsea, TN36 4AG. Location of vineyard: Opp lay-by off A269 just outside Winchelsea | t: 01797 226216 | www.wickhammanor.co.uk

---

Oxfordshire

Childrey Manor Vineyard

An award winning Oxfordshire based Winemaker. Received a Highly Commended Award in the English and Welsh Wines of the Year 2007 and a Bronze medal in the 2008 awards for their Childrey Manor 2007.

a: Childrey Manor, Wantage, Oxfordshire, OX12 9PQ
t: 01235 751244

Oxfordshire

Chiltern Valley Vineyard

Set in an area of outstanding natural beauty, Old Luxters is home to 'Chiltern Valley Wines', its vineyard, winery, brewery and cellar shop. Winning over 70 trophies, awards and commendations.

a: Old Luxters, Hambleden, Henley-on-Thames, Oxfordshire, RG9 6JW | t: 01491 638330
www.chilternvalley.co.uk

East Sussex

Chingley Oast Vineyard

Dating back to 1850 and originally converted in the late 1970's, more recently, the property has been extensively refurbished. Set back from the road along a private drive - area of 'Outstanding Natural Beauty'.

a: Chingley Manor Oast, Flimwell, Wadhurst, East Sussex,
TN5 7QA
t: 01580 879528

Buckinghamshire

Claydon Vineyard

In 1997 twenty six families cleared some abandoned allotments and planted 200 vines of Rondo and Seyval Blanc. The white wine was crisp with a hint of Lavender. The Rondo produced a really deep red.

a: 3 Sandhill Farm, Middle Claydon, Buckinghamshire, MK18 2LD. Location of vineyard: The Allotments, Botolph Claydon, Buckinghamshire | t: 01296 730730

London

Clocktower Vineyard

Hazel and her husband own what they believe is the only working vineyard in central London. 3 years of hard work and set on two allotments in Isleworth - they produced their first bottles of year 2000 wine.

a: Twickenham Road, Redlees Park, Isleworth, London, TW7 6DW

Hampshire

Coach House Vineyard

Started in 1989 by Rodger and Margaret Marchbank. Producing rose and dry white wine. The wines are produced by Roger in the winery at Setley Ridge Vineyard in Brockenhurst.

a: Salisbury Road, West Wellow, Romsey, Hampshire, SO51 6BW
t: 01794 323345

Hampshire

Cottonworth Vineyard

Planted in 2005 and further plantings each year until 2010 they have doubled in size from 4.8 hectares to 8. Produce sparkling pink and white wines. To be sold locally. Plan to produce 50,000 botttles a year!

a: Fullerton Farms, Cottonworth, Andover, Hampshire, SP11 7JX
t: 01264 860221

East Sussex

Court Garden Vineyard

In 2005 we planted our first section of vineyard in a south facing field. A total of 6 acres planted. In 2009 our first wine had arrived in the farm shop for sale, namely, Court Garden Sparkling Wine.

a: Orchard Lane, Ditchling, East Sussex, BN6 8TH
t: 01273 844479
www.courtgardensfarm.co.uk

Hampshire

Court Lane Vineyard

Planted in 1978 and operating as a small family concern. In 1993 a winery was built which produces around 2000 bottles a year. The wines are mainly medium dry and available from the winery.

a: Ropley, Alresford, Hampshire, SO24 0DE
t: 01962 773391
www.ukvines.co.uk/vineyards/courtlane.htm

Hampshire

Danebury Vineyard

Danebury Vineyard, situated in Hampshire, England, produces white wine and sparkling wine characterised by their clean, crisp and fruity flavour. Wine tasting and wine cellar.

a: Nether Wallop, Stockbridge, Hampshire, SO20 6JX
t: 01264 781851
www.danebury.com

East Sussex

Davenport Vineyard

Organic managed vineyards in Kent and East Sussex producing premium dry white and sparkling English wines by Will Davenport who is one of the more serious and talented winegrowers in the UK today.

a: Limney Farm, Castle Hill, Rotherfield, East Sussex, TN6 3RR | t: 01892 852380
www.davenportvineyards.co.uk

Buckinghamshire

Daws Hill Vineyard

Daws Hill Vineyard produces high quality English sparkling wine using the Methode Traditionelle..

a: Town End Road, Radnage, High Wycombe, Buckinghamshire, HP14 4DY | t: 01494 483358
www.dawshillvineyard.co.uk

Hampshire

Deans Farm Vineyard

Grape varieties: Pinot Noir.

a: Weston, Petersfield, Hampshire, GU32 3NP
t: 01730 269111

London

Decanter Magazine Vineyard

As silly as this sounds we thought this was worth a mention... a total of 6 vines on the 10th floor of IPC Media's Blue Fin Building, outside Decanter's tasting room.

a: Blue Fin Building, 110 Southwark Street, London, SE1 0SU | t: 02031 485000
www.decanter.com

Surrey

Denbies Wine Estate

An all weather destination, the "Indoor Wine Experience" tours operate all year, the Outdoor Vineyard Train, March - November. A popular day out and business venue for local visitors.

a: London Road, Dorking, Surrey, RH5 6AA
t: 01306 876616
www.denbies.co.uk

East Sussex

Ditchling Vineyard

See entry for for Plumpton College for contact details. Vineyard rented by Plumpton College.

a: Beacon Road, Ditchling, East Sussex, BN6 8XB

Buckinghamshire

Dropmore Vineyard

Based on the site of historic Dropmore House at Burnham Beeches. Just under 1 hectare. Grape varieties: Bacchus, Ortega, Chardonnay, Pinot noir, Pinot Meunier. Visits by appointment.

a: Brook End Farmhouse, Dropmore Road, Littleworth Common, Buckinghamshire, SL1 8NF
t: 01628 664376

Hampshire

Dunley Vineyard

Grape varieties: Auxerrois, Phenix, Regent, Pinot Noir Précoce, Dunkelfelder.

a: Dunley House, Dunley, Whitchurch, Hampshire, RG28 7PU
t: 01256 892876

Hampshire

East Meon Vineyard

Grape varieties: Chardonnay, Pinot Noir

a: The Court House, East Meon, Hampshire, GU32 1NJ
t: 01730 823274

Kent

East Sutton Vine Garden

Grape varieties: Pinot Noir, Bacchus, Reichensteiner.

a: Brissenden, East Sutton Road, Headcorn, Maidstone, Kent, ME17 3DU
t: 01622 844811

West Sussex

Ebernoe Vineyard

Producing around 800-1000 bottles of dry white wine a year for friends and family. Grape varieties: Seyval Blanc and MT. currently on 1 hectare of land.

a: Petworth, West Sussex, GU28 9LH
t: 01428 707269
www.twitter.com/NatSchooler

Kent

Elham Valley Vineyard

Since 1995 the vineyard has been run by the Vale of Elham Trust, providing work and recreational opportunities in the East Kent area for adults with learning disabilities. Tours can be arranged.

a: Breach, Barham, Canterbury, Kent, CT4 6LN
t: 01227 832022 | www.visitsoutheastengland.com/site/things-to-do/elham-valley-vineyard-p68303

East Sussex

English Wine Centre

No vineyard on this site but there is a wine shop that sells a large selection of English wines.

a: Alfriston Roundabout, Alfriston, East Sussex, BN26 5QS
t: 01323 870164
www.englishwine.co.uk

Hampshire

Exton Park Estate Vineyard

Planted in 2003 on 4.85 hectares. In 2010 the vineyard size grew to 12 hectares. Grape varieties: Chardonnay, Pinot Noir, Pinot Meunier. Currently building a winery and wine available for sale in 2012.

a: Exton, Southampton, Hampshire, SO32 3NW
t: 01489 877834

Buckinghamshire

Fawley Vineyard

Produces still and sparkling English wines. Over 1,000 vines grown in two and a half acres vineyard. The wine is produced by Chiltern Valley vineyard.

a: The old Forge, Fawley Green, Henley-on-Thames, Buckinghamshire, RG9 6JA | t: 01491 577998
http://www.chilternsaonb.org/site_details.asp?siteID=243

Surrey

Fernhurst Vineyard

Fernhurst Vineyard Sparkling Red Wine made by James & Cathy Lane. A surprisingly light "Champagne" style Pinot Noir. Very delicate palate, an ideal summer aperitif.

a: Gospel Green Cottage, Haslemere, Surry, GU27 3BH. Location of vineyard: GU27 3NW
t: 01428 654120

Oxfordshire

Floreys Vineyard

Owned by Abbey Vineyards. Please see Abbey Vineyards, East Midlands for more information. Future plans consist of a winery and shop. Grape varieties: Regent, Chardonnay, Solaris, Acolon.

a: c/o Abbey Vineyards, Irnham Grange, Irnham Road, Corby Glen, Grantham, Lincolnshire, NG33 4NE. Location of vineyard: OX7 | t: 01476 550191 | www.tandsnurseries.com

East Sussex

Forstal Farm Vineyard

Grape varieties: Chardonnay, Pinot Noir, Pinot Meunier.

a: Old House Farm Lane, Peasmarsh, East Sussex, TN31 6YD
t: 02073 036321

London

Forty Hall Vineyard

The project is in its infancy – the first two acres are planted but we need to raise funds to plant up the remaining land. We will produce a range of still and sparkling wines of the highest quality.

a: Forty Hall Farm, Forty Hill, Enfield, London, EN2 9HA
t: 02088 001358
www.fortyhallvineyard.org.uk

Kent

Friday Street Vineyard

Grape varieties: Chardonnay, Pinot Noir, Meunier.

a: Friday Street Farm, East Sutton, Maidstone, Kent, ME17 3DD
t: 01622 842162

Surrey

Godstone Vineyard

Overlooking the beautiful Surrey countryside, and established in 1985, June Deeley and her family look forward to providing a warm welcome to you, whenever you choose to visit. Wine shop & tasting bar.

a: Flower Farm, Flower Lane, Godstone, Surrey, RH9 8DE. Location of vineyard: RH9 8DQ | t: 01883 744590
www.godstonevineyards.com

Surrey

Goose Green Vineyard

A few test vines were planted in 2003 with a following 130 planted in 2005. Two wines are made: Autum Gold and a bottle fermented sparkling wine. Grape varieties: Phoenix, Orion, Pinot Noir.

a: c/o 292 Stafford Road, Wallington, Surrey, SM6 8PN. Location of vineyard: Baddington, Croydon, CR0 4TB
t: 02086 881797

Oxfordshire

Grange Farm Vineyard

The winery here also produces organic apple and pear juices.

a: Swerford, Chipping Norton, Oxfordshire, OX7 4AX
t: 01608 737313

Surrey

Greyfriars Vineyard

We are a small vineyard, established in 1989, on the south facing slopes of the Hogs Back Ridge. Our vineyard grows Chardonnay and Pinot Noir and produces renowned white and bubbly wines.

a: Greyfriars Farm, The Hogs Back, Puttenham, Guildford, Surry, GU13 1AG | **t:** 01483 813712
www.greyfriarsvineyard.com/

Kent

Groombridge Place Vineyard

We provide a truly exceptional location for Corporate Services. Wines include the dry white wine made from grapes grown in the estate vineyard. English wine tasting's can be arranged.

a: Grrombridge, Tunbridge Wells, Kent, TN3 9QG
t: 01892 861444
www.groombridge.co.uk

Kent

Gusbourne Estate Vineyard

The estate is owned by Andrew Weeber. The first vintage releases were presented at the EWP Trade Tasting in 2006 and in two styles. A ground breaking new winery is planned for the near future.

a: Kenardington Road, Appledore, Ashford, Kent, TN26 2BE | **t:** 01233 758666
www.ukvines.co.uk/vineyards/gusbourne.htm

Buckinghamshire

Hale Valley Vineyard

We make a single wine each year, blending all the grapes together. All so far have been still, dry whites, with the exception of the sparkling wines in 1998 and 2000.

a: Boddington East, Hale Lane, Wendover, Buckirmghamshire, HP22 6NQ | **t:** 01296 623730
www.ukvines.co.uk/vineyards/hale.htm

West Sussex

Halnaker Vineyard

Grape varieties: Chardonnay, Pinot Noir, Pinot Meunier.

a: Thicket Lane, Halnaker, Chichester, West Sussex, PO18 0QS
t: 01903 730140

Hampshire

Hambledon Vineyard

The first commercial vineyard in England since the dissolution of the monasteries by Henry VIII in 1537. The wine currently produced can be purchased at The Peoples Market and the village grocer.

a: Mill Down, Hambledon, Hampshire, PO7 4RY
t: 01239 2632066

Kent

Harbourne Vineyard

A small family owned and run vineyard and winery using traditional methods and minimum intervention to produce handmade wines in Kent England.

a: Wittersham, Tenterden, Kent, TN30 7NP. Location of vineyard: High Halden, Tenterden, Kent, TTN26 3HD
t: 01797 270420 | www.harbournevineyard.co.uk

Kent

Harden Vineyard

Planted around 30 years ago. 3 hectares in size. The owner Grape varieties: Reichensteiner, Schönburger, Regent Pinot noir Précoce.

a: Harden Farm, Grove Road, Tonbridge, Kent, TN11 8DX
t: 01892 870221

Hampshire

Hattingley Valley Vineyard

A 7.3 hectare site, planted in 2008. The first harvest will be in 2011. The grapes will be transported to the Winery-Wield Yard turned into a premium sparkling wine, by two highly acclaimed winemakers.

a: Kings Farm, Lower Wield, Alresford, Hants, SO24 9RX. Location of vineyard: GU34 5NQ | **t:** 01256 389188
www.kingsfarm.co.uk/vineyard/Vineyard.htm

Oxfordshire

Hendred Vineyard

Located on the edge of the village of East Hendred, our vineyard sits in 9 acres of English countryside. With Seyval Blanc, Madeleine Angevine and Pinot Noir vines we produce quality still and sparkling wines.

a: Reading Road (entrance off Allins Lane), East Hendred, Wantage, Oxfordshire, OX12 8HR | **t:** 01235 820081
www.hendredvineyard.co.uk

East Sussex

Henners Vineyard

Classic Champagne varieties Pinot Noir, Chardonnay, and Pinot Meunier have been planted, with a selection of clones and rootstocks to give an assemblage of flavours and aromas to the finished wine.

a: The Granary, Ladham Road, Goudhurst, Kent, TN17 1LS. Location of vineyard: BN27 1QJ | t: 01323 831746
www.hennersvineyard.co.uk

East Sussex

Herons Ghyll Estate

Grape varieties: Huxelrebe, Reichensteiner.

a: Newnham Park, Chillies Lane, Crowborough, East Sussex, TN6 3TB | t: 07956 388272
www.heronsghyllestate.co.uk

Hidden Spring Vineyard

Welcome to Hidden Spring Vineyard and Orchards; 23 acres of working smallholding and campsite in the Sussex countryside. We produce wines from our vines, juice and cider from our apples and pears

a: Vines Cross Road, Horam, East Sussex, TN21 0HG
t: 01435 812640
www.hiddenspring.co.u

Surrey

High Clandon Vineyard

Grape varieties: Chardonnay, Pinot Noir, Pinot Meunier.

a: Clandon Downs, High Clandon, Surry, GU4 7RP
t: 01483 225660

West Sussex

Highdown Vineyard

Discover our newly opened tea room, serving freshly cooked food. Why not have a glass of wine with your lunch. The vineyard leads onto the Downs so its the perfect place to start a walk! Shop & tatsings.

a: Littlehampton Road, Ferring, West Sussex, BN12 6PG
t: 01903 500663
www.highdown-vineyard.co.uk

East Sussex

Hobdens Vineyards

Welcome to the very early days of our new vineyard. Our aim is to produce delicious, craftsman-made sparkling wines from carefully selected Pinot Noir and Pinot Gris grapes.

a: Hobdens, Wellbrook Hall, Mayfield, East Sussex, TN20 6HH
www.hobdensvineyards.com

Kent

Horsmonden Vineyard

Davenport Vineyards is relatively new (for a vineyard), but rapidly becoming a leader in the English wine scene. Planted in 1991 they now have 12 acres of vines.

a: Davenport Vineyards, Limney Farm, Castle Hill, East Sussex, TN6 3RR. Location of vineyard: Hazel Street Farm, Horsmonden, Kent, TN12 8EF

Kent

Hush Heath Estate Vineyard

A perfectly manicured vineyard, shielded from the modern world by 400 acres of ancient, virgin woodland. There isn't pink champagne in the whole world quite like it.

a: Cranbrook, Kent, TN17 2NG
t: 02074 799500
www.hushheath.com

Surrey

Iron Railway Vineyard

It was established by John Dickin in 1983 on part of the old horse drawn railway, and has grown over the years. A variety of fruit is grown, including apples and grapes. The vineyard produces its own wines.

a: 11 Vincent Road , Coulsdon, Surrey CR5 3DH. Location of vineyard: RH1 3BA | t: 01737 551829
www.squidoo.com/iron-railway-vineyard

Hampshire

Jays Farm Vineyard

Produces Seyval Blanc wine under the Embley brand which is sold by the case from the vineyard. Winner of the Thames & Chilterns Asociation Guest Award 2001 for Embley 2000 dry

a: Embley Lane, East Wellow, Hampshire, SO51 6DN
t: 01794 511314
www.ukvines.co.uk/vineyards/jaysfarm.htm

Hampshire
Jenkyn Place Vineyard
A small and exclusive estate. The vineyard has been created with excellence in mind and has been designed and planted to produce top-quality English sparkling wines.

a: Hole Lane, Bentley, ALTON, Hants, GU10 5LU
t: 02077 363102
www.jenkynplacevineyard.co.uk

Kent
Kempes Hall Vineyard
Planted in 1976.
Grape varieties: Chardonnay, Schönburger, Seyval Blanc.

a: Kemps Corner, Wye, Ashford, Kent, TN25 4ER
t: 01233 812217

Kent
Kit's Coty Vineyard
Owned by Chapel Down, the Kit's Coty site is just off Bluebell Hill near Aylesford. The vineyard contains Chardonnay and Pinot Noir sparkling varietals and is the finest site for "Champagne" style grapes.

a: Pilgrims Way, Eccles, Aylesford, Maidstone, Kent, ME20 7EF
www.englishwinesgroup.com

Kent
Lamberhurst Vineyard
Set amongst 20 acres of beautiful countryside. Experience a walk around the vineyard, a guided tour together with wine tasting, or simply to enjoy fine wholesome, local food available at the Bistro.

a: The Down, Lamberhurst, Kent, TN3 8ER
t: 01892 890412 | www.visitkent.co.uk/explore/thedms.asp?dms=13&venue=3090648

Hampshire
Laverstoke Park Vineyard
The vineyard currently comprises of 9 hectares of Chardonnay, Pinot Noir and Pinot Meunier. Within each of these varieties clones were selected for their suitability to produce quality organic sparkling wine.

a: Laverstoke Park Farm, Overton, Hampshire, RG25 3DR
t: 01256 772659
www.laverstokepark.co.uk

Hampshire
Leckford Estate Vineyard
The Waitrose vines will grow for 3 years before the first crop, followed by a 2 year wine-making and maturation cycle for the production of a high quality sparkling wine, ready on Waitrose shelves by 2014.

a: The Estate Office, Leckford, Stockbridge, Hampshire, SO20 6JF. Location of vineyard: SO20 6JG | t: 01264 810585
www.waitrose.com/ourcompany/leckfordestate.aspx

Oxfordshire
Linch Hill Vineyard
Grape varieties: Seyval Blanc, Phoenix.

a: Linch Hill, Stanton Harcourt, Oxfordshire, OX29 5BB
t: 07775 583737

Kent
Little Knoxbridge Vineyard
Planted in 1983 both still and sparkling wines are made, mainly for home consumption.

a: Cranbrook Road, Staplehurst, Kent, TN12 0EU
t: 01580 893643

Hampshire
Little West End Farm Vineyard
A small grower from Avize, Champagne, planted 3 hectares of Chardonnay and Pinot Noir near Hambledon in Hampshire. There is a small winery on the farm.

a: 14 Route d'Oger, 51190 Avize France. Location of vineyard: Little West End Farm, Chideen, Hambledon, Hampshire, P07 4TE | t: +33 (0)326 577704

West Sussex
Lurgashall Winery
Transformed using time-honoured recipes, hand-gathered elderflowers, rose petals and the sap of the silver birch tree - to name but a few of the fresh, natural ingredients we use.

a: Lurgashall Winery, Lurgashall, West Sussex, GU28 9HA
t: 01428 707292
www.lurgashall.co.uk

Buckinghamshire
Magpie Lane Vineyard
Owned by Abbey Vineyrads. Please see Abbey Vineyards, East Midlands for more information. Future plans consist of a winery and shop. Grape varieties: Pinot Noir, Pinot Meunier, Chardonnay, Ortega.

a: c/o Abbey Vineyards, Irnham Grange, Irnham Road, Corby Glen, Grantham, Lincolnshire, NG33 4NE. Location of vineyard: HP7 0LU | t: 01476 550191 | www.tandsnurseries.com

Buckinghamshire
Manor Fields Vineyard
Planting began in 2004/2005.
Varities include: Chardonnay, Pinot Gris, Pinot Meunier and Pinot Noir. These will be used to make sparkling wine.

a: Northcroft, Weedon, Aylesbury, HP22 4NR
t: 01296 641178
www.manorfieldsvineyard.co.uk

Kent
Marden Organic Vineyard
The first vintage was produced in 2007. In 2009 a sparkling and still Chardonnay wine were made. Produce around15,000-20,00 bottles a year. Grape varieties: Chardonnay, Pinot Noir, Pinot Meunier.

a: Herbert Hall Wines Ltd, Poultry Farm, Plain Road, Marden, Tonbridge, TN12 9LS
t: 07956 163519

Hampshire
Marlings Vineyard
Here at Marlings Vineyard, we have a passion for English Wine. We grow the grapes and make the wine at our family home in the heart of the beautiful New Forest, Hampshire.

a: Mead End Road, Sway, Hampshire, SO41 6EE
t: 01590 681606
www.newforestwine.co.uk

Kent
Mayshaves Vineyard
The vineyard was planted in 1982.
Grape varieties: MT, Reichensteiner, Seyval Blanc. A dry white wine is made from the grapes which is enjoyed by friends and family.

a: Mayshaves Farm, Woodchurch, Ashford, Kent, TN26 3PT
t: 01233 820286

Oxfordshire
Meadowgrove Vineyard
A family home on the outskirts of Wantage in the glorious Vale of the White Horse. We make our wine from the grapes we grow, which we share with our friends and family. Not sold commercially.

a: Meadowgrove, Letcombe Road, Wantage, Oxon, OX12 9NA | t: 01235 767913
www.meadowgrove.com

Kent
Meopham Valley Vineyard
The 2 hectare vineyard grows a substantial range of grapes and makes English White, Red, Rosé and sparkling wines. David and Pauline Grey set up Meopham Valley Vineyard in 1991.

a: Norway House, Wrotham Road, Meopham, DA13 0AU
t: 01474 812727
www.meophamvalleyvineyard.co.uk

East Sussex
Methersham Vineyard
Once a commercial vineyard that in recent years has been neglected. Now under new ownship since May 2009 the vineyard is not expected to produce a harvest until 2012. Holiday accomodation on the horizon.

a: Hobbs Lane, Beckley, TN31 6TX
t: 01797 260491

London
Mill Hill Village Vineyard
A non-commercial vineyard planted between 1986-1993. Winning a number of non-commercial wine awards.

a: 68 Millway, Mill Hill, London, NW7 3QY
t: 02089 592214

East Sussex
Mount Harry Vines
The grapes are only grown and picked here. They are then sent and used by Ridgeview Estate. Grape varieties: Chardonnay, Pinot Noir, Pinot Meunier.

a: Mount Harry House, Ditchling Road, Offham, Lewes BN7 3QW
t: 01273 474456

Kent

Mount Vineyard

Situated in the idyllic village of Shoreham in Kent. The vineyard is open a few days a year for customers and is well worth a visit but by appointment only. Award winning wines.

a: The Mount, Church Street, Shoreham, Sevenoaks, TN14 7SD | t: 01959 524008
www.themountvineyard.co.uk

Kent

Mystole Members Vineyard

Grape varieties: Bacchus, Dornfelder, Regent, Kerner, Seyval Blanc, Pinot Noir, Chardonnay.

a: The Orangery, Mystole, Canterbury, Kent, CT4 7DB
t: 01227 738348

Kent

National Fruit Collection - Brogdale

Offering visitors a fun day out to experience the beauty of the countryside, sample the healthy lifestyle options of local Kent produce. Come visit our market place of shops and crafts.

a: Brogdale Farm, Brogdale Road, Faversham, Kent, ME13 8XZ | t: 01795 536250
www.brogdalecollections.co.uk

West Sussex

Netherland Vineyard

Nyetimber's Netherland vineyard.
Grape varieties: Pinot Noir, Chardonnay, Pinot Meunier.

a: Nyetimber Vineyard, Gay Street, West Chiltington, RH20 2HH. Location of vineyard: Tillington, Petworth, West Sussex, GU28 0PQ | t: 01798 813989 | www.nyetimber.com

---

East Sussex

New House Farm Vineyard

Care of Carr Taylor.
Please see Carr Taylor for more information.

a: Carr Taylor Wines Lts. Wheel Lane, Westfield, Hastings, East Sussex, TN35 4SG. Location of vineyard: TN32 5UB
t: 01424 752501 | www.carr-taylor.co.uk

Berkshire

North Court Farm Vineyard

Grape varieties: MA, Reichensteiner, Schönburger, Huxelrebe.

a: 100b High Street, Hampton, Middlesex, TW12 2ST. Location of vineyard: North Court Farm, Wick Hill, Finchampstead, Berkshire, RG40 3SN | t: 02089 796550

Hampshire

Northbrook Springs

Northbrook Springs is a modern working vineyard, producing a range of award-winning white wines. Trade and Retail Sales.Visitors are welcome to walk and picnic in the vineyard

a: Beeches Hill, Bishops Waltham, Southampton, Hampshire, SO32 1FB
t: 01489 892659

West Sussex

Nutbourne Lane Vineyard

Nyetimber's Nutbourne Lane Vineyard.
Grape varieties: Pinot Noir, Reichensteiner, Bacchus, Schönburger, Huxelrebe, MT, Rondo.

a: Nyetimber Vineyard, Gay Street, West Chiltington, RH20 2HH. Location of vineyard: Nutbourne, Pulborough, West Sussex, RH20 2HS | t: 01798 813989 | www.nyetimber.com

---

West Sussex

Nutbourne Vineyards

First planted in 1980 and there are now 18 acres of vines in production. Producing award winning Sparkling and Still Wines in the heart of West Sussex, England.

a: Gay Street, Nr Pulborough, West Sussex, RH20 2HE
t: 02076 273800
www.nutbournevineyards.com

West Sussex

Nyetimber Vineyard

A new era for English wine began in 1988 when the first Nyetimber vineyards were planted in the heart of West Sussex. The largest vineyard in the UK, the Nyetimber Estate comprises 438 acres.

a: Nyetimber Vineyard, Gay Street, West Chiltington, RH20 2HH | t: 01798 813989
www.nyetimber.com

London
Olding Manor Vineyard

As lovers of English Wine, for some time we have harboured ambitions to establish a grand vineyard in Kent. It measures just 0.01hectares and is based on the St Mary's Road Allotments.

a: 42 Pitfold Road, Lee, London, SE12 9HX. Location of vineyard: SE12 0TF | t: 02076 523151
www.oldingmanor.co.uk

Oxfordshire
Pheasants Ridge Vineyard

The Gilbeys inherited their 1.5 acre vineyard when they bought their present house. Producing both dry white and sparkling wines. The wine is available either via the vineyard or from the Gilbey restaurants.

a: Hambelden, Henley on Thames, RG9 6SN
t: 01491 576087
www.gilbeygroup.com

Surrey
Port Lympne Vineyard

Set in 15 acres of beautiful landscaped terrain which include a vineyard, figary, chessboard and the stripe garden. Vistors can enjoy breathtaking panoramic views from the Trojan stairway.

a: Bunch Lane, Haslemere, Surrey, GU27 1AJ
t: 01303 264647
www.totallywild.net/portlympne

Hampshire
Priors Dean Vineyard

Visitors are welcome to see the vines by appointment throughout the year, but access is only on foot via a steep rough track so it is necessary to be fit and active, a small picnic site is available by arrangement.

a: 5 St Mary's Road, Liss, Hampshire, GU33 7AH. Location of vineyard: Buttons Lane, Slebounre, Alton, Hants, GU34 3SD
t: 01730 894147 | www.priorsdeanvineyard.co.uk

East Sussex
RidgeView Wine Estate

RidgeView Estate is dedicated solely to the production of the highest quality sparkling wine from traditional Champagne varieties and methods. Tours and tastings available.

a: Fragbarrow Lane, Ditchling Common, East Sussex, BN6 8TP | t: 01444 241441
www.ridgeview.co.uk

Surrey
Painshill Park Vineyard

An award-winning vineyard, initially flourishing in the 18th century, the two-and-a-half acres were replanted 15 years ago with Pinot Noir, Chardonnay and Seyval Blanc grapes to produce their three wines.

a: Portsmouth Road, Cobham, Surrey, KT11 1JE
t: 01932 868113
www.painshill.co.uk

East Sussex
Plumpton College Vineyard

Open to the public, but only to groups by prior arrangement. The wine produced at the College is for sale at many local outlets. Provides courses in all aspects of wine.

a: Ditchling Road, Nr Lewes, BN7 3AE
t: 01273 890454
www.plumpton.ac.uk

Surrey
Primrose Hill Vineyard

Grape varieties: Orion, Phoenix, Regent, Rondo, Seyval Blanc.

a: Bunch Lane, Haslemere, Surrey, GU27 1AJ
t: 01428 643360

West Sussex
Redfold Farm Vineyard

Grape varieties: Chardonnay, Pinot Noir, Pinot Meunier.

a: Nutbourne Lane, Nutbourne, Pulborough, West Sussex, RH20 2HS
t: 01798 817202

West Sussex
River Walk Vineyard

Nyetimber's River Walk Vineyard.
Grape varieties: Ortega, Solaris, Pinot Noir.

a: Nyetimber Vineyard, Gay Street, West Chiltington, RH20 2HH. Location of vineyard: GU28 9BG | t: 01798 813989
www.nyetimber.com

West Sussex
Rock Lodge Vineyard
See Plumton College entry.

a: Plumpton College, Ditchling Road, Nr Lewes, BN7 3AE. Location of vineyard: Scaynes Hill, Haywards Heath, West Sussex, RH17 7NG | t: 01273 890454

West Sussex
Roman Villa Vineyard
Nyetimber's Roman Villa Vineyard.
Grape varieties: Pinot Noir, Chardonnay, Pinot Meunier.

a: Nyetimber Vinyard, Gay Street, West Chiltington, West Sussex, RH20 2HH. Location of vineyard: RH20 1PQ
t: 01798 813989 | www.nyetimber.com

East Sussex
Rosemary Farm Vineyard
Grapes are only grown and picked here. They are then sent to Chapel Down Wines to be used. Grape varieties: Chardonnay, Pinot Noir, Pinot Meunier.

a: Rosemary Lane, Flimwell, Wadhurst, East Sussex, TN5 7PT | t: 07710 111800

Isle of Wight
Rosemary Vineyard
One of the largest producers of English Wine, covering 30 acres. From full-bodied english red wines, ciders and bottle fermented sparkling wines to liqueurs, country wines and refreshing apple juice.

a: Smallbrook Lane, Ryde. Isle of Wight, PO33 4BE
t: 01983 811084
www.rosemaryvineyard.co.uk

Oxfordshire
Rossi Regatta Vineyard
Grape varieties: Unknown.

a: Benham Orchard, Benhams Lanes, Fawley, Oxfordshire, RG9 6JG

Isle of Wight
Rossiters Vineyard
The 10 acre vineyard was planted from 1990 onwards, and is now producing a variety of excellent wines. Enjoy a walk through the vineyards, taste our wines in our wine shop and view our working winery.

a: Main Road, Wellow, Isle of Wight, PO41 0TE
t: 01983 761616
www.rossitersvineyard.com

Hampshire
Rother Valley Vineyard
Rother Valley Vineyard, an English wine producer based in the heart of the South Downs on the Sussex / Hampshire border.

a: Rother Valley Vineyard, Rother Farm, Elsted, Midhurst, Hampshire, GU29 0JS | t: 01730 816888
www.rothervalleyvineyard.co.uk

London
Saint Andrew's Vineyard
Grape varieties: Rondo, Dornfelder, Pinot noir, Schönburger, MA.

a: 24 Bolton Road, London, NW10 4BG. Location of vineyard: Dors Close Allotments adjacent to NW9 8DE
t: 02089 613029

Kent
Sandhurst Vineyard
Our vineyard consists of Bacchus, Reichensteiner and Schönberger grapes for white wine production and Rondo, Dornfelder for red wine. A warm welcome is extended to visitors for B&B at Hoads Farm.

a: Hoads Farm, Crouch Lane, Sandhurst, Cranbrook, Kent, TN18 5PA | t: 01580 850296
www.sandhurstvineyards.co.uk

East Sussex
Sculdown Vineyard
A small certificated campsite that accepts just five caravans or motorhomes – ideal for when you want to get away from it all.

a: Broad Oak - Sculdown Vineyard & Orchard, Chitcombe Road, Broad Oak, Rye, East Sussex, TN31 6EX
t: 01424 883127

East Sussex

Sedlescombe Organic Vineyard

England's first organic wine producers Roy and Irma cook have set themselves a new challenge... Biodynamic cultivation. Visit the vineyard and winery and taste some remarkable wines.

a: Hawkhurst Road, Cripp's Corner, Sedlescombe, Robertsbridge, East Sussex, TN32 5SA | t: 01580 830715
www.englishorganicwine.co.uk

Hampshire

Setley Ridge Vineyard

We grow the grapes, make the wine and bottle all on site, but at all times we try to be sensitive to the environment in which we work and are rewarded with a rich diversity of flora and fauna for us to appreciate.

a: Lymington Road, Brockenhurst, Hampshire, SO42 7UF
t: 01590 622246
www.setleyridge.co.uk

Buckinghamshire

Shardeloes Vineyard

An 18th-century landscape park and woodland. The site originally occupied 390 hectares, though the surrounding areas of parkland have largely been returned to agriculture.

a: Shardeloes Farm, Cherry Lane, Amersham, Buckinghamshire, HP7 0QF | t: 01494 433333
www.shardeloesfarm.com

East Sussex

Sheffield Park Vineyard

Established for 33 years. We are situated in the victorian kitchen garden of Sheffield Park House. We produce are own sparkling wine 'Sifelle' from our 3 acre vineyard.

a: The Walled Garden, Sheffield Park, Uckfield, East Sussex, TN22 3QX | t: 01825 790775
www.sheffieldparkvineyard.co.uk

Surrey

Shere Vineyard

Planted in 2007 with the first crop in 2009. The grapes are only grown and picked here. They are then sent to Bookers to be used. Grape varieties: Bacchus, Chardonnay, Pinot Noir.

a: Winterfold End, Hound House Road, Shere, Surrey, GU5 9JJ
t: 01483 203491

Hampshire

Somborne Valley Vineyard

Somborne Valley is a relatively recent planting of 20 acres on the Hoplands Estate, set in the picturesque Somborne Villages of Hampshire. Wines are made by Three Choirs and are listed on the estate website.

a: Hoplands Estate, Kings Somborne, Stockbridge, Hampshire, SO20 6QH | t: 01794 388547
www.ukvines.co.uk/vineyards/somborne.htm

Hampshire

Sour Grapes Vineyard

Unique, original wine labels for gifts & special occasions. Our fully automated on line web site is currently under construction – but our wine and labels are up and running.

a: Oak Tree House, Michelmersh, Romsey, Hampshire, SO51 0NQ | t: 01794 367300
www.sourgrapesvineyard.co.uk

West Sussex

Southlands Valley Vineyard

Grape varieties: Chardonnay, Pinot Noir, Pinot Meunier.

a: Mitchbourne Farm, Malthouse Lane, Ashington, West Sussex, RH20 3EU
t: 01903 892203

Oxfordshire

Springfield Vineyard

A red and white wine is produced here and enjoyed by friends and family. Grape varieties: MA, Seyval Blanc, Triomphe.

a: Springfield Farm, Howe Road, Watlington, Oxfordshire, OX49 5EL
t: 01491 612095

East Sussex

Springfields Vineyard

A private estate of some 20 acres and the first vineyard in the UK to be registered with the Bio Dynamic Agricultural Association. Planting of over 10,000 vines from 2007 present.

a: Deerview Farm, Down Street, Piltdown, East Sussex, TN22 3XX | t: 01825 713421
www.springfieldsvineyard.co.uk

Kent
Squerryes Court Vineyard
Learn about the newly planted vineyard at Squerryes and taste a selection of English wines, some of them award winners. Cost per person £8.50 (includes admission to the house and gardens.

a: Squerryes Estate Office, 2 The Granary, Westerham, Kent, TN16 2DT. Location of vineyard: TN16 2DT | t: 01959 562345
www.squerryes.co.uk

West Sussex
Standen Vineyard
Planted in 2000 with the grape varieties: Auxerrois, Seyval Blanc and Reichensteiner. In 2008, 500 bottles of sparkling white wine were produced. Consumed by friends and family only.

a: Standen Farm, Standen, West Sussex, RH19 4NE
t: 01342 328835

Kent
Stanford Bridge Vineyard
Grape varieties: Chardonnay, Pinot Noir.

a: Stanford Bridge House, Pluckley, Ashford, Kent, TN27 0RU

Berkshire
Stanlake Park Wine Estate
A comprehensive selection of finest quality English wine to suit every palate and taste. A 150 acre Wine Estate in the heart of the Thames Valley with a cellar shop selling award-winning locally-produced wine.

a: Twyford, Reading, berkshire, RG10 0BN
t: 01189 340176
www.stanlakepark.com

West Sussex
Stopham Vineyard
Planted in 2007 with 21,000 vines. Producing still white, rosé and sparkling wines. We produced 15,000 bottles in 2010 and hope to produce 35,000 bottles on average each year when fully established.

a: Stopham, Pulborough, West Sussex, RH20 1EG
t: 01273 566826
www.stophamvineyard.co.uk

West Sussex
Storrington Priory Vineyard
Planted in 2006 on land we own near our cemetery. We grow 2 varieties of grape: Pinot Noir and Chardonnay. We also planted 70 table grapes - a white Danlass, and 2 red - Alphonse and Cardinal.

a: Our Lady of England Priory, School Lane, Storrington, West Sussex, RH20 4LN | t: 01903 742150
www.norbertines.co.uk

Kent
Surrenden Vineyard
Established in 1986 and 1987 – is reputed to be the first UK vineyard to plant the Champagne varieties specifically for the production of bottle-fermented sparkling wine.

a: Walnut Tree Farm, Swan Lane, Little Chart, Ashford, Kent, TN27 0ES
t: 01233 840214

Kent
Syndale Valley Vineyards
Planted on the site of an earlier Roman one. Grape varieties: Pinot Noir, Chardonnay, Pinot Blanc, Pinot Meunier, Bacchus.

a: Parsonage Farm, Seed Road, Newnham, Sittingbourne, Kent, ME9 0NA
t: 01795 890693

Kent
Tenterden Vineyard
See Chapel Down Wines for more information.

a: Small Hythe, Tenterden, Kent, TN30 7NG
t: 01580 766111

Kent
Terlingham Vineyard
Planted in 2006. We grow three classic champagne varieties: Pinot Noir, Pinot Meunier and Chardonnay plus Seyval Blanc for sparkling. Bacchus for still white and Rondo and Dornfelder for rose and red.

a: Terlingham Manor Farm, Gibraltar Lane, Hawkinge, Kent, CT18 7AE | t: 01303 892743
www.terlinghamvineyard.co.uk

Berkshire

Theale Vineyard

An artificial hill was fashioned with topsoil and planted with Chardonnay vines imported from Champagne in 2000. Managed by award-winning sparkling wine producer RidgeView Wine Estate.

a: Laithwaites, New Aquitaine, Exeter Way, Theale, Reading, Berkshire, RG7 4PL
t: 01189 030903

Surrey

Thorncroft Vineyard

A small family business that started out on a small farm near Leatherhead in the 1980's. All our drinks are made from quality ingredients to the best possible recipes created at home by founder Guy Woodall.

a: Thorncroft Drive, Leatherhead, Surrey, KT22 8JD
t: 01642 791792
www.thorncroftdrinks.com

Kent

Throwley Vineyard

Planted in 1986, we are consistently winning international awards for our wines including rare Gold medals in the International Wine and Spirit Competition and International Wine Challenge.

a: The Old Rectory, Throwley, Faversham, Kent, ME13 0PF
t: 01795 890276
www.throwleyvineyard.co.uk

East Sussex

Ticehurst Vineyard

Grape varieties: Reichenstener, MT, Kerner, Schönburger, Dornfelder, Dunkelfelder.

a: Burnt House Farm, Burwash Weald, Etchingham, East Sussex, TN5 7HE. Location of vineyard: TN5 7HE
t: 01424 441979

West Sussex

Tinwood Vineyard

Owned by the Tukker family, 25% owners of the RidgeView Estate. Grape varieties: Chardonnay, Pinot Noir, Pinot Meunier.

a: Groves Farm Office, Colworth, Chichester, West Sussex, PO20 2DX. Location of vineyard: PO18 0NE
t: 01243 788478

Hampshire

Titchfield Vineyard

Planted in 1991 and producing the first vintage in 1996. The vine varieties were chosen for their ability to ripen with good sugar levels in the English climate. All wines are produced and bottled on the estate.

a: Misty Haze, Brownish Lane, Hampshire, PO14 4NZ
t: 01489 895773
www.titchfieldvineyard.co.uk

West Sussex

Tullens Vineyard

Located in Pulborough West Sussex Tullens Fruit Farm was founded in the 1950s as one of the Country's first pick-your-own farms. Our produce is sold directly to the public through Tullens Farm Shop.

a: Tullens Fruit Farm, Pickhurst Lane, Pulborough, West Sussex, RH20 1DA | t: 01798 872108
www.tullens.co.uk

Buckinghamshire

Tyringham Hall Vineyard

First harvest due in 2011.
Grape varieties: Chardonnay, Pinot Noir, Pinot Meunier.

a: Tyrubgham Hall, Tyringham, Newport Pagnell, Buckinghamshire, MK16 9EX
t: 02072 350422

West Sussex

Upperton Vineyard

Upperton Vineyards is commited to producing the highest quality sparkling wine from traditional Champagne varieties and methods.

a: Upperton Farm, Tillington, Petworth, West Sussex, GU28 0RD
t: 01798 343958

West Sussex

Upperton Vineyard (Nyetimber)

Nyetimber's Upperton Vineyard.
Grape varieties: Pinot Noir, Reichensteiner, Bacchus, Schönburger, Huxelrebe, MT, Rondo.

a: Nyetimber Vineyard, Gay Street, West Chiltington, RH20 2HH. Location of vineyard: GU28 9BG | t: 01798 813989
www.nyetimber.com

Surrey
Virginia Water Vineyard
Grape varieties: Merlot.

a:Laithwaites, Unit1, London Road, Virginia Water, Surrey,
GU25 4QU
t: 01189 030903

Hampshire
Waitrose Estate
Waitrose already own a 4,000-acre farm, The
Leckford Estate on the river Test in Hampshire.
Waitrose's very own English sparkling wine is
expected on the supermarket's shelves in 2014.

www.waitrose.com

West Sussex
Warnham Vale Vineyard
Planted in 1990. We produce a clean crisp dry white.
Happy Valley is a blend of Seyval and Schönburger
and The Gap is made from Reichensteiner which has
been lightly oaked in French barrels.

a: The Old Barn,, Northlands Road, Warnham, West Sussex,
RH12 3SQ | t: 01306 627603
www.thetroddengrape.co.uk/warnham_vale.html

Surrey
Warren Farm Vineyard
Grape varieties: Bacchus, Schönburger, Rondo,
Pinot Noir Précoce.

a: Warren Farm House, Warren Road, Guilford, Surrey,
GU1 2HF
t: 02031 162959

Hampshire
Webb's Land Vineyard
An eight-acre vineyard situation in the Hampshire
countryside and surrounded by Wickham Golf Course.
Organised 'Tour & Tasting' events for parties of 50 or
more. Please call or email us.

a: Webbs Land, Tanfield Lane, Wickham, Hampshire,
PO17 5NS | t: 01329 833633
www.webbsland.com

Hampshire
Westward House Vineyard
The vineyard is not currently in use although it is still
looked after every year.

a: Silchester Road, Little London, Tadley, Hampshire,
RG26 5EX
t: 01256 851599

Kent
Westwell Wines
Perfectly located on the chalk Downs, we produce
exclusive, quality sparkling wines made from the
classic Champagne varieties as well as a new clone
of Ortega for our still wines.

a: Westwell Wines, Westwell Lane, Nr. Charing, Kent,
TN25 4NG | t: 01622 862102
www.westwellwines.co.uk

Kent
White Horse Vineyard
Please see entry under Terlingham vineyard.

a: Terlingham Manor Farm, Gibraltar Lane, Hawkinge, Kent,
CT18 7AE
t: 01303 892743

Hampshire
Wickham Vineyards
Come and visit the vineyard and winery. Enjoy our
audio tour. Find out about grape growing and the
making of award winning wines. Enjoy a free tasting
and experience the delights of Vatika Restaurant.

a: Botley Road, Shedfield, Southampton, Hampshire,
SO32 2HL | t: 01329 834042
www.wickhamvineyard.com

Hampshire
Winchester Vineyard
The Winchester Vineyard is a community of people
committed to living out the words and works of Jesus.
We want to love and serve each other as a church
and the city around us.

a: 20 Arthur Road, Winchester, Hampshire, SO23 7EA
t: 01962 863492
www.winvin.org.uk

Surrey

Wisley Vineyard at the RHS Garden

The 16 acre fruit field is a major part of the fruit department at Wisley, and is home to a multitude of plants and trees. Wisley vineyard began producing wine in 2006. Producing around 300 bottles.

a: RHS Wisley Gardens, Wisley Lane, Wisley, Woking, Surrey, GU23 6QB | t: 01483 224234
www.rhs.org.uk

West Sussex

Wiston Estate Winery

Widely regarded as one of the most exciting new sparkling wine enterprises in the UK today. Established in 2008 exclusively for the production of traditional method English sparkling wines.

a: Dermot Sugrue, Wiston Estate Winery, North Farm Washington, West Sussex | t: 01903 877845
www.wistonestate.com

Hampshire

Wooldings Vineyard

The brainchild of the late Charles Cunningham, murdered in Indonesia while on holiday in 2002. Based in a hidden valley in Hampshire and superbly positioned to produce English wines.

a: Coates and Seely Ltd. Northington House, Overton, Hampshire, RG25 3DJ. Location of vineyard: Wooldings Farm, Whitchurch, Hampshire, RG28 7QT | t: 01256 771461

Kent

Wootton Park Vineyard

Up until 1999 Wotton Park Vineyard was producing award winning wines. Since the change of ownership it now been greatly reduced in size and produces wine only for personal consumption.

a: The Gables, Wootton, Canterbury, Kent, CT4 6RT
t: 01303 844334

Kent

Wrangling Lane Vineyard

Grape varieties: Seyval Blanc, Bacchus, Rondo, Pinot Noir.

a: 187 Wood Road, Heybridge, Maldon, Essex, CM9 4AU. Location of vineyard: Great Buckland, Luddesdown, Gravesend, Kent, ME13 | t: 07967 585632

West Sussex

Wychwood House Vineyard

Grape varieties: Huxelrebe, Schönburger, Faberrebe, Bacchus, Dornfelder.

a: Shermanbury, Horsham, West Sussex, RH13 8HE
t: 01403 710328

Oxfordshire

Wyfold Vineyard

Planted in 2003 and completed in 2006. The first wines were produced in 2009. The grapes are sent to RidgeView to be vinified.

a: Wyfold Lodge, Wyfold, Oxfordshire, RG4 9HU
t: 01491 680495

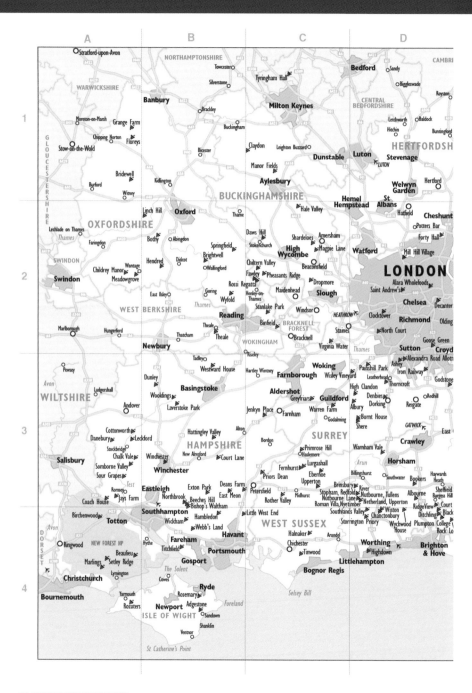

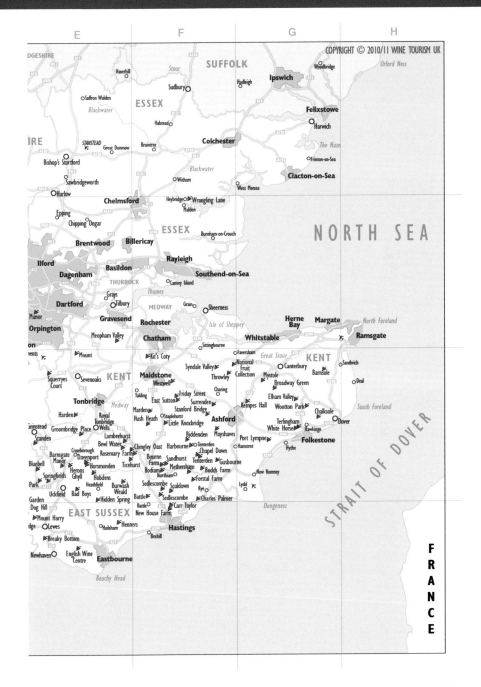

BERKSHIRE

Legoland

At LEGOLAND Windsor there's Land of the Vikings - and at its heart the biggest, wildest, wettest ride in the park, Vikings' River Splash! Join the Viking fleet and set sail for a white water voyage through turbulent rapids! Prepare for a soaking as you encounter mythical sea monsters, race through raging waters and thunder down churning waterfalls. Back on dry land unravel the mystery of Loki's Labyrinth, our Nordic-themed hedge maze.

a: Winkfield Road, Windsor, Berkshire, SL4 4AY
t: 08705 040404 | www.legoland.co.uk

BERKSHIRE

Windsor Castle

Windsor Castle is the oldest and largest occupied castle in the world and the Official Residence of Her Majesty The Queen. Its rich history spans almost 1000 years. The Castle covers an area of about 5 hectares (13 acres).

a: Windsor, Berkshire, SL4 1NJ
t: 02077 7660304 | www.royalcollection.org.uk

EAST SUSSEX

1066 Battle Abbey and Battlefield

An abbey founded by William the Conqueror on the site of the Battle of Hastings. Battlefield views and new visitor centre with film and interactive exhibition.

a: High Street, Battle, East Sussex, TN33 0AD
t: 014240 775705 | www.english-heritage.org.uk

EAST SUSSEX

Drusillas Zoo Park

Drusillas Park offers an opportunity to get nose to nose with nature with hundreds of exotic animals from monkeys and crocodiles to penguins and meerkats. Go Wild! Go Bananas! and Amazon Adventure are paradise for anyone who needs to let off steam and Thomas the Tank Engine offers a train service 362 days a year. Don't miss close encounters in Lemurland, or our brand new Adventure Maze Quest – Eden's Eye.

a: Alfriston Road, Alfriston, East Sussex, BN26 5QS
t: 01323 874100 | www.drusillas.co.uk

EAST SUSSEX

Lewes Castle & Barbican Museum

High above the medieval streets stands Lewes Castle, begun soon after 1066 by William de Warenne as his stronghold in Sussex and added to over the next 300 years, culminating in the magnificent Barbican. Steep climbs to the top of this and the adjacent keep are rewarded with spectacular views. Next door, in Barbican House Museum, explore the archaeological history of Sussex and the changing exhibitions in the upper gallery.

a: Barbican House, 169 High Street, Lewes, East Sussex BN7 1YE
t: 01273 486290 | www.sussexpast.co.uk

EAST SUSSEX

Royal Pavilion

The spectacular seaside palace of the Prince Regent (George IV) transformed by John Nash between 1815 and 1822 into one of the most dazzling and exotic buildings in the British Isles.

a: 4/5 Pavilion Buildings, Brighton, East Sussex, BN1 1EE
t: 03000 290900 | **www.brighton-hove-rpml.org.uk/RoyalPavilion/Pages/home.aspx**

EAST SUSSEX

Sea Life Centre

Fancy diving beneath the sea without getting wet? You'll come eyeball to eyeball with everything from shrimps to sharks, and learn tons of great stuff from SEA LIFE experts. So go on, take the plunge and visit Brighton SEA LIFE centre soon!

a: Brighton Sea Life Centre, Madeira Drive, Brighton, East Sussex, BN2 1TB
t: 01273 604234 | **www.sealifeeurope.com**

HAMPSHIRE

Paultons Family Theme Park

Paultons Family Theme Park in Hampshire, on the edge of the New Forest, offers a great family day out with over 50 different attractions and rides included in the price. The variety of things to see and do includes thrilling and gentle rides, dinosaurs, museums, animated shows, play areas, exotic birds and other fun activities for all ages in garden setting.

a: Ower, nr. Romsey, The New Forest, Hampshire, SO51 6AL
t: 02380 814442 | **www.paultonspark.co.uk**

HAMPSHIRE

Portsmouth Historic Dockyard

Visit the world famous historic ships at the home of the Royal Navy. Go aboard HMS Victory, HMS Warrior 1860 and see the Mary Rose Museum for the best day out in the South of England. Portsmouth Harbour's leading attraction also includes the National Museum of the Royal Navy, Action Stations and Harbour Tours. The Historic Dockyard is a great place to experience 800 years of naval history surrounded by working docks and historic buildings.

a: Visitor Centre, Victory Gate, HM Naval Base, Portsmouth, Hampshire, PO1 3LJ.
t: 023 9283 9766 | **www.historicdockyard.co.uk**

HAMPSHIRE

Winchester Cathedral

Winchester Cathedral tells the story of more than 1,000 years of history, faith and worship. Treasures include the 12th-century Winchester Bible, medieval carvings and contemporary sculptures. It is the burial place of Jane Austen and Saxon Kings. Major events for 2010 included a new exhibition to celebrate the life of Jane Austen and her Hampshire home. Free entry for children under 16 with family and free children's trail.

a: Cathedral Office, 1 The Close, Winchester, Hampshire, SO23 9LS
t: 01962 857200 | **www.winchester-cathedral.org.uk**

The Needles Park

ISLE OF WIGHT

The Isle of Wight´s premier visitor attraction and is situated at Alum Bay overlooking the Island´s most famous landmark, The Needles Rocks and Lighthouse. Every year, nearly half a million people visit to view these jagged chalk stacks and lighthouse, the unique multi coloured sand cliffs and enjoy the Park´s facilities, including the spectacular chairlift. The Needles Park is a fantastic place to visit with all the family.

a: Alum Bay, Isle of Wight, PO39 0JD
t: 08717 200022 | **www.theneedles.co.uk**

Chartwell

KENT

Once upon a time, the family home of Sir Winston Churchill from 1924. The rooms are kept as they were during his lifetime and offer an insight into both his domestic and political life. Photographs, books and personal possessions, including his famous cigars, evoke his career, personality and family. Museum and exhibition rooms contain displays, sound recordings and collections of memorabilia. Many of Sir Winston´s own paintings are on view in his studio.

a: Westerham, Kent, TN16 1PS
t: 01732 868381 | **www.nationaltrust.org.uk**

Dover Castle

KENT

Dover Castle boasts 2000 years of history and includes the newly developed The Great Tower, a Roman Lighthouse and a Saxon Church. Enjoy a Hidden Dover Castle tour or enter the Secret Wartime Tunnels deep beneath the famous White Cliffs.

a: Castle Hill Road, Dover, Kent, CT16 1HU
t: 01303 211067 | **www.english-heritage.org.uk/daysout/properties/dover-castle**

Hever Castle & Gardens

KENT

Romantic 13th century moated castle, once Anne Boleyn's childhood home. Magnificently furnished interiors, spectacular award winning gardens. Miniature Model House Exhibition, Yew Maze, unique Splashing Water Maze.

a: Edenbridge, Kent, TN8 7NG
t: 01732 865224 | **www.hevercastle.co.uk**

Leeds Castle and Gardens

KENT

Historic Leeds Castle set in 500 acres of beautiful parkland, some of its many attractions include; Knights Realm playground, Castle Craft Cafe; Dog Collar Museum; Bird Aviary; Falconry; Gardens; Vineyard; Gift shops; Restaurant and cafe.

a: Maidstone, Kent, ME17 1PL
t: 01622 765400 | **www.leeds-castle.com**

Blenheim Palace

OXFORDSHIRE

Birthplace of Sir Winston Churchill and home to the Duke of Marlborough, Blenheim Palace, one of the finest baroque houses in England, is set in over 2,000 acres of landscaped gardens.

a: Woodstock, Oxfordshire, OX20 1PX
t: 01993 811091 | www.blenheimpalace.com

Didcot Railway Centre

OXFORDSHIRE

Didcot Railway Centre is home to a collection of over twenty Great Western Railway steam locomotives based in the original engine shed or under restoration in the locomotive works, together with Great Western carriages and wagons. Brunel's original broad gauge railway has been recreated with a replica of the Fire Fly locomotive dating from 1840. There are Steamdays and special events throughout the year when you can ride on the steam trains.

a: Didcot, Oxfordshire, OX11 7NJ
t: 01235 817200 | www.didcotrailwaycentre.org.uk

RHS Garden Wisley

SURREY

Stretching over 240 acres of glorious garden, Wisley demonstrates the best in British gardening practices, whatever the season. Plant centre, gift shop and restaurant.

a: Woking, Surrey, GU23 6QB
t: 08452 609000 | www.rhs.org.uk/wisley

Thorpe Park

SURREY

The nation's thrill capital! We live for adrenaline fuelled rides. Go from 0 to 80 in under 2 seconds, survive a death defying beyond vertical drop, spin through 10 insane loops... and that's just for starters! With over 30 rides, THORPE PARK is the place to get your adrenaline pumping!

a: Staines Road, Chertsey, Surrey, KT16 8PN
T: 01932 577123 | www.thorpepark.com

Chessington World of Adventures

SURREY

With exciting rides & roller coasters, a Zoo, SEA LIFE Centre and Safari Themed Hotel - Chessington really is Britain's Wildest Adventure. Our Lands: Forbidden Kingdom; Land of the Dragons; Market Square; Mexicana; Mystic East; Pirates Cove; Toytown; Transylvania; Wild Asia. Our Zoo's: Wanyama Village & Reserve; Lorikeet Lagoon; Trail of the Kings; SEA LIFE Centre; Children's Zoo; Creepy Caves; Monkey & Bird Garden; Penguin Cove & Otters; Sealion Bay

a: Leatherhead Road, Chessington, Surrey, KT9 2NE
t: 08716 634477 | www.chessington.com

⚐Food & Wine Festivals
South East & London

EAST SUSSEX

Brighton & Hove Food and Drink Festival | September/October
www.brightonfoodfestival.com
Address: Brighton & Hove, East Sussex

EAST SUSSEX

Eastbourne Beer Festival | October
www.eastbournebeerfestival.co.uk
Address: Held at the Winter Garden, East Sussex | **Tel:** 01323 412000 | **email:** info@goaheadevents.com

---

EAST SUSSEX

Hastings Seafood and Wine Festival | September
Address: Hastings Old Town, Rock-a-nore Road, Hastings, East Sussex, TN34 3AR
Tel: 01424 451066 | **email:** hic@hastings.gov.uk

EAST SUSSEX

Hove Champagne Festival | June
www.hovechampagnefestival.co.uk
Address: Hove Lawns, Brighton and Hove, East Sussex | **Tel:** 01273 778811 | **email:** info@goaheadevents.com

---

EAST SUSSEX

Plumpton College Open Day | 14th May 2011
www.plumpton.ac.uk
Address: Plumpton College, Ditchling Road, Nr Lewes, East Sussex, BN7 3AE | **Tel:** 01273 890454

EAST SUSSEX

The Glynde Food & English Wine Festival | 16th July 2011 - 17th July 2011
www.glynde.co.uk
Address: Glynde Place, Glynde, East Sussex, BN8 6SX | **Tel:** 01273 858224 | **email:** subscribe@glynde.co.uk

---

HAMPSHIRE

The Hampshire Food Festival | 1st July 2011 - 31 July 2011
www.hampshirefare.co.uk
Address: Hampshire | **Tel:** 01962 847098 | **email:** sophie.boxall@hants.gov.uk

---

LONDON

Real Food Festival | 5th May 2011 - 8th May 2011
www.realfoodfestival.co.uk
Address: Earls Court, London, SW5 9TA

LONDON

Taste of Christmas | December
www.tasteofchristmas.com
Address: Excel, London | **Tel:** 02072 443164 | **email:** vickys@brandevents.co.uk

---

LONDON

Taste of London Festival | 16th June 2011 - 19th June 2011
www.tastefestivals.com/london
Address: Regents Park, London | **Tel:** 02074 711080

LONDON

Toast Festival | 10th June 2011 - 12th June 2011
www.toastfestivals.co.uk
Address: London | **Tel:** 08712 30559 | **email:** info@goaheadevents.com

WEST SUSSEX

South of England Agricultural Show | 9th June 2011 - 11th June 2011
www.seas.org.uk
Address: Ardingly, West Sussex, RH17 6TL | **Tel:** 01444 892700 | **email:** seas@btclick.com

WEST SUSSEX

Festive Food & Drink Fayre | 3rd December 2011 - 4the December 2011
www.seas.org.uk
Address: Ardingly, West Sussex, RH17 6TL | **Tel:** 01444 892700 | **email:** seas@btclick.com

☐ Notes:

....
....
....
....
....
....
....
....
....
....
....
....
....
....
....
....
....
....
....
....
....
....
....
....
....
....
....
....
....
....
....
....
....

East

 England

Essex, Hertfordshire, Bedfordshire, Cambridgeshire, Norfolk, Suffolk

East

The East covers Essex, Hertfordshire, Bedfordshire, Cambridgeshire, Norfolk and Suffolk and is based around the ancient kingdom of East Anglia; it has just over 30 wine estates.

Beautiful, timber-framed villages, traditional market towns, rolling countryside and unspoilt coastline - this is England as you always thought it should be and right on London's doorstep.

You can visit the famous University City of Cambridge, with its ancient colleges, magnificent King's College Chapel and go punting on the river. The medieval city of Norwich is dominated by its cathedral and 12th century castle. There's Colchester - Britain's oldest recorded town, St. Albans, with its cathedral and the rich treasures of Verulamium, the third city of Roman Britain.

The Broads are Britain's largest nationally protected wetland, whilst The Fens, stretching out from The Wash, are noted for their dramatic skies and sweeping views. To the west, the rolling Dunstable Downs offer chalk life flora and fauna. All offer fantastic wildlife and are amongst the UK's best places for bird-watching.

The coastline comprises unspoilt sandy beaches, tiny fishing villages, crumbling cliffs, estuaries, shingle spits and Britain's best mudflats and salt marshes. Here smugglers inns nestle close to the

waters where Lord Nelson learnt to sail. Enjoy the fun-packed family resorts of Great Yarmouth and Southend, alongside idyllic coastal towns such as Southwold and Cromer.

Inland, explore the inspirational landscapes of our artists, authors and filmmakers - such as Constable Country, where Britain's greatest landscape painter was born and worked. Picturesque medieval villages and fine Georgian towns are the legacy of a prosperous past. Newmarket is internationally renowned for being the historic home of horseracing.

> ## 'This is England as you always thought it should be and right on London's doorstep.'

Discover the spectacular colours and delicate fragrances of some of Britain's finest gardens, and magnificent treasure houses such as Woburn Abbey, Hatfield House, Blickling Hall and Royal Sandringham - alongside ancient castles, steam trains, museums and a rich aviation and maritime heritage.

Selected wineries
Chilford Hall (Cambridgeshire)
Gifford's Hall Vineyard (Suffolk)
Shawsgate Vineyard (Suffolk)

Chilford Hall

Chilford Hall's 20-acre vineyard is the only commercial vineyard in Cambridgeshire and has been in operation in Linton since 1972, with the first vintage being produced in 1974. The estate is famous for sparkling and still rosé and white wines, and produced its first Granta Valley red wine in 2008 which sold out within six weeks.

The vineyard, comprising of free draining "flinty" soil and overlaying chalk, is situated on a south west facing slope to maximise the sunshine available during the summer months. The first vines were planted in 1972 and are trained in a wide row and tall trellised system. This allows a larger leaf area to be exposed to the sunlight and the roots to spread widely in the generous soil space. This system of vine management ultimately intensifies the sweetness of the grapes. The local microclimate enables the fruit to ripen to the optimum sugar and acidity levels.

Gifford's Hall Vineyard

Gifford's Hall is located in the village of Hartest between Bury St Edmunds and Sudbury in Suffolk. They currently have 12 acres of vines under cultivation with five grape varieties; Madeleine Angevine, Reichensteiner, Bacchus, Rondo and Pinot Noir. They are one of the largest producers of Madeleine Angevine.

They are able to offer their customers good quality, clean grapes that have achieved gold medal status. The Gifford's Hall vineyard was planted around 20 years ago and the vines are now approaching their prime. The grapes are sold to vineyards in Suffolk, Essex, Kent and Dorset

Shawsgate Vineyard

One of East Anglia's oldest, commercial vineyards producing a range of white, red, rosé and quality sparkling wines.

At Shawsgate they are passionate about their wines which are made to very high standards in their own on-site winery. They have many regional, national and international awards to their name. They produce a range of wines from dry through to medium sweet white alongside two styles of red wine. When visiting you will also find occasional and small batch wines which could include oaked wines, vintage wines (over 10 years), light reds and rosé. They are currently in the process of preparing their first sparkling wine for sale.

Selected destinations:
Cambridge: Visit Cambridge and explore the historic college buildings, plus a wide range of attractions and museums. Take a short break and enjoy the surrounding areas.

Colchester: 2000 years of history snuggles up to 21st-century culture making the place burst with everything you need for a day trip, short break or longer stay.

Ipswich: England's oldest, continuously settled Anglo-Saxon town - with medieval streets and architectural gems - from the decorative plasterwork of the 'Ancient House' (c.1670), to Sir Norman Foster's award-winning Willis Corroon building. Peterborough's 3,000 years of heritage and an extensive choice of leisure, shopping and activity pursuits provide a dynamic experience for leisure and business visitors alike.

The Norfolk and Suffolk Broads: Britain's largest protected wetland and third largest inland waterway, with the status of a national park. It is home to some of the rarest plants and animals in the UK. The Broads Authority was set up in 1989, with responsibility for conservation, planning, recreation and waterways.

 **East**

Map	Wine estate	Tel number	Opening times
D3	Bardfield Vineyard	01371 810776	Wine tastings and sales at vineyard all year
E3	Brook Farm Vineyard	01787 248590	By appointment only
B4	Broxbournebury Vineyard	02088 862168	By appointment only
E3	Carters Vineyard	01206 271136	Easter Monday-Oct, Mon-Fri 11.00-17.00
E2	Chapel Field Vineyard	01953 602749	Not open to the public
C3	Chilford Hall Vineyard	01223 895600	Mar-Oct Mon-Fri 10.00-17.30,
			Nov-Feb Fri-Sun By appointment only
D4	Clayhill Vineyard	08002 118515	By appointment only
D4	Coggeshall Vineyard	01371 851509	Not open to the public
D1	Congham Vineyard	01485 600153	Not open to the public
C3	Coton Orchard Vineyard	07808 161945	Not open to the public
E2	Crown Vines	01379 741081	Not open to the public
C2	Elysian Fields Vineyard	01353 662722	By appointment only
D4	Felsted Vineyard	01245 361504	Mon-Sun 10.00-16.00pm
A4	Frithsden Vineyard	01442 878723	Open to the public
D3	Giffords Hall Vineyard	01284 830799	By appointment only
C3	Gog Magog Vineyard	01223 844075	Not open to the public
C4	Gravel Lane Vineyard	02088 855888	Not open to the public
C4	Hazel End Vineyard	01279 812377	Not open to the public,
			wine purchases can be collected from the vineyard
B4	Herts Oak Farm Vineyard	01992 448537	Not open to the public
E2	Heveningham Hall	01986 798151	Not open to the public
D3	Hilders Field	01787 376800	Not open to the public
D3	Ickworth Vineyard	01284 723399	Jun-Oct Second Sun of the month 11.00-16.00
D3	Kemp's Vineyard	01359 271497	Not open the public
E2	Knettishall Vineyard	07968 106549	By appointment only
E3	Melton Lodge Vineyard	----------------	Not open to the public
E4	Mersea Island Vineyard	01206 385900	Cafe and shop open Wed-Sun 10.30-16.00
B4	Mimram Valley Vineyard	01438 714395	Not open to the public
C4	Moat House Vineyard	01920 468733	By appointment only
D4	New Hall Vineyards	01621 828343	
E2	Oak Hill Vineyard	01379 586868	Not open to the public
E3	Old Rectory Vineyard	01394 386339	Not open to the public
D3	Ollivers Farm Vineyard	01787 237642	Not open to the public
E4	Potash Vineyard	01206 734734	Not open to the public
E2	Railway Vineyard	01953 602749	Not open to the public
D4	Robert Fleming Wines	01621 828837	Not open to the public
D3	Russetts Vineyard	01799 599775	Not open to the public
C3	Saffron Grange Vineyard	01799 516678/97	Not open to the public
D4	Saint Mary Magdalen Vineyard	01277 651315	Not open to the public
D3	Sandyford Vineyard	01799 586586	Open to the public

Map	Wine estate	Tel number	Opening times
E3	Shawsgate Vineyard	01728 724060	Mon-Sat 10.00-17.00
E3	Shotley Vineyard	01329 834042	Mon-Sat 10.30-17.30, Sun 11.30-17.00
D2	South Pickenham Estate Vineyard	01760 756376	Not open to the public
E3	Staverton Vineyard	01394 460271	By appointment only
E1	Sustead Lane Vineyard	01476 550191	Not open to the public
E2	Tas Valley Vineyard	01476 550191	By appointment only
E2	Thelnetham Vineyard	01379 890739	By appointment only
E2	Valley Farm Vineyards	01986 785535	Mon-Fri 11.00-18.00, Closed January & February
B3	Warden Abbey Vineyard	01462 816226	By appointment only, wine store open all year
C4	Wareside Wines	01920 468733	By appointment only
E3	Willow Grange Vineyard & Winery	01449 760612	By appointment only
E2	Wyken Vineyard	01359 252372	Open to the public

Essex

Bardfield Vineyard

The vineyard was planted in 1990 using varieties of Bacchus and Reichensteine. Bardfield Vineyard was the winner of the 1998 "East Anglian Wine of the Year Award" with the Bardfield Dry 1996 Vintage.

a: Great Lodge, Great Bardfield, Essex, CM7 4QD
t: 01371 810776
www.thegreatlodgeexperience.com

Suffolk

Brook Farm Vineyard

Lavenham Heritage Products is the brand name for the items we produce at Brent Eleigh. We aim to sell products of the highest quality at a fair price using methods which meet the best ethical standards.

a: Cock Lane, Brent Eleigh, Sudbury, Suffolk, CO10 9PB
t: 01787 248590
www.lavenhamheritageproducts.co.uk

Hertfordshire

Broxbournebury Vineyard

Growing Seyval Blanc, Gamay Hatif, and Pinot Noir. Wines featured on our wine lists include white, red and sparkling. Martin Knight is a true local enthusiast and we are proud to support him.

a: Park Avenue, Palmers Green, London, N13 5PG. Location of address: Cock Lane, Hoddesdon, Hertfordshire, EN11 8LS
t: 02088 862168

Essex

Carters Vineyard

Carter's is an enchanting place comprising of 40 acres of vines, wildflower meadows, lakes and woodlands. We produce a range of fine English wines, several of which are award winners.

a: Green Lane, Boxted, Colchester, Essex, CO4 5TS
t: 01206 271136
www.cartersvineyards.co.uk

Norfolk

Chapel Field Vineyard

Planted in 2002 with its first bottles of wine on sale in Feb 2011 on a comercial level. Producing 2 rosé, 2 white, 2 red and a sparkling wine. Grape varieties: Bacchus, Pinot Noir Précoce, MA, Rondo.

a: Pilgrim's Barn, Chapel Road, Spooner Row, Wymondham, Norfolk, NR18 9LN. t: 01953 602749
www.chapelfieldsvineyard.co.uk

Cambridgeshire

Chilford Hall Vineyard

Planted in 1972 and currently harvesting 18 acres. Conference and event facilities, Weddings, Exhibitions, Bistro and a winery where processing and fermentation takes place.

a: Balsham Road, Linton, Cambridge, Cambridgeshire, CB21 4LE | t: 01223 895600
www.chilfordhall.co.uk

Essex

Clayhill Vineyard

A 12 acre site with 10 acres of vineyard. There are 15,300 vines in total which were planted by hand! Varieties include Pinot Noir and Chardonnay which produce sparkling wines, roses and stills.

a: 3 Tyle Cottages, Lower Burnham Road, Latchingdon, Chelmsford, Essex, CM3 6HE. Location of vineyard: CM3 6HF | t: 08002 118515 | www.clayhillvineyard.co.uk

---

Essex

Coggeshall Vineyard

A 5 acre site with 1 of these in vines. The grape variety is Faberrebe and the vines are over 25 years old.

a: Danes Vale, Wethersfield, Essex, CM7 4AH. Location of vineyard: West Street, Coggeshall, Essex, CO6 1NS
t: 01371 851509

Norfolk

Congham Vineyard

Planted in 2006 with the first harvest in 2009. Grape varietiy: Rondo, Acolon, Orion, Phoenix. The wine is produced mainly for firends and family but has been trialled in local shops and pubs.

a: Heath House, Hillington, King's Lynn, Northfolk, PE31 6BZ
t: 01485 600153

Cambridgeshire

Coton Orchard Vineyard

Coton Orchard is a patchwork of apple and plum trees, strawberry fields, green pastures and 1 acre vineyard cultivated with Reichensteiner, Madeliene Angevine, Muller Thurgau vines.

a: Madingley Road, Coton, Cambridge, Cambridgeshire, CB23 7PJ | t: 07808 161945
www.cotonorchard.com

Norfolk

Crown Vines

Planted in 2003. Making a róse wine for friends and family. Produce on average 300-500 bottles annually. Grape varieties: Seyval Blanc, MA, Pinot noir, Rondo, Regent.

a: Crown Farm House, 25 Mill Road, Burston, Northfolk, IP22 5TW
t: 01379 741081

Cambridgeshire

Elysian Fields Vineyard

Elysian Fields White is a still, medium dry table wine, with a well developed fruit flavour. We have recently planted 500 red grape vines and have been producing red and rose wines since 2007 vintage.

a: Bedwell Hey Farm, Ely Road, Little Thetford, Ely, Cambridgeshire, CB6 3HJ | t: 01353 662722
www.elysianfieldsvineyard.co.uk

Essex

Felsted Vineyard

Wine and beers may be bought along with other local produce. Children welcome, animals to view depending on time of year.

a: Crix Green, Felsted, Essex, CM6 3JT
t: 01245 361504

Hertfordshire

Frithsden Vineyard

Grubbed up in 1990s and closure in 2001, it did not look good but in 2005, Simon and Natalie Tooley bought the site and in 2006, 5000 vines were planted and grew exceptionally well in the following years.

a: Frithsden, Hemel Hempstead, Hertfordshire, HP1 3DD
t: 01442 878723
www.frithsdenvineyard.co.uk

Suffolk

Giffords Hall Vineyard

Giffords Hall vineyard was planted around 20 years ago and the vines are now approaching their prime. Madeleine Angevine, Bacchus, Reichensteiner, Rondo and Pinor Noir all do well here.

a: Hartest, Bury St Edmunds, Suffolk, IP29 4EX
t: 01284 830799
www.giffordshall.co.uk

Cambridgeshire

Gog Magog Vineyard

Gog Magog vineyard was first planted in 1995 and had it's first harvest in 1997 producing a still Chardonnay. Since 2002 they started making sparkling wine.

a: Great Shelford, Cambridge, Cambridgeshire, CB22 5AN
t: 01223 844075
www.gogmagogvineyard.co.uk

Essex

Gravel Lane Vineyard

Planted in 2008. First harvest expected in 2011. A new venture for owner, 'Graham' who is in it purely for the love of the outdoors & country. Grape varieties: Pinot Noir Précoce, Bacchus, Schönburger, Acolon.

a: 1-7 Garman Lane, Tottenham, London, N17 0UR
Location of vineyard: Gravel Lane, Chigwell, Essex, IG7 6DQ
t: 0288 855888 | www.gravellanevineyard.co.uk

Hertfordshire

Hazel End Vineyard

The first experiments with vine growing began in 1976. Grape varieties: Bacchus, Huxelrebbe, Muller-Thurgau, Reichensteiner. These four varieties blend well to produce a light, aromatic and dry finish.

a: Hazel End Farm, Bishop's Stortford, Herts, CM23 1HG
t: 01279 812377
www.corylet.com

Hertfordshire

Herts Oak Farm Vineyard

Grape varieties: Bacchus, Reichensteiner, Dunkelfelder, Regent Rondo Acolon, Nero. Schönburger, Acolon.

a: 165 High Road, Broxbournebury, Hertfordshire, EN10 7BT.
Location of vineyard: Beaumont Road, Wormley, West End, Broxbourne, Hertfordshire, EN10 7QJ | t: 01992 448537

Suffolk

Heveningham Hall

Privately owned 18th century Heveningham Hall is not open to the public but is interesting to drive by and see the extent of the work gone into re-creating the Capability Brown designed landscape.

a: Country Fair Trust, Heveningham Hall, Heveningham, Suffolk, IP19 0PN | t: 01986 798151
www.countryfair.co.uk

Suffolk

Hilders Field

An organic vineyard which was planted by hand in 2003 consisting of 380 Triomphe vines.
The wine made here is purely for friends and family.

a: School Lane, Borley, Sudbury, Suffolk, CO10 7AE
t: 01787 376800

Suffolk

Ickworth Vineyard

planted in 1995 with Bacchus and Auxerrois vines. The west side was planted in 1996 with Rondo along with 70 Pinot Noir vines. We produce, sparkling, rose, red and white wine.

a: Fortlands Sicklesmere Road, Bury St Edmunds, Suffolk, IP33 2BN. Location of vineyard: IP29 5QE
t: 01284 723399 | www.ickworthvineyard.co.uk

Suffolk

Kemp's Vineyard

2009 was a cracking year. We had a good summer and this produced one of the best harvests for some years. We produce four wines, our Estate Reserve, Harvest Blend, single varietal wine and a rosé.

a: The Winery, Dales Meadow, Bury St Edmunds, Suffolk, IP29 4EY | t: 01359 271497
www.winehub.co.uk/acatalog/giffords.html

Suffolk

Knettishall Vineyard

Grape varieties: Bacchus, Pinot Noir, Auxerrois.

a: Hall Farm, Heath Road, Knettishall, Diss, Suffolk, IP22 2TQ
t: 07968 106549

Suffolk

Melton Lodge Vineyard

Grape varieties: Bacchus, Pinot Noir Reichensteiner, Siegerrebe.

a: Melton, Woodbridge, IP12 1LU

Essex

Mersea Island Vineyard

A family run business committed to providing high class Bed & Breakfast accommodation and weekly Holiday Lets, quality English Wines, own made Beers and informative Vineyard Tours & suppers.

a: Rewsalls Lane, East Mersea, Colchester, CO5 8SX
t: 01206 385900
www.merseawine.com

Hertfordshire

Mimram Valley Vineyard

Grape varieties: Bacchus, Huxelrebe, MA, Reichensteiner.

a: The Garden House, Tewin Water, Welwyn, Hertfordshire, AL6 0AB
t: 01438 714395

Hertfordshire

Moat House Vineyard

Planted in 2005 by hand on 0.4 hectares of land. Grape varieties: Pinot Noir Précoce, Bacchus. The first big harvest was in 2009 and produced 700 bottles of wine. Sold locally in wine shop/restaurant.

a: New Hall Green, Wareside, Hertfordshire, SG12 7SD
t: 01920 468733

Essex

New Hall Vineyards

Our 67 hectare vineyard is one of the oldest and largest English Wine Producer's in the Country.
First established by the Greenwood family in Purleigh, 1969. Producing 250,000 bottles each year!

a: Chelmsford Road, Purleigh, Chelmsford, CM3 6PN
t: 01621 828343
www.newhallwines.co.uk

Suffolk

Oak Hill Vineyard

Family run business in the centre of the Fressingfield. With an award-winning vineyard and a beautiful converted granary, as holiday accomodation, Oak Hill is ideal for a comfortable break in the country.

a: Willow House Vineyard, Fressingfield, Eye, IP21 5PE
t: 01379 586868
www.oak-hill.co.uk

Suffolk
Old Rectory Vineyard
Grape varieties: Seyval Blanc, Rondo.

a: The Street, Bredfield, Woodbridge, Suffolk, IP13 6AX
t: 01394 386339

Essex
Ollivers Farm Vineyard
Ollivers Farm B&B is a 17th century farmhouse set in fields in a quiet rural location. We have 1.5 acres of landscaped gardens and vineyard. Beautiful views of surrounding countryside.

a: Toppesfield, Halstead, Essex, CO9 4LS
t: 01787 237642
www.essex-bed-breakfast.co.uk

Essex
Potash Vineyard
Grape varieties: Bacchus, Reichensteiner, Dornfelder, Pinot Noir.

a: Abberton Road, Layer de la Haye, Colchester, Essex, CO2 0JX
t: 01206 734734

Norfolk
Railway Vineyard
Owned by Chapel Field Vineyard. Please see Chapel Field Vineyard for more information.
Grape varieties: Bacchus, Pinot Noir, Précoce, MA, Rondo.

a: c/o Pilgrim's Barn, Chapel Road, Spooner Row, Wymondham, Norfolk, NR199LN. Location of vineyard: Junction of A11 and Wymondham Road, Spooner Row, NR19 | t: 01953 602749

Essex
Robert Fleming Wines
Grape varieties: Bacchus, Pinot Blanc, Pinot Noir, Chardonnay.

a: Roundbush Farm, Mundon, Maldon, Essex, CM9 6NP
Location of vineyard: CM3 6RW
t: 01621 828837

Essex
Russetts Vineyard
Grape varieties: Phoenix, Bacchus, Auxerrois, Pinot Noir, MA.

a: Bumpstead Road, Hampstead, Saffron Walden, Essex, CB10 2PW
t: 01799 599775

Essex
Saffron Grange Vineyard
An up and coming vineyard based on the borders of Cambridgeshire and Essex. As the vineyard is only at very early stages we have yet to produce any wines. In May 2009 5,000 vines were planted.

a: Rowley Hill Farm, Little Waldon, Saffron Waldon, Essex, CB10 1UZ | t: 01799 516678/97
www.saffrongrange.com

Essex
Saint Mary Magdalen Vineyard
Grape varieties: MT, Huxelrebe, Seyval Blanc, Pinot Noir, Gagarin Blue, Pinot gris, Chardonnay.

a: 143 High Street, Billericay, Essex, CM11 2TR
t: 01277 651315

Essex
Sandyford Vineyard
Sandyford Vineyard is a 2 acre part of our 400-acre family farm. The vineyard was planted in 1999. producing quality white, red, rose and sparkling wines, several of which have won UK wine industry awards.

a: Salix Farm, Great Sampford, Saffron Walden, Essex, CB10 2QE | t: 01799 586586
www.sandyfordvineyard.co.uk

Suffolk
Shawsgate Vineyard
One of East Anglia's oldest commercial vineyards producing a range of white, red, rosé and quality sparkling wines. We make dry through to medium sweet white alongside two styles of red wine.

a: Badingham Road, Framlingham, Woodbridge, Suffolk, IP13 9HZ | t: 01728 724060
www.shawsgate.co.uk

Suffolk

Shotley Vineyard

Grapes are grown, picked and delivered to Wickham Vineyards. See Wickham Vineyards, S.East & London. Grape varieties: Pinot Noir, Rondo, Bacchus, Ortega Reichensteiner, Chardonnay, Auxerrois, Seyval.

a: c/o Wickham Vineyards, Botley Road, Shedfield, Southampton, Hampshire, SO32 2HL. Location of vineyard: IP9 1EP | t: 01329 834042 | www.wickhamvineyard.com

Norfolk

South Pickenham Estate Vineyard

Grape varieties: MT, Seyval Blanc, Huxelrebe, Schönburger.

a: The Estate Office, South Pickenham Norfolk, PE37 8DZ
t: 01760 756376

Suffolk

Staverton Vineyard

Grape varieties: Bacchus, MT, Ortea, Reichensteiner.

a: The Rookery, Eyke, Woodbridge, Suffolk, IP12 2RR
t: 01394 460271

Norfolk

Sustead Lane Vineyard

Owned by Abbey Vineyards. Please see Abbey Vineyards, East Midlands for more information. Future plans consist of a winery and shop. Grape varieties: Bacchus, Chardonnay, Pinot noir.

a: c/o Abbey Vineyards, Irnham Grange, Irnham Road, Corby Glen, Grantham, Lincolnshire, NG33 4NE. Location of vineyard: NR11 8RR | t: 01476 550191 | www.tandsnurseries.com

Norfolk

Tas Valley Vineyard

Owned by Abbey Vineyards. Please see Abbey Vineyards, East Midlands for more information. Winery on-site, plans for a shop. Grape varieties: Bacchus, Reichensteiner, MT

a: c/o Abbey Vineyards, Irnham Grange, Irnham Road, Corby Glen, Grantham, Lincolnshire, NG33 4NE. Location of vineyard: NR16 1LW | t: 01476 550191 | www.tandsnurseries.com

Norfolk

Thelnetham Vineyard

Grape varieties: MT, Bacchus.

a: Thelnetham House, High Street, Norfolk, IP22 1JL
t: 01379 890739

Suffolk

Valley Farm Vineyards

Come stay with us in idyllic surroundings of blissful tranquillity. Located on 14 acres of vineyards that produce fine English wines using only sustainable viticultural practices.

a: Wissett, Halesworth, Suffolk, IP19 0JJ
t: 01986 785535
www.valleyfarmvineyards.com

Bedfordshire

Warden Abbey Vineyard

Planted in 1986 on the site of a 12th century vineyard attached to a Cistercian Abbey, our first vintage was 1990. Every year since then one or more of our wines have won awards.

a: Southill Park, Biggleswade, Bedfordshire, SG18 9LJ
t: 01462 816226
www.wardenwines.co.uk

Hertfordshire

Wareside Wines

The vineyard is approximately one acre planted with Pinot Noir and Bacchus. We produce an English sparkling wine as well as our Bacchus being made into a single vineyard wine.

a: Findon, new Hallm Wareside, Hertfordshire, SG12 7SD
t: 01920 468733
www.waresidewines.com

Suffolk

Willow Grange Vineyard & Winery

Grape varieties: MT, Optima, Ortega.

a: Street Farm, Stone Street, Crowfield, Ipswich, Suffolk, IP6 9SY
t: 01449 760612

Suffolk

Wyken Vineyard

A 1200-acre farm which includes a 7-acre vineyard producing award-winning wines, including the English Wine of the Year. The vineyard restaurant, The Leaping Hare, is located in our 400-year-old barn.

a: Wyken Road, Stanton, Bury St Edmunds, IP31 2DW
t: 01359 252372
www.wykenvineyards.co.uk

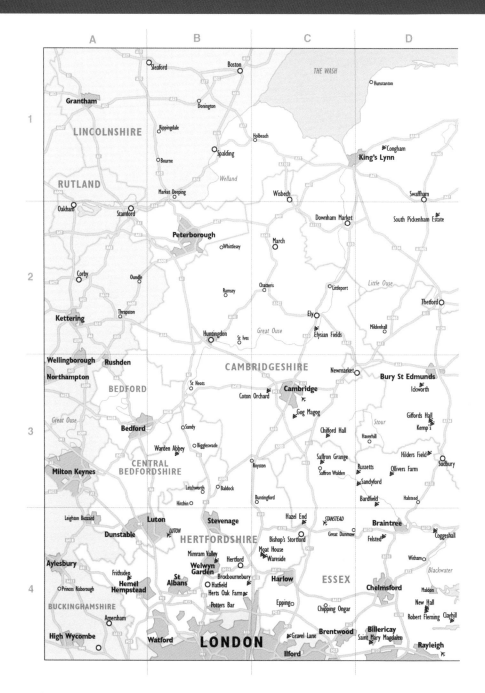

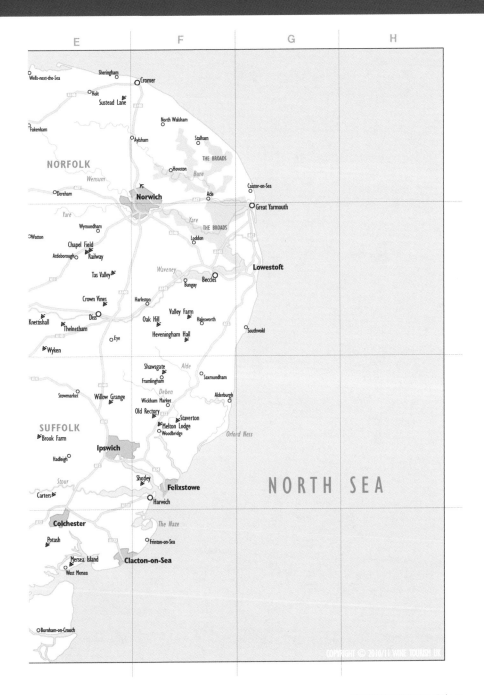

BEDFORDSHIRE

Bodyflight

The World's largest indoor skydiving wind tunnel. Enjoy flight in the wind tunnel made famous by Daniel Craig in scenes from the 2008 James Bond film. The Bodyflight wind tunnel at a diameter of 5m (16.4ft) and a flight area 8m (26.25ft) tall, offers flyers real space to manoeuvre! Producing up to 4000 HP of airflow, our size, power and air quality is unrivalled. All types of flyers are welcome from whether you're a complete beginner or a world champion!

a: Building 36, Twinwoods Business Park, Twinwoods Road, Clapham, Bedfordshire
t: 0845 200 2960 | **www.bodyflight.co.uk**

BEDFORDSHIRE

Woburn Abbey

Home of the Duke of Bedford, a treasure house with outstanding collections of art, furniture, silver, gold and extensive gardens. Set in a beautiful 3,000 acre deer park, Woburn Abbey has been home to the Dukes of Bedford for over 300 years, and is currently occupied by the 15th Duke and his family. Touring the Abbey covers three floors. Purchase an official guide book or audio tour to ensure you will make the most of your experience.

a: Woburn, Bedfordshire, MK17 9WA
t: 01525 290333 | **www.woburn.co.uk**

CAMBRIDGESHIRE

Fitzwilliam Museum

World-class collections of works of art and antiquities spanning centuries and civilisations. Highlights include masterpieces of painting from the fourteenth century to the present day, drawings and prints, sculpture, furniture, armour, pottery and glass, oriental art, illuminated manuscripts, coins and medals and antiquities from Egypt, the Ancient Near East, Greece, Rome and Cyprus. Fascinating Egyptian, Greek, Roman and other antiquities and so much more.

a: Trumpington Street, Cambridge CB2 1RB
t: 01223 332900 | **www.fitzmuseum.cam.ac.uk**

CAMBRIDGESHIRE

Imperial War Museum

With its air shows, unique history and atmosphere, nowhere else combines the sights, sounds and power of aircraft quite like Duxford. Duxford is a former Royal Air Force fighter base and Europe's leading aviation museum, with many original period buildings such as the Control Tower and hangars still in use, alongside state of the award-winning exhibition buildings including Airspace and the American Air Museum.

a: Duxford, Cambridge, Cambridgeshire, CB22 4QR
t: 01223 835000 | **www.duxford.iwm.org.uk**

CAMBRIDGESHIRE

Kings College Chapel

King's College Chapel is a masterpiece of English craftsmanship. It's part of one of the oldest Cambridge colleges sharing a wonderful sense of history and tradition with the rest of the University. It was founded by Henry VI in 1441, and includes an elaborate fan-vault ceiling, magnificent stained-glassed windows and Ruben's masterpiece, The Adoration of the Magi. There's also an exhibition in the northern side chapels showing how the chapel built.

a: Cambridge, Cambridgeshire, CB2 1ST
t: 01223 331212 | **www.kings.cam.ac.uk**

Audley End House and Gardens

ESSEX

Built by Thomas Howard, Earl of Suffolk to entertain King James - Audley End is one of England's most magnificent stately homes. Enjoy over 30 lavishly decorated room interiors by Robert Adam. See the restored historic stables, complete with resident horses and a Victorian groom. Children can let loose in our brand new themed play area next to our new Cart Yard Café which is already proving very popular with visitors.

a: Saffron Walden, Essex, CB11 4JF
t: 01799 522842 | **www.english-heritage.org.uk**

Colchester Zoo

ESSEX

Colchester Zoo is now one of the finest Zoos in Europe due to a constant programme of development and recently won the coveted "Large Visitor Attraction of the Year" Award from the East of England Tourist Board. With over 270 species to see, set in 60 acres of beautiful parkland and lakes, Colchester Zoo is well worth a visit. There are also over 50 daily displays including the unique opportunity to feed the elephants and giraffes yourself!

a: Maldon Road, Stanway, Colchester, Essex, CO3 0SL
t: 01206 331292 | **www.colchester-zoo.com**

Hatfield House

HERTFORDSHIRE

Splendid Jacobean House and Garden in a spectacular countryside setting. Childhood home of Elizabeth I. Built by Robert Cecil, 1st Earl of Salisbury and Chief Minister to King James I; from 1607 to 1611. There is a marvellous collection of pictures, furnishings and historic armour on display. The estate has been in the Cecil family for 400 years - one of England's foremost political families. Hatfield House is the home of the 7th Marquis of Salisbury.

a: Hatfield, Hertfordshire, AL9 5NQ
t: 01707 287010 | **www.hatfield-house.co.uk**

Mersea Island

MERSEA ISLAND

Britain's most easterly inhabited island. Located around eight miles from Colchester in Essex, Mersea Island is situated between the estuaries of the Colne and Blackwater rivers. This unique place is the most easterly inhabited island in the British Isles. Boasts a population of around seven thousand people. If you're thinking about coming to Mersea, don't forget to book your place to stay early. Its well worth planning your holiday here!!!

www.mersea-island.com

Blickling Hall

NORFOLK

A Jacobean redbrick mansion with a garden, orangery, parkland and lake. Spectacular long gallery, plasterwork ceilings and fine collections of furniture, pictures and books. Walks. There is also a display of fine tapestries and furniture, a picnic area, shop, restaurant, plant centre, second-hand bookshop, exhibitions and full events programme.

a: Blickling, Norwich, Norfolk, NR11 6NF
t: 01263 738030 | **www.nationaltrust.org.uk**

Norfolk Lavender

NORFOLK

Large landscaped grounds set around an historic mill. Lavender distillery, national lavender collection, herb garden and new rare breed animal centre. See many varieties of lavender and a large miscellany of herbs. Hear about the harvest and the ancient process of lavender distillation. The Countryside Gift Shop stocks the full range of Norfolk Lavender's famous products. There is also a tearoom that specialises in cream teas, freshly-baked cakes and lunches.

a: Caley Mill, Heacham, King's Lynn, Norfolk, PE31 7JE
t: 07787 550286 | **www.norfolk-lavender.co.uk**

Sainsburys Centre for Visual Arts

NORTHFOLK

Houses the Robert and Lisa Sainsbury collection in a breathtaking Norman Foster building, with works by Picasso, Bacon and Henry Moore also displayed. The Sainsbury Centre is one of around a hundred university museums in the UK which are regularly open to the public. Sir Robert and Lady Lisa Sainsbury donated their collection of world art to the University of East Anglia in 1973 and the Sainsbury Centre first opened its doors to visitors in 1978.

a: University of East Anglia, Norwich, NR4 7TJ
t: 01603 593199 | **www.scva.org.uk**

Seal watching at Blakeney

NORTHFOLK

Without going out into the open sea, our experienced skipper's take you to known areas frequented by seals. However, we ask that you appreciate that we do not control, or attempt to influence their natural behaviour, or habitat, in order to see them. Here you may observe both common and grey seals from the boat, basking near the water's edge. Our experienced crews will tell you all about the lives of these delightful creatures, and take you in very close.

a: Turnstone Cottage, Old Post Office Yard, Westgate Street, Blakeney, Northfolk, NR25 7NQ
t: 08000 740754 | **www.norfolksealtrips.co.uk**

RSPB Minsmere Nature Reserve

SUFFOLK

One of the UK's premier nature reserves, offering excellent facilities for people of all ages and abilities to experience close views of wildlife in beautiful scenery. Our volunteer guides will help you to discover more, perhaps you prefer to simply stroll around the beautiful RSPB countryside walks, enjoying the stunning scenery. In the visitor centre there is a tearoom. Browse the RSPB shop, which stocks a wide range of bird food, feeders, books, gifts and binoculars.

a: 7Westleton, Saxmundham, Suffolk, IP17 3BY
t: 01728 648281 | **www.rspb.org.uk**

Sutton Hoo Burial Site

SUFFOLK

Sutton Hoo, (National Trust) is an Anglo-Saxon royal burial site overlooking the River Deben in Suffolk, plus exhibition hall. This hauntingly beautiful 103-hectare (255-acre) estate, with far-reaching views over the river Deben, is home to one of the greatest archaeological discoveries of all time. Walk around the ancient burial mounds and discover the incredible story of the ship burial of an Anglo-Saxon king and his treasured possessions.

a: Sutton Hoo, Woodbridge, Suffolk, IP12 3DJ
t: 01394 389700 | **www.nationaltrust.org.uk**

🏳Food & Wine Festivals
East

CAMBRIDGESHIRE

The Free Cambridge Food & Garden Festival | September
www.oakleighfairs.co.uk
Address: CB1 1JF, Cambridgeshire | **Tel:** 0800 141 2823 | **email:** web-contact@oakleighfairs.co.uk

CAMBRIDGESHIRE

Feast East | 4th March 2011 - 6th March 2011
www.feasteast.co.uk
Address: Chilford Hall, Linton, Cambridgeshire, CB21 4LE | **Tel:** 01473 785883 | **email:** enquiries@tastesofanglia.com

ESSEX

Christmas Food & Craft Show | 26th November 2011 - 27th November 2011
www.theessexfoodshow.co.uk | **Address:** on B1018 between Braintree and Witham, Essex, CM77 8PD
Tel: 01621 773403 | **email:** contact@theessexfoodshow.co.uk

ESSEX

Colchester Carnival Oyster Fair | 3rd September 2011
www.colchesterfoodanddrinkfestival.co.uk
Address: Castle Park, Colchester, Essex, CO1 1UD | **Tel:** 01206 525527 | **email:** don.quinn@ntlworld.com

ESSEX

Colchester Food & Drink Festival | 25th June 2011 - 26th June 2011
www.colchesterfoodanddrinkfestival.co.uk
Address: Castle Park, Colchester, Essex, CO1 1UD | **Tel:** 01206 525527 | **email:** don.quinn@ntlworld.com

ESSEX

The Essex Food Show (Spring) | 14th May 2011 - 15th May 2011
www.theessexfoodshow.co.uk | **Address:** on B1018 between Braintree and Witham, Essex, CM77 8PD
Tel: 01621 773403 | **email:** contact@theessexfoodshow.co.uk

ESSEX

The Essex Food Show (Autum) | 8th October 2011 - 9th October 2011
www.theessexfoodshow.co.uk | **Address:** on B1018 between Braintree and Witham, Essex, CM77 8PD
Tel: 01621 773403 | **email:** contact@theessexfoodshow.co.uk

SUFFOLK

Helmingham Hall Food & Drink Festival | 6th August 2011 - 7th August 2011
www.colchesterfoodanddrinkfestival.co.uk
Address: Helmingham Hall, Helmingham, Suffolk | **Tel:** 01206 525527 | **email:** don.quinn@ntlworld.com

SUFFOLK

The Melford Hall Food & Drink Festival | 23rd July 2011 - 24th July 2011
www.colchesterfoodanddrinkfestival.co.uk
Address: Melford Hall, Braintree, Suffolk, CO10 9AA | **Tel:** 01206 525527 | **email:** don.quinn@ntlworld.com

NORFOLK

Norfolk food festival | September
www.norfolkfoodfestival.co.uk
Address: Norfolk | **email:** mail@maryruddpr.co.uk

Notes:

West Midlands

 England

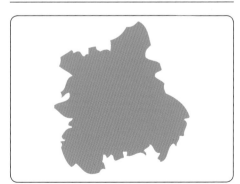

Herefordshire, Shropshire, Staffordshire, Warwickshire, West Midlands, Worcestershire

West Midlands

The West Midlands covers Herefordshire, Shropshire, Staffordshire, Warwickshire, West Midlands and Worcestershire and has nearly 40 wine estates in the region.

The West Midlands is at the hub of Britain's road network, so exploring every last bit of it is made very easy! No need to have to fly into London as the international airport at Birmingham is right in the centre of the region. Birmingham also offers a world-class cultural scene, superb shopping, top attractions, fantastic nightlife, major international events and exhibitions.

Take some time to visit the Cotswolds, taking in the many honey-coloured villages. The potteries of Staffordshire to the north of the region are juxtaposed with Shakespeare's Stratford-upon-Avon and the nearby, lesser-known parts of Warwickshire. Close by lies the Black Country - a visit here will reveal a rich seam of art, crafts, tradition and culture with modern architectural design sitting alongside villages from the Victorian era.

Explore the counties of Herefordshire and Shropshire along the beautiful borderlands of England and Wales, sampling the myriad of excellent restaurants and locally produced food. Don't forget to discover the real taste of the countrysideby sampling Herefordshire's famous cider. In Worcestershire you can find fine churches,

historic buildings and a thriving arts scene with internationally acclaimed festivals and events.

Selected wineries
Halfpenny Green Vineyard (Staffordshire)
Ludlow Vineyard (Shropshire)
Wroxeter Roman Vineyard (Shropshire)

Halfpenny Green Vineyard
The Complete English Wine Experience! The Vineyard is open to the public where individuals or small groups can follow the self-guided vineyard trail. This follows a relaxing route through the vineyard. Information boards describe many of the French, German and Hybrid varieties planted. After touring the vineyard the visitor can inspect the Winery, taste the wines and visit their Gift Shop, Craft Centre and Conservatory Tea Rooms. No need to book for the vineyard trail just turn up and enjoy a relaxing visit.

The first half acre was planted in 1983 and by 1991 a further 22 acres had been added. In 2005, 3 acres of Bacchus were added. The vineyard is situated 250ft above sea level with well-sheltered south facing slopes and light, sandy, free-draining soil.

Ludlow Vineyard

Ludlow Vineyard is located in Clee St Margaret, on the lower slopes of the Brown Clee Hill, near Ludlow in South Shropshire. There is a vineyard, orchards with apples and walnuts and a Distillery.

The product range encompasses wine, spirits, cider, apple juice and green walnuts (fresh and pickled). The vineyard is spread over 10 acres, and has about 8,000 vines. The main white grape varieties are Madeleine Angevine (a Riesling derivative), Seyval and Solaris, but there is also Phoenix, Madeleine Sylvaner, Kernling and Ortega, and red varieties including Rondo, Regent and Triomphe. Ludlow Vineyard is in a remote location and is not currently open to the public, but visitors are welcome by appointment in the summer.

Wroxeter Roman Vineyard

Planted in 1991 Wroxeter Roman Vineyard is truly a "Taste of Shropshire" Situated next to the Roman city of Viroconium it is the close of a 2000 year arc which sees modern methods twinned with the newer vine varieties, this unique blend means the highest quality wine can be grown.Both the Vineyard and the city are within 10 minutes of the M54, Shrewsbury, Telford and the world heritage site of Ironbridge. Wroxeter Roman Vineyard specialises in giving interesting, informative tours that are fun for everyone.

Selected destinations:

Birmingham: A dynamic business city, offering a world class cultural scene, a diverse and lively mix of shopping, attractions, nightlife, major international events and exhibitions.

Coventry: Has the best of both worlds with its prominent history and cinematic countryside combined with vibrant city life and multi-million pound regeneration.

Hereford: Agricultural county town; with its Norman cathedral, a large chained library and the world-famous Mappa Mundi exhibition.

Ludlow: Perched on a cliff above the picturesque River Teme in south Shropshire in one of the most unspoiled parts of rural England. Ludlow was described by John Betjeman as "the loveliest town in England" and by Country Life as "the most vibrant small town in the Country".

'Explore the counties of Herefordshire and Shropshire along the beautiful borderlands of England and Wales, sampling the myriad of excellent restaurants and locally produced food.'

Shrewsbury: The county town of Shropshire and features breezy, black and white 'magpie' half-timbered houses. Set amidst glorious countryside near to the Welsh Borders, it is one of England's finest medieval market towns. Charles Darwin was born and educated in Shrewsbury and all around you will find reminders of his association with the town.

Stoke-on-Trent: Home to the world's greatest pottery manufacturers, the city boasts visitor centres, ceramic museums and factory shops, plus excellent leisure and entertainment.

Stratford-upon-Avon: is William Shakespeare's home town with a glorious river setting, five houses associated with Shakespeare, The RSC Courtyard Theatre and first class shopping and dining.

Worcester: Full of history and surrounded by beautiful countryside. Situated on the banks of the River Severn the city has a rich and varied heritage to explore.

West Midlands

Map	Wine estate	Tel number	Opening times
B6	Astley Vineyards	01299 822907	Mon, Thur, Sat 10.00-17.00, Sun 12.00-17.00, Other times by appointment
B7	Backbury House Vineyard	01432 850255	By appointment only
C6	Bearley Vineyard	02476 468062	Not open to the public
B7	Beeches Vineyard	01306 886124	By appointment only
B6	Broadfield Court Vineyard	01568 797483	10.30-15.30 Winter, 10.00-16.30 Easter-Summer
C4	Buzzard Valley Vineyard	01213 081951	Open to the public
B7	Castle Brook Vineyard	01989 562770	Not open to the public
B6	Church Farm Vineyard	01905 620283	
B5	Clee Hills Vineyard	----------------	Not open to the public
B6	Coddington Vineyard	01531 640668	Mar-Dec Thu-Sun, Bank Holidays 2.00-17.00, other times by appointment
A3	Commonwood Vineyard	01939 236193	By appointment only
A6	Croft Castle Vineyard	01568 780246	Open to the public
B7	Four Foxes Vineyard	01432 850065	Not open to the public
B6	Frome Valley Vineyard	01885 490768	By appointment only
A4	Habberley Vineyard	01743 790144	Not open to the public
B5	Halfpenny Green Vineyard	01384 221122	Mon-Sun 9.30-17.00
A5	Hargrove Estate	01694 771722	Not open to the public
C6	Heart of England Vineyard	01789 750565	By appointment only
C6	Hunt Hall Farm Vineyard	01789 750349	Not open to the public
B5	Ludlow Vineyard	01584 823356	Not open to the public
A7	Lulham Court Vineyard	01981 251107	Open to the public
A5	Morville St. Gregory Vineyard	01584 841021	By appointment only
B6	Nash Vineyard	01905 821397	Not open to the public
B7	Old Grove House Vineyard	01989 770754	Not open to the public
B7	Pengethley Manor Vineyard	01989 730211	Open to the public
B6	Rose Bank Vineyard	01905 451439	By appointment only
B7	Sparchall Vineyard	01432 850800	By appointment only
C4	Spring Cottage Vineyard	01922 454447	Not open to the public
A7	Sunnybank Vineyard and Vine Nursery	01981 240256	
B7	Tarrington Court Vineyard	01432 890632	By appointment only
B3	Tern Valley Vineyard	01630 639688	By appointment only
B7	Tiltridge Vineyard	01684 592906	Mon-Fri 9.00-17.00
B7	Townsend Farm Vineyard	01989 563772	Not open to the public
A7	Treago Vineyard	01981 580208	Not open to the public
C6	Welcombe Hills Vineyard	01789 731071	By appointment only
B4	Wroxeter Roman Vineyard	01743 761888	Mon-Sat 9.00-17.00, Sun 10.30-16.30

Worcestershire

Astley Vineyards

Established in the 1970's by viticultural pioneers Michael and Betty Bache. The vineyards are close to the River Severn. Over 85% of all Astley wines ever produced have won an award!

a: Astley, Stourport-onSevern, Worcester, DY13 0RU
t: 01299 822907
www.astley-vineyards.co.uk

Herefordshire

Backbury House Vineyard

Grape varieties: Phoenix, Seyval Blanc.

a: Checkley, Hereford, Herefordshire, HR1 4NA
t: 01432 850255

Warwickshire

Bearley Vineyard

Following on from our successful first harvest in 2008, 2009 resulted in more than double the crop of Pinot Noir Précoce and Regent grapes. Now Producing around 1,500 bottles of red wine a year.

a: The Beeches, Snitterfield Road, Bearley, Stratford-upon-Avon, Warwickshire, CV37 0SR
t: 02476 468062

Herefordshire

Beeches Vineyard

A small, family-run vineyard producing fine English red, rosé and white wines. We're very pleased to be producing fine English wines and hope that you enjoy them as much as we do.

a: Beeches, Upton Bishop, Herefordshire, HR9 7UD
t: 01306 886124
www.beechesvineyard.com

Herefordshire

Broadfield Court Vineyard

Why not drop in to our shop and café to taste some of our wines. We offer wine-tasting tours including lunches, teas and suppers for up to 50 people. wine with lunch or supper.

a: Bowley Lane, Bodenham, Herefordshire, HR1 3LG
t: 01568 797483
www.broadfieldcourt.co.uk

Staffordshire

Buzzard Valley Vineyard

We grow and make 14 wines on site (including sparkling) we have a world wine shop that also sells Whiskies, Brandies, Ports, Sherry, Liqueurs as well as non-alcoholic drinks.

a: 37 Shirrall Drive, Drayton Bassett, Tamworth, Staffordshire, B78 3EQ | t: 01213 081951
www.buzzardvalley.co.uk

Herefordshire

Castle Brook Vineyard

The South facing slopes and thin slightly acidic soil are perfect for growing the Chardonnay, Pinot Noir and Pinot Meunier grapes required to produce the finest fizz.

a: Cobrey Farms, Coughton, Ross-on-Wye, Herefordshire, HR9 5SG | t: 01989 562770
www.cobrey.co.uk/wine.html

Worcestershire

Church Farm Vineyard

A small vineyard on the property of Church Farm Oast House that comprises a mixture of Richenstiener, Kurnling and Bacchus grape varieties.

a: Church Lane, Shrawley, Worcestershire, WR6 6TS
t: 01905 620283

Shropshire

Clee Hills Vineyard

Grape varieties: MA, Seyval Blanc, Reichensteiner, Rondo, Regent, Léon Millot.

a: Clee St. Margaret, Craven Arms, Shropshire, SY7 9DT

Herefordshire

Coddington Vineyard

A well established English vineyard, having been planted mainly in 1985. It is situated a few miles west of the Malvern Hills in an area of outstanding natural beauty.

a: Ledbury, Herefordshire, HR8 1JJ
t: 01531 640668
www.coddingtonvineyard.com

Shropshire
Commonwood Vineyard

First planted in 2002, it has now expanded to include red vines. Wines are made in the small winery on site. Both red and white wines are produced, with plans for sparkling wine in the near future

a: Weavers Loft, Commonwood, Nonely, Wem, Shropshire, SY4 5SJ | t: 01939 236193
www.ukvines.co.uk/vineyards/wem.htm

Herefordshire
Croft Castle Vineyard

A late16th century stately home built on the remains of a 14th century medieval castle. There is a vineyard and walled gardens beside the house. If the day is clear you can see 14 counties from the top.

a: Yarpole, Leominster, Herefordshire, HR6 9PW
t: 01568 780246
www.britainexpress.com/attractions.htm?attraction=3606

Herefordshire
Four Foxes Vineyard

First planted in 1985. The 8 acre site faces SSE. A shop and cafe were built in the 90s. The vineyard was bought by Peter Crilly who renamed it Four Foxes. Produces red and varietal white wines.

a: Longworth Lane, Bartestree, Hereford, Herefordshire, HR1 4BX | t: 01432 850065
http://www.ukvines.co.uk/vineyards/fourfoxes.htm

Herefordshire
Frome Valley Vineyard

We produce a range of white wines to suit all tastes from dry to medium sweet. They are light and fruity. They are ideal as an aperitif or as an accompaniment to fish or white meat.

a: Paunton Court, Bishops Frome, Herefordshire, WR6 5BJ
t: 01885 490768
www.fromewine.co.uk

Shropshire
Habberley Vineyard

Grape varieties: Phoenix, Rondo, Solaris

a: Habberley, Shrewsbury, Shropshire, SY5 0TR
t: 01743 790144

Staffordshire
Halfpenny Green Vineyard

The first ½ acre planted in 1983. By 1991 a further 22 acres had been added. In 2005 3 acres of Bacchus were added. Situated 250ft above sea level. Book a tour, see our tea rooms or visit the craft centres.

a: Tom Lane, Bobbington, Staffordshire, DY7 5EP
t: 01384 221122
www.halfpenny-green-vineyards.co.uk

Shropshire
Hargrove Estate

Grape varieties: Siegerrebe, Bacchus, Phoenix, Regent.

a: Wall-under-Heywood, Church Stretton, Shopshire, SY6 7DP | t: 01694 771722

Warwickshire
Heart of England Vineyard

Planted in 1995 the wines have been entered for the UKVA and Mercian Association competitions, and are doing well, with the Red (Rondo/Triomph) being best Mercian non-white wine in 2002.

a: Welford Hill, Welford-on-Avon, Warwickshire, CV37 8AE
t: 01789 750565
www.ukvines.co.uk/vineyards/heart.htm

Warwickshire
Hunt Hall Farm Vineyard

4 Hectares of various grape varieties.

a: Hunt Hall Lane, Welford-on-Avon, Stratford-on-Avon, Warwickshire, CV37 8HE | t: 01789 750349

Shropshire
Ludlow Vineyard

Spread over 10 acres, 8,000 vines. The main white grape variety is Madeleine Angevine (a Riesling derivative), but we also have Seyval Blanc, Solaris, Phoenix, Madeleine Sylvaner, Kernling and Ortega.

a: Wainbridge House, Clee St Margaret, Craven Arms, SY7 9DT | t: 01584 823356
www.ludlowvineyard.co.uk

Herefordshire
Lulham Court Vineyard
A three acre vinyard, surrounded by the wonderful Wye valley. Producing wine since 1984. Varieties: Muller Thurgau Reichensteiner and Seyval Blanc. Range: dry to medium in still and brut in the spakling.

a: Lulham, Nr Madley, Hereford, HR2 9JQ
t: 01981 251107
www.lulhamcourtvineyard.co.uk

Shropshire
Morville St. Gregory Vineyard
Early wines have produced encouraging results. In 2005 Richard Rallings received the Mercian Vineyards Association cup for the small-volume producer of the year.

a: Valentine Cottage, Aston Munslow, Craven Arms, Shropshire, SY7 9EW | t: 01584 841021
www.ukvines.co.uk/vineyards/morgreg.htm

Worcestershire
Nash Vineyard
Produce wine for friends and family only.
Grape varieties: Reichensteiner, Regent, Rondo, Seyval Blanc, Bacchus, Phoenix.

a: The Nash, Kempsey, Worcester, Worchestershire, WR5 3PB | t: 01905 821397

Herefordshire
Old Grove House Vineyard
Produce wine for friends and family only.
Vineyard consists of around 100 vines.
Grape varieties: Triomphe, Rondo, Phoenix.

a: Llangrove, Ross-on-Wye, Herefordshire, HR9 6HA
t: 01989 770754

Herefordshire
Pengethley Manor Vineyard
Planted in 1993 and now around 1.5 acres in size. Producing sparkling wine for the hotel. The wine is professionally made for us at Three Choirs Vineyard at Newent in Gloucestershire.

a: Pengethley Park, Nr Ross-on-Wye, HR9 6LL
t: 01989 730211
www.pengethleymanor.co.uk

Worcestershire
Rose Bank Vineyard
Rose Bank wines taste delicious, and as they are local, have a tiny carbon-footprint!
Establish your green credentials by buying Rose Bank!

a:257 Droitwich Road, Fernhill Heath, Worcester, Worcestershire, WR3 7UH | t: 01905 451439
www.rosebankvineyard.co.uk

Herefordshire
Sparchall Vineyard
Grape varieties: Bacchus, Pinot Noir, Regent, Rondo, Seyval Blanc.

a: Sparchall Farm, Tarrington, Hereford, Herefordshire, HR1 4EY
t: 01432 850800

West Midlands
Spring Cottage Vineyard
Planted in 2000 on an allotment. Produce a white, red, róse and sparkling wine for friends and family. News of a second site planted! Grape varieties: Rondo, Triomphe, Pinot Noir, MA, Phoenix, Seyval Blanc.

a: 6 Highfield Way, Walsall, West Midlands, WS9 8XF.
Location of vineyard: Allotments, Green Lane, Walsall, West Midlands, WS4 1RT | t: 01922 454447

Herefordshire
Sunnybank Vineyard and Vine Nursery
We sell small quantities of one year old rooted vines on their own rootstock and bare wood cuttings for your own propagation. Supplied while the vines are dormant between mid Nov-Mar each year.

a: Cwm Barn, Rowlestone, Herefordshire, HR2 0EE
t: 01981 240256
www.sunnybankvines.co.uk

Herefordshire
Tarrington Court Vineyard
Produces between 400-800 bottles of Tarrington Court wine annually with the assistance of Three Choirs Vineyard, occupies around a quarter of an acre on a sloping, south facing site.

a: Tarrington Court, Tarrington, Hereford, Herefordshire, HR1 4EX
t: 01432 890632

Shropshire

Tern Valley Vineyard

Situated on the sunny slopes of the River Tern in Shropshire. We are one of England's newest Vineyards. We aim to produce award-winning, world-class wines in the heart of the English countryside...

a: Hall Farm, Tern Hill, Market Drayton, Shropshire, TF9 3PU
t: 01630 639688
www.ternvalleywine.com

Worcestershire

Tiltridge Vineyard

A small family-run concern which began life in the Springs of 1988/89 when the two vineyards were planted. Our first commercial crop was picked in 1991 and we have been open to the public since 1992.

a:Upper Hook Road,, Upton-upon-Severn, Worcestershire, WR8 0SA | t: 01684 592906
www.elgarwine.com/wine.html

Herefordshire

Townsend Farm Vineyard

Grape varieties: Regent, Rondo, Phoenix, Seyval Blanc.

a: Brampton Abbotts, Ross-on-Wye, Herefordshire, HR9 7JE
t: 01989 563772

Herefordshire

Treago Vineyard

Produces Treago branded award-winning red, white and sparkling wines.

a: St Weonards, Hereford, Herefordshire, HR2 8QBL
t: 01981 580208

Warwickshire

Welcombe Hills Vineyard

Welcombe Hills is owned and run by Chris and Jane Gallimore. Both former teachers of English they decided to follow their love of viticulture and established the vineyard in 2001.

a: Vine Cottage, Kings Lane, Snitterfield, Stratford on Avon, CV37 0QB | t: 01789 731071
www.welcombehills.co.uk

Shropshire

Wroxeter Roman Vineyard

Planted in 1991 Wroxeter Roman Vineyard is truly a "Taste of Shropshire". Modern methods twinned with the newer vine varieties create a unique blend which creates the highest quality wine that can be grown.

a: Wroxeter, Shrewsbury, Shropshire, SY5 6PQ
t: 01743 761888
www.wroxetervineyard.co.uk

Narrowboats at Etruria, Staffordshire

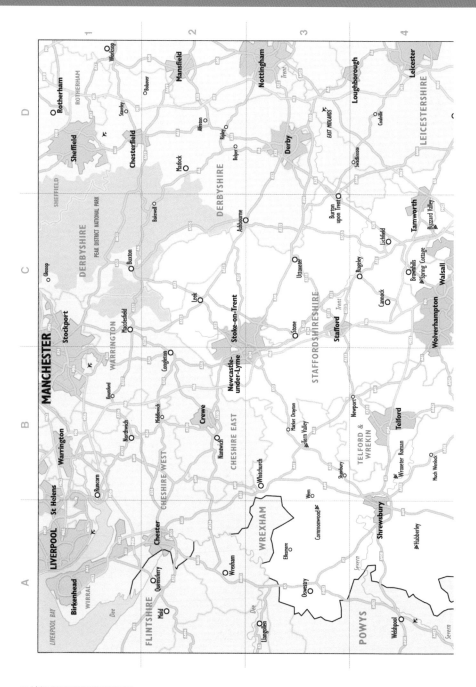

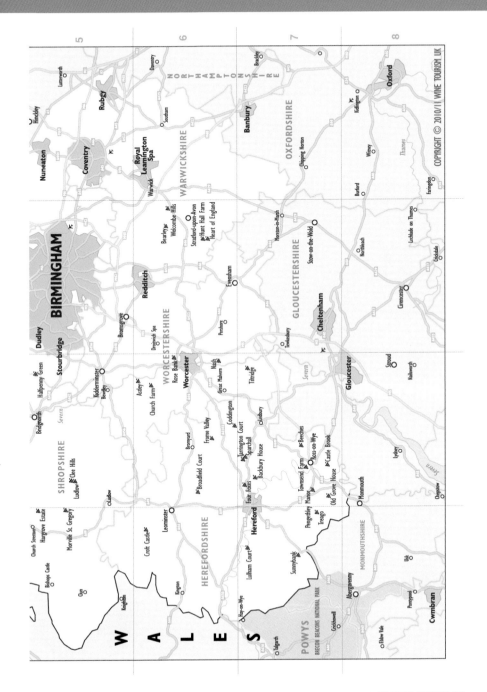

Ironbridge Gorge Museums

SHROPSHIRE

Whether you are interested in fine china, decorative tiles, fun interactives or a Victorian recreated town, it's all to be found in this stunning World Heritage Site. Step back in time at Blists Hill Victorian Town. Visit Coalport China Museum, Marvel at the world's first cast iron bridge and check out our most interactive attraction yet, Enginuity. Here you can pull a real locomotive and control the flow of a river to generate electricity.

a: Coalbrookdale, Telford, Shropshire, TF8 7DQ
t: 01952 884391 | **www.ironbridge.org.uk**

Wroxeter Roman City

SHROPSHIRE

Wroxeter (or 'Viroconium') was the fourth largest city in Roman Britain. It began as a legionary fortress and later developed into a thriving civilian city. Though much still remains below ground, today the most impressive features are the 2nd-century municipal baths, and the remains of the huge wall dividing them from the exercise hall in the heart of the city. There is a site museum and audio tour available.

a: Wroxeter, Shropshire, SY5 6PH
www.english-heritage.org.uk

Amerton Farm

STAFFORDSHIRE

Amerton Farm first opened to the general public in 1984, when ice cream was made and the old cowshed was turned into a Tea Room. Prior to that cream, half a pig and eggs were sold from the farmhouse door. Today well over 400,000 visitors a year arrive at Amerton Farm & Craft Centre to taste the many delights or search for that special gift from the Craft Centre. Amerton Farm is an exciting and adventurous place for children!!

a: Stowe by Chartley, Staffordshire, ST18 0LA
t: 01889 270294 | **www.amertonfarm.co.uk**

Hereford Light Infantry Museum

HEREFORDSHIRE

The Herefordshire Light Infantry Museum tells the story of the Herefordshire Light Infantry in campaigns such as Gallipoli, Egypt and Palestine. It also describes their inception as the Herefordshire Rifle Volunteers raised in 1860, and in modern times, their involvement in the arrest of Admiral Doenitz at the end of World War 2.

a: Harold Street, Hereford, Herefordshire, HR1 2QX
t: 01432 950328 | **www.armymuseums.org.uk**

Amazing Hedge Puzzle

HEREFORDSHIRE

Planted over twenty years ago by brothers Lindsay and Edward Heyes, the fun of the aMazing Hedge Puzzle has made it Herefordshire's most popular private tourist attraction.

a: Symonds Yat West, Ross-on-Wye, Herefordshire HR9 6DA, England
t: 01600 890360 | **www.mazes.co.uk**

WEST MIDLANDS

Red House Glass Cone

Take a self guided tour through the glassworks including the underground passages and tunnels. A spiral staircase allows you to walk up through the core of the glass furnace onto a viewing platform. Skilled craftspeople will be on hand to demonstrate glassmaking skills and answer questions. Built at the end of the 18thC, it is one of only four cones surviving in the UK. With the aid of film, audio guides, you can explore its 200 years of history.

a: High Street, Wordsley, Stourbridge, West Midlands, DY8 4AA
t: 01384 3812750 | **www.dudley.gov.uk**

WARWICKSHIRE

The Master's Garden, Lord Leycester Hospital

Behind the ancient buildings of the Lord Leycester Hospital lays the tranquil oasis of the 600 year old Master's Garden. The Lord Leycester Hospital is not a medical establishment. The word hospital is used in its ancient sense meaning "a charitable institution for the housing and maintenance of the needy, infirm or aged". For nearly 200 years it was the home of Warwick's medieval Guilds. So it remains today as an independent charity for ex-Servicemen and their wives.

a: High Street, Warwick, Warwickshire, CV34 4BH
t: 01926 491422 | **www.lordleycester.com**

WARWICKSHIRE

The Webb Ellis Rugby Football Museum

The Webb Ellis Rugby Football Museum is the site of the first rugby football workshop and houses a fabulous collection of international rugby memorabilia built up over the last hundred years. The museum is opposite Rugby School in the original building where James Gilbert, boot and shoemaker, made the first rugby footballs in 1842. This tradition still continues today, giving it the accolade of having the longest continuous association with the game of rugby.

a: 5 St. Matthews Street, Rugby, Warwickshire, CV21 3BY
t: 01788 567777 | **www.rugby.gov.uk**

WARWICKSHIRE

Warwick Castle

Our history stretches back almost 1,100 years. In 914AD. Ethelfleda, daughter of Alfred the Great ordered the building of a 'burh' or an earthen rampart to protect the small hill top settlement of Warwick from Danish invaders. Where you can immerse yourself in a thousand years of jaw-dropping history. Where ancient myths and spell-binding tales will set your imagination alight and your hair on end. Where princesses are pampered and maidens are wooed.

a: Warwick, Warwickshire, CV34 4QU
t: 08712 652000 | **www.warwick-castle.com**

WEST MIDLANDS

Birmingham Sea Life Centre

Fancy diving beneath the sea without getting wet? You'll come eyeball to eyeball with everything from shrimps to sharks, and learn tons of great stuff from SEA LIFE experts. So go on, take the plunge and visit Birmingham SEA LIFE centre soon!

a: 3A Brindley Place, Birmingham, West Midlands, B1 2JB
t: 01216 436777 | **www.sealifeeurope.com**

Cadbury World

WEST MIDLANDS

Discover the history of Cadbury at Cadbury World, from its social pioneering to the perfection of the recipe for Cadbury Dairy Milk; first launched in 1905, and still a market leader today. Find out all there is to know about making chocolate, and amaze yourself with the brand stories and brand timeline that show how many Cadbury brands have been favourites since the early 1900s.

a: Linden Road, Bournville, West Midlands, B30 2LU
t: 0121 451 4198 | **www.cadbury.co.uk**

Coventry Cathedral

WEST MIDLANDS

Coventry Cathedral is an internationally renowned place of worship and pilgrimage. St Michael's Hall Treasury houses treasures from the old and new Cathedrals including the original charred cross. Coventry Cathedral has been a place of worship for over 900 years. To walk from the ruins of the old Cathedral into the splendour of the new is to walk from Good Friday to Easter, from the ravages of human self-destruction to the glorious hope of resurrection.

a: 1 Hill Top, Coventry, West Midlands, CV1 5AB
t: 02476 521200 | **www.coventrycathedral.org.uk**

Coventry Transport Museum

WEST MIDLANDS

The world's largest collection of British road transport located in the birthplace of British transport. Offering everything from 'bone shaking' cycles to land speed record cars. Coventry is the birthplace of the British cycle and motor industry. The Museum's collection includes over 240 cars, commercial vehicles and buses, 94 motorcycles, 200 cycles, 25,000 models and around 1 million archive and ephemera items.

a: Millennium Place, Hales Street, Coventry, West Midlands, CV1 1JD
t: 02476 234270 | **www.transport-museum.com**

Dudley Zoo & Castle

WEST MIDLANDS

Dudley Zoo is home to some of the world's rarest and exotic animals with many endangered species. Dudley Castle was founded around 1071 and during the year many re-enactments and archery demonstrations are held here. From lions and tigers to snakes and spiders there's something for all ages at Dudley Zoo. Picnic in the courtyard or dine in our licensed restaurant and pick up a souvenir from the safari gift shop before you leave.

a: 2 The Broadway, Dudley, West Midlands, DY1 4QB
t: 01384 215313 | **www.dudleyzoo.org.uk**

Priory Visitor Centre

WEST MIDLANDS

Priory Gardens are a haven of peace and tranquillity in the centre of Coventry on the site of the first cathedral. Visitors to the city centre have already voted with their feet and decided that the new Priory Gardens are the ideal place to while away a few moments, right in the heart of the city centre. The Priory Gardens is part of the Phoenix Initiative, is a haven of peace and tranquillity on the site of Coventry's first cathedral, St Mary's.

a: Priory Visitor Centre, Priory Gardens, Coventry, West Midlands, CV1 5EX
t: 02476 552242 | **www.theherbert.org**

Food & Wine Festivals
West Midlands

SHROPSHIRE

Ludlow Food Festival | September
www.foodfestival.co.uk
Address: Ludlow, Shropshire | **Tel:** 01584 873957 | **email:** info@foodfestival.co.uk

SHROPSHIRE

Oswestry Food & Drink Festival | July
www.oswestryfoodfestival.co.uk
Address: Oswestry Town Centre, Oswestry, Shropshire | Tel: 08453 300232

STAFFORDSHIRE

Stone Food & Drink Festival | October
www.stonefooddrink.org.uk
Address: Stone, Staffordshire | **Tel:** 01785 816955

WARWICKSHIRE

BBC Summer Good Food Show | 15th June 2011 - 19th June 2011
www.bbcgoodfoodshowsummer.com
Address: NEC Birmingham, Warwickshire | **Tel:** 08445 811341 | **email:** bbcgoodfoodshow@haymarket.com

WARWICKSHIRE

Coventry and Warwickshire Food and Drink Awards | Back in 2012!!!
www.foodanddrink2009.co.uk
Address: Coventry, Warwickshire | **Tel:** 01926 412136 | **email:** tourism@warwickshire.gov.uk

WARWICKSHIRE

Good Food Show Winter | November
www.bbcgoodfoodshow.com
Address: NEC Birmingham, Warwickshire | **Tel:** 08445 811341 | **email:** bbcgoodfoodshow@haymarket.com

WARWICKSHIRE

Royal Leamington Spa Food & Drink Festival | 10th September 2011 - 11th September 2011
www.leamingtonfoodfestival.co.uk
Address: Royal Pump Room and Gardens, Leamington Spa, Warwickshire | **Tel:** 01926 470634

WARWICKSHIRE

Taste of Birmingham Cannon Hill Park | June
www.taste.visitbirmingham.com
Address: Cannon Hill Park, Birmingham, Warwickshire | **Tel:** 01212 025024 | **email:** info@marketingbirmingham.com

☐ Notes:

....

....

....

....

....

....

....

....

....

DERBYSHIRE

Add: The Events Office, Renishaw Hall, Renishaw, Sheffield, S21 3WB
Tel: 01246 432310 | **Fax:** 01246 430760
Email: enquiries@renishaw-hall.co.uk
www.renishaw-hall.co.uk

Postcode (GPS): S21 3WB
Map Reference: B2

Renishaw Hall Vineyard

Opening times: Vineyard: By appointment only.
Renishaw Hall is now open at Christmas.
Apr-Sep Wed-Sun 10.30-16.30 and bank holidays.

TOP THREE WINES

❖ Dry white & sparkling wine

Introduction:

Renishaw Hall and gardens have been in the Sitwell family
for many years, the owner, Alexandra Hayward continues to
welcome visitors to the extensive Italianate gardens, woodland
and Georgian Courtyard where visitors can enjoy the café,
galleries, museum and shop. The autumn highlight is the tour
with the vineyard manager followed by an estate wine tasting.

Renishaw Vineyard grows the
varieties Madeleine Angevine and
Seyval Blanc. The dry white wine is a
blend of these varieties with a floral,
fruity character. The quality sparkling
wine is made exclusively from Seyval
Blanc alone with a crisper taste.

wine
Tourism UK

East Midlands

✚ England

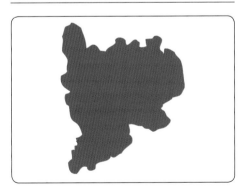

Derbyshire, Leicestershire, Rutland, Northamptonshire, Nottinghamshire, Lincolnshire

East Midlands

East Midlands covers Derbyshire, Leicestershire, Rutland, Northamptonshire, Nottinghamshire and Lincolnshire, and has nearly 30 wine estates in the region.

You may already know of some of this regions treasures such as the the infamous Robin Hood, the Peak District National Park and Silverstone, but there are many more just waiting to be discovered.

Magnificent castles and stately homes provide a unique glimpse into the past plus inspiring countryside with sweeping green hills and dramatic rocky outcrops; cosmopolitan cities combining shopping with night life; historic market towns; majestic gardens and locations that have inspired movie makers.

Venture across the dramatic landscape of the Peak District National Park or the rolling Lincolnshire Wolds. Look skywards to catch a glimpse of the exhilarating Red Arrows practising in their homeland skies, and then go underground to hear the echoes in deep caverns and caves.

Prefer to live it up? Make for historic Lincoln, Nottingham, Derby or Leicester where fine Asian cuisine is spicily sumptuous. Seek out traditional local fares too - delicious cheeses, gingerbread and the famous Melton Mowbray pork pies.

Selected wineries
Welland Valley Vineyard (Northampton)
Eglantine Vineyard (Nottinghamshire)
Fleurfields Vineyard (Northampton)

Welland Valley Vineyard
Welland Valley Vineyard is a 2 acre English Vineyard established in 1991 on a sheltered south facing slope 3 miles south west of Market Harborough on the Leicestershire and Northamptonshire county boundary. The soil is well drained loam over Jurassic clay. Although further north than most English vineyards it is nearly always free from damaging spring frosts and rainfall is low. They grow a very varied selection of French and German vine varieties comprising the following white varieties: Bacchus, Madeleine Angevine, Phoenix, Reichensteiner, Seyval Blanc, Solaris and Orion. The red varieties grown are: Acolon, Dornfelder, Regent and Rondo. A spread of different flowering and ripening times lessens the risks of adverse weather.

Their ethos is to produce quality wine using traditional methods combined with modern equipment in as natural a way as possible. A variety of award winning estate bottled wines are made including white, red and rosé as well as bottle fermented sparkling.

Eglantine Vineyard

The inspiration for Eglantine Vineyard came from a Black Hamburg vine which had been taken, as a cutting, from the Great Vine of Hampton Court in 1935. Eglantine Vineyard was first planted in 1979 on south facing slopes, in the parish of Costock, at a time when English vineyards were entering a period of significant expansion. Research stations around the world had been developing new and earlier ripening varieties of vines, which meant that it was possible to grow and harvest grapes successfully in the East Midlands. Eglantine Vineyard has had 30 years of experience of growing vines and making wine in Nottinghamshire.

There are about four thousand vines in the vineyard, the main variety being the Madeleine Angevine, a highly reliable vine which sets fruit every year and always ripens well - despite the vagaries of the English climate.

Wines are made in the purpose-built winery; sweet, sparkling and dry white wines, rosé, red wine and a cherry wine, as well as mead from home-produced honey.

Fleurfields Vineyard

Fleurfields occupies a south-facing slope overlooking Pitsford Reservoir in Northamptonshire. Planted in 2002, the first wine was produced in 2005 when 4500 bottles of sparkling, white and rosé were produced. Unlike many vineyards in the UK, Fleurfields is not relying exclusively on the local market. Some of their wine goes to France where is has been well received. It is also sold in Northampton (Partridges) and in Greens Restaurant in Collingtree.

Selected destinations:

Derby: A vibrant and cosmopolitan city with a fantastic heritage and an exciting future. Experience cutting edge culture, shopping and entertainment, all in the heart of a compact city where history combines with a very modern atmosphere. Derby is the UK's most central city, so it's easy to get to from all directions!

Leicester: Cosmopolitan and cultured, historic but futuristic, buzzing yet relaxed. Unusual shops, fine restaurants, a vibrant nightlife and a strong cultural diversity have all contributed to Leicester's recent style revolution.

Lincoln: Lincoln's Historic Bailgate area is an ideal place to spend a day. Wander the streets, enjoy the smart boutiques, independent shops and unique specialist stores. Stop for lunch or dinner in one of the many excellent restaurants, bars and pubs flanked by cobbled streets and the newly improved Bailgate york stone pathways. The area is defined by the architcecural delights and magnificence of Lincoln Cathedral. This splendid Gothic building is Lincoln's main highlight and should not be missed. The Bailgate is in the north of Lincoln city and is signposted on major routes as Historic Lincoln.

'Venture across the dramatic landscape of the Peak District National park or the rolling Lincolnshire Wolds.'

The Peak District: Britain's first National Park, with open moorland, attractive valleys and a fascinating historical and cultural heritage. This unique and diverse region is home to some of the country's finest stately homes, enchanting market towns and picturesque villages.

Rutland: England's smallest county, its greatest length north to south is only 18 miles and west to east 17 miles. It is the smallest (in terms of population) normal unitary authority in mainland England. Oakham, the county town of Rutland, is a delightful market town full of boutique shops and great cafés.

East Midlands

Map	Wine estate	Tel number	Opening times
C4	Abbey Vineyards	01476 550191	By appointment only
B6	Chevelswarde Vineyard	01858 575309	Mon-Fri 9.00-18.00
B4	East Bridgeford Vineyard	01476 550191	Not open to the public
B4	Eglantine Vineyard	01509 852386	10.00-18.00, contact before to ensure it is open
B6	Fleurfields Vineyard	01604 880197	By appointment only
C5	Good Earth Vineyard	01780 762859	Not open to the public
B7	Harlestone Allotment Vineyard	01604 616679	Not open to the public
B6	High Cross Vineyard	01455 209116	Not open to the public
C6	Kemps Vineyard	01933 623497	Not open to the public
B5	Keyham Vineyard	01476 550191	Not open to the public
B5	Kingfishers' Pool Vineyard	01162 078701	Not open to the public
C3	Lincoln Vineyard	01522 873542	Mon-Sun 10.00-17.00
B5	Manor Farm Vineyard	01455 822657	Not open to the public
C3	Mill Lane Vineyard	01522 788784	Not open to the public
C7	New Lodge Vineyard	01604 811311	By appointment only
C5	Old Oak Vineyard	01476 550191	Not open to the public
B6	Ravensthorpe Vineyard	01604 770463	Not open to the public
B2	Renishaw Hall Vineyard	01246 432310	Apr-Sep
B4	River Walk Vineyard	01476 550191	Not open to the public
A5	Sealwood Cottage Vineyard	01283 761371	Not open to the public
C1	Somerby Vineyards	01652 629162	Not open to the public
C5	South Shore Vineyard	01476 550191	Not open to the public
C2	Three Sisters Vineyard	08454 735539	By appointment only
C5	Tixover Vineyard	01572 823912	By appointment only
B7	Vernon Lodge Vineyard	01327 350077	By appointment only
B4	Walton Brook Vineyard	07779 622858	Not open to the public
B6	Welland Valley Vineyard	01858 434591	By appointment only
B7	Windmill Vineyard	01327 262023	Sat-Sun, Easter-Oct

Lincolnshire

Abbey Vineyards (T&S Nurseries)

Currently own 9 vineyards across the East Midlands, East & S.East. At present, Tas Valley Vineyard is the only one producing wine (see Tas Valley Vineyard, East) Plans for wineries/shops on each of the others.

a: Irnham Grange, Irnham Road, Corby Glen, Grantham, Lincolnshire NG33 4NE | **t:** 01476 550191
www.tandsnurseries.com

Leicestershire

Chevelswarde Vineyard

Our one-acre vineyard, on a south-east facing slope in South Kilworth was started in 1973. Our vines are grown organically and our winemaker makes the wine as 'Dry' or 'Medium Dry.

a: Chevel House, The Belt, South Kilworth, Lutterworth, Leicestershire, LE17 6DX | **t:** 01858 575309
www.chevelswardeorganics.co.uk

Nottinghamshire

East Bridgeford Vineyard

Owned by Abbey Vineyards. Please see Abbey Vineyards for more information. Future plans consist of a winery and shop. Grape varieties: Pinoit Noir, Riesling, Bacchus, Triomphe.

a: c/o Abbey Vineyards, Irnham Grange, Irnham Road, Corby Glen, Grantham, Lincolnshire, NG33 4NE. Location of vineyard: NG13 8LP | **t:** 01476 550191 | www.tandsnurseries.com

Nottinghamshire

Eglantine Vineyard

First planted in 1979 on south facing slopes, in the parish of Costock. There are four thousand vines in the vineyard. Grape variety: Madeleine Angevine - sweet, sparkling and dry white wines, rosé, red wine.

a: Ash Lane, Costock, Loughborough, Nottinghamshire, LE12 6UX | **t:** 01509 852386
www.eglantinevineyard.web.officelive.com

Northamptonshire

Fleurfields Vineyard

Fleurfields occupies a south-facing slope overlooking Pitsford Reservoir in Northamptonshire. Planted in 2002, the first wine was produced in 2005 when 4500 bottles of sparkling, white and rosé were produced.

a: Hill Farm House, Brixworth, Northamptonshire, NN6 9DQ
t: 01604 880197
www.fleurfields.co.uk

Lincolnshire

Good Earth Vineyard

A small vineyard which was planted in May 2007 in the centre of England, near Peterborough.

a: 9 Lea View, Ryhall, Stmford, Lincolnshire, PE9 4HZ. Location of vineyard: Stamford, Lincolnshire, PE9 2QH
t: 01780 762859 | www.an-english-vineyard.blogspot.com

Northamptonshire

Harlestone Allotment Vineyard

A Micro-Vineyard on an allotment. The allotment is a long way from sunny California or France but with global warming and climate change it may do just fine!

a: 10 Lower Harlestone, Northampton, Northamptonshire, NN7 4EW | **t:** 01604 616679
www.myallotment.com

Leicestershire

High Cross Vineyard

Grape varieties: Solaris, Regent.

a: Tanglewood, 1 Main Road, Claybrooke Magna, Leicester, Leicestershire, LE17 5AJ. Location of vineyard: LE17 5
t: 01455 209116

Northamptonshire

Kemps Vineyard

The vineyard contains four main grape varieties - Madeleine Angevine, Bacchus, Reichensteiner and Rondo (a modern red grape used exclusively for rosé wine).

a: Church Street, Hargrave, Northamptonshire, NN9 6BW
t: 01933 623497
www.winehub.co.uk/acatalog/giffords.html

Leicestershire

Keyham Vineyard

Owned by Abbey Vineyards. Please see Abbey Vineyards for more information. Future plans consist of a winery and shop. Grape varieties: Seyval Blanc, Rondo, Solaris, Ortega, Acolon.

a: c/o Abbey Vineyards, Irnham Grange, Irnham Road, Corby Glen, Grantham, Lincolnshire NG33 4NE Location of vineyard: LE7 9JU | **t:** 01476 550191 | www.tandsnurseries.com

Leicestershire

Kingfishers' Pool Vineyard

An amateur vineyard consisting of 550 vines.
First harvest is anticipated in 2010.

a: 43 Westfield Lane, Rothley, Leicestershire, LE7 7LH
t: 01162 078701

Leicestershire

Manor Farm Vineyard

Grape varieties: Regent, Rondo.

a: Main Street, Botcheston, Leicester, LE9 9FF
t: 01455 822657

Northamptonshire

New Lodge Vineyard

Small vineyard situated just outside the village of
Earls Barton on a gentle slope, overlooking the Nene
Valley facing South. Established in 2000 with
approximatly 400 vines producing a dry white wine.

a: Northampton Road, Earls Barton, NN6 0HF
t: 01604 811311
www.newlodgevineyard.co.uk

Northamptonshire

Ravensthorpe Vineyard

A non-commercial vineyard consisting of over 100
vines. The wine varieties are Bacchus and Ortega. All
wine is consumed by friends and family and of course
the owners. No intention of going commercial!

a: The Hollows, Ravensthorpe, Northamptonshire, NN6 8EN
t: 01604 770463

Nottinghamshire

River Walk Vineyard

Owned by Abbey Vineyards. Please see Abbey
Vineyards for more information. Future plans consist
of a winery and shop. Grape varieties: Ortega,
Solaris, Pinot Noir.

a: c/o Abbey Vineyards, Irnham Grange, Irnham Road, Corby
Glen, Grantham, Lincolnshire, NG33 4NE. Location of vineyard:
NG13 9 | t: 01476 550191 | www.tandsnurseries.com

Lincolnshire

Lincoln Vineyard

Lincoln Medieval Bishops Palace - discover the
fascinating history of this building and its residents.
Climb the stairs to the Alnwick tower, see the
contemporary heritage garden and vineyard.

a: Bishop's Palace, Minster Yard, Lincoln, LN1 1DH
t: 01522 873542 | www.english-heritage.org.uk/daysout/prop-
erties/lincoln-medieval-bishops-palace

Lincolnshire

Mill Lane Vineyard

Planted in 2006.
Grape varieties: Regent, Rondo, Bacchus,
Pinot Noir Précoce, Phoenix.

a: Brantedge Farm, Webourn Road, Brant Broughton,
Lincolnshire,LN5 0SP
t: 01522 788784

Rutland

Old Oak Vineyard

Owned by Abbey Vineyards. Please see Abbey
Vineyards for more information. Future plans consist
of a winery and shop. Grape varieties: Pinot Noir,
Chardonnay, Reichensteiner, Regent.

a: c/o Abbey Vineyards, Irnham Grange, Irnham Road, Corby
Glen, Grantham, Lincolnshire, NG33 4NE. Location of vineyard:
LE15 | t: 01476 550191 | www.tandsnurseries.com

Derbyshire

Renishaw Hall Vineyard

Renishaw's vineyard was planted in the upper pasture
in 1972. Of the many varieties planted in the 70's only
Seyval remains. In 1997-2002 a programme of
replanting was started. First crop went on sale in 2006.

a: Sheffield, Derbyshire, S21 3WB
t: 01246 432310
www.sitwell.co.uk/renishaw_vineyard.htm

Derbyshire

Sealwood Cottage Vineyard

Grape varieties: Ortega, Solaris, Rondo, Regent.

a: Seal Wood Lane, Linton, Swadlincote, Derby, Derbyshire,
DE12 6PA | t: 01283 761371

Lincolnshire

Somerby Vineyards

Somerby Vineyards is a small vineyard with the emphasis on quality. In 2006 we planted 150 vines. In 2007/8 we planted a further 3,000 vines - Orion, Ortega, Phoenix, Regent, Rhondo and Solaris.

a: Manor House, Somerby Green, Somerby, Lincolnshire, DN38 6EY | t: 01652 629162
www.somerbyvineyards.com

Rutland

South Shore Vineyard

Owned by Abbey Vineyards. Please see Abbey Vineyards for more information. Future plans consist of a winery and shop. Grape varieties: Bacchus, Reichesnteiner.

a: c/o Abbey Vineyards, Irnham Grange, Irnham Road, Corby Glen, Grantham, Lincolnshire NG33 4NE. Location of vineyard: LE15 8RN | t: 01476 550191 | www.tandsnurseries.com

Lincolnshire

Three Sisters Vineyard

The Three Sisters Vineyard is located in the small village of Claxby, just off the A46 (Grimsby) road, approximately 5 miles north of Market Rasen in Lincolnshire. A total of approx. 1650 vines.

a: The Laurels, Mulberry Road, Claxby, Market Rasen, Lincolnshire, LN8 3YS | t: 08454 735539
www.three-sisters-vineyard.co.uk

Rutland

Tixover Vineyard

At around 2 acres (0.8 of a hectare) it is an almost insignificant area for a commercial vineyard. Planted to Pinot Noir, Pinot Grigio/Gris and Pinot Bianco in 2004 with around 1,500 per acre.

a: The Knoll, 103 Main Street, Lyddington, Rutland, LE15 9LS
Location of vineyrad: LE15 9LS
t: 01572 823912

Northamptonshire

Vernon Lodge Vineyard

Unique in Britain - a community vineyard. The site occupies 0.3 acres in Mike Dean's garden, with neatly trellised grapes running East/West down to a small winery. None is sold. Visitors welcome.

a: Tiffield, Towcester, Northamptonshire, NN12 8AB
t: 01327 350077
www.ukvines.co.uk/vineyards/vernon.htm

Leicestershire

Walton Brook Vineyard

Planted in May 2009 we have over 2500 vines that will shortly be in production. Existing varieties include Seyval Blanc, Solaris, Regent and Madeline Angevine. Trial plantings of new grape varieties in 2010.

a: Horseleys Farm, Burton-on-theWolds, Loughborough, Leicestershire, LE12 5TQ
t: 07779 622858

Northamptonshire

Welland Valley Vineyard

A two acre English Vineyard established in 1991 producing a variety of award winning estate bottled wines including white, red and rosé regional wines and bottle fermented quality sparkling.

a: Vine Lodge, Marston Trussell, Marker Harborough, LE16 9TX | t: 01858 434591
www.welland-vineyard.com

Northamptonshire

Windmill Vineyard

The highest windmill in England, 665 feet above sea level, producing wines from grape varieties grown in England. As well as wine, we produce cider and perry from our own orchards. Shop and tastings onsite.

a: Windmill Hill Farm, Hellidon, Daventry, Northamptonshire, NN11 8LG | t: 01327 262023
http://www.ukvines.co.uk/vineyards/helidon.htm

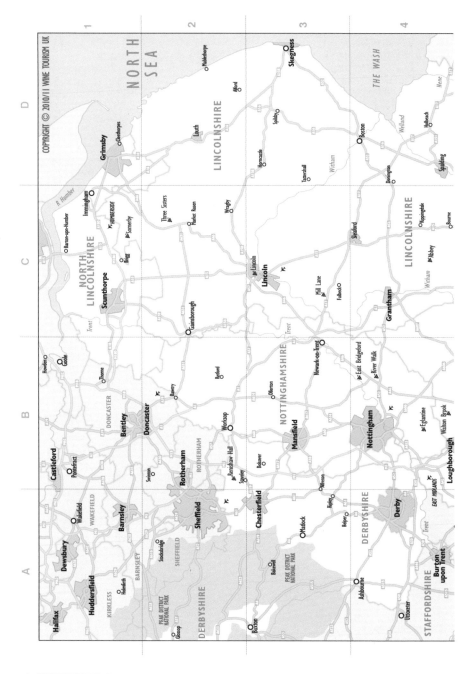

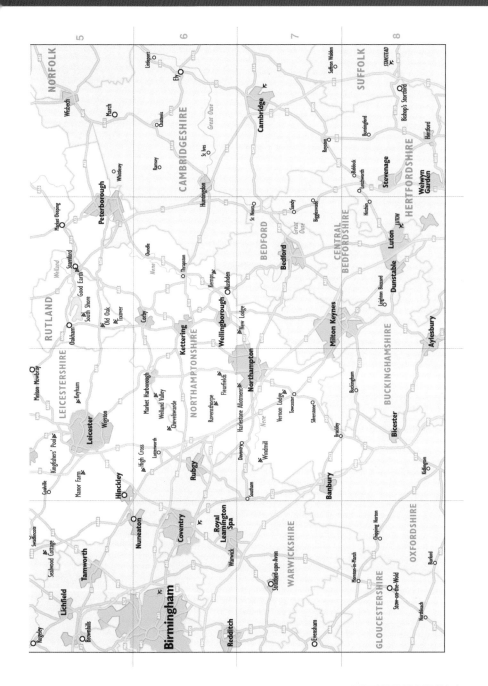

Mr Straw's House

NOTTINGHAMSHIRE

This ordinary house was the home of the Straw family, who threw nothing away for more than 60 years and lived without many of the modern comforts. Step back in time to the 1920s and find out how a grocer's family lived in this market town. This ordinary semi-detached house, with original interior decorations from 1923, was the home of the Straw family. Household objects spanning 100 years can still be seen exactly where the owners left them.

a: 5-7 Blyth Grove, Worksop, Nottinghamshire, S81 0JG
t: 01909 482380 | **www.nationaltrust.org.uk/main/w-mrstrawshouse**

Wistow Maize Maze (Winner of Leicestershire's "best visitor attraction")

LEICESTERSHIRE

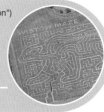

Enjoy a great day out exploring one of the country's largest maize mazes, set in 8 acres of living maize and sunflower crop. It's great exercise for mind and body! See if you can unravel the QUIZ TRAIL and find all 10 boards hidden amongst the 3 miles of paths. The maze also incorporates 10ft high bridges and viewing towers which give visitors stunning 3D panoramic views over the maze and the beautiful surrounding countryside.

a: Leicestershire, LE8 0QF
www.wistow.com/maze.asp

Lyveden New Bield

NORTHAMPTONSHIRE

Lyveden is a remarkable survival of the Elizabethan age. Begun by Sir Thomas Tresham to symbolise his Catholic faith, Lyveden remains incomplete and virtually unaltered since work stopped on his death in 1605. Discover the mysterious garden lodge and explore the Elizabethan garden with spiral mounts, terracing and canals. Wander through the new orchard, explore the Lyveden Way, a circular path through meadows, woodland and villages.

a: Near Oundle, Northamptonshire, PE8 5AT
t: 01832 205358 | **www.nationaltrust.org.uk/main/w-lyvedennewbield**

Treak Cliff Cavern

DERBYSHIRE

An underground wonderland of stalactites, stalagmites, rocks, minerals and the unique mineral Blue John Stone. Blue John Stone is found nowhere in the world but amongst the rocks of Treak Cliff Hill, Castleton. Blue John Stone can now be found in only two caverns: Treak Cliff Cavern and Blue John Cavern. This mineral, a colour banded form of fluorspar, is so beautiful that it has been prized for many hundreds of years.

a: Castleton Gift Shop, Cross Street, Castleton, Hope Valley, S33 8WH
t: 01433 620571 | **www.bluejohnstone.com**

78 Derngate (Winner of the 2009 Enjoy England Excellence Award)

NORTHAMPTON

Recognized as the place to visit in Northampton. The house was remodelled by the world-famous designer and architect, Charles Rennie Mackintosh in his iconic Modernist style. The Gallery is free to enter, selling and showing the best in contemporary craft. The Dining Room, the in-house boutique-style restaurant, serves a full range of delicious contemporary cuisine, while the gift & craft shop offers a unique shopping experience.

a: 78 Derngate, Northampton, NN1 1UH
t: 01604 603407 | **www.78derngate.org.uk**

Chatsworth

DERBYSHIRE

Chatsworth is one of Britain's best loved historic houses and estates. It offers something for everyone to enjoy, from famous works of art and the spectacular fountains in the garden to the finest shopping, food and drink and many miles of free walks. The home of the Duke and Duchess of Devonshire is set in the magnificent landscape of Derbyshire's Peak District National Park, and is seen in the recently released film of 'Pride and Prejudice'.

a: Bakewell, Derbyshire, DE45 1PP
t: 01246 582204 | **www.chatsworth.org**

National Space Centre (Awarded Gold, Enjoy England Awards 2009)

LEICESTER

The UK's largest attraction dedicated to space. From the moment you catch sight of the Space Centre's futuristic Rocket Tower you'll be treated to hours of breathtaking discovery and interactive fun. Home to the UK's largest 360° planetarium, the National Space Centre is a hands-on, interactive journey through six stunning galleries, Rocket Tower and S.I.M ride that offers an experience that is out of this world.

a: Exploration Drive, Leicester, Leicestershire, LE4 5NS
t: 01162 610261 | **www.spacecentre.co.uk**

Newstead Abbey

NOTTINGHAMSHIRE

A beautiful historic house set in a glorious landscape of gardens and parkland. Founded as a monastic house in the late twelfth century, Newstead became the seat of the Byron family in 1540. The most famous owner, the poet Lord Byron, sold the property in 1818 to his friend Colonel Thomas Wildman. Newstead Abbey remained a private country house until 1931, when it was presented to the Nottingham Corporation for the public to enjoy.

a: Newstead Abbey Park, Nottingham, NG15 8NA
t: 01623 455900 | **www.newsteadabbey.org.uk**

Sherwood Forest

NOTTINGHAMSHIRE

Once part of a royal hunting forest, Sherwood Forest Country Park covers 450 acres and incorporates some truly ancient areas of native woodland. Slender birch trees grow alongside more than one thousand veteran oaks; most of which are over 500 years old. The largest and most famous of these is the Major Oak, linked throughout the world to Sherwood's legendary hero Robin Hood.

a: Edwinstowe, Mansfield, Nottinghamshire, NG21 9HN
t: 01623 823202 | **www.nottinghamshire.gov.uk/sherwoodforestcp**

Rutland Belle

RUTLAND

A cruise aboard the Rutland Belle allows you to enjoy the sights of Rutland Water whilst listening to commentary highlighting points of interest. The Rutland Belle can carry up to 110 passengers, with 60 places in the under-cover saloons. Drinks are available on board. Rutland Water is set in three thousand acres of beautiful English countryside. Around the twenty-five mile perimeter of the lake are four parking and leisure areas.

a: Whitwell Harbour, Rutland Water, Whitwell, Rutland, LE15 8BL
t: 01572 787630 | **www.rutnet.co.uk**

LINCOLNSHIRE

Lincoln Cathedral

Lincoln Cathedral is visible from 25 miles away and is a distinguished landmark which is even more stunning close up. Take a guided floor or roof tour; see the imposing West Front with its Romanesque Frieze. Marvel at the wonderful 14th century stone carvings on the choir screen or visit the famous library, one of only two designed by Sir Christopher Wren. Visitors are always welcome to join in any of the daily services.

a: Minster Yard, Lincoln, Lincolnshire, LN2 1PX
www.lincolncathedral.com

LEICESTERSHIRE

Twinlakes Park

Set in beautiful countryside with 14 family rides, 10 play zones and 100,000 sq.ft. of indoor play. There are an unbelievable variety of attractions for the whole family from the Buffalo Stampede Coaster to water zapping Bumper Boats and from white knuckle Gladiators Galleon to the cute Wild West city. The awesome indoor venture centres including Master Blaster arenas and the scary Trauma Tower ride. There's also hundreds of animals and birds to see!

a: Melton Spinney Road, Melton Mowbray, Leicestershire, LE14 4SB
t: 01664 567777 | **www.twinlakespark.co.uk**

STAFFORDSHIRE

Claymills Victorian Pumping Station

Claymills has four large beam engines, two working, five Lancashire boilers, steam powered engineering workshops with blacksmiths forge and steam hammer, early steam powered dynamo house and fourteen other auxiliary steam engines. All engines are original to the pumping station.

a: Meadow Lane, Stretton, Burton-on-Trent, Staffordshire, DE13 0DA
t: 01283 509929

LEICESTERSHIRE

Bosworth Battlefield Visitor Centre

The site of the Battle of Bosworth in 1485, the decisive battle of the War of the Roses where Richard III lost his life and his crown to the future Henry VII. Re-live history from interactive displays to battle re-enactments. Children and adults can handle weapons and armour in the detailed exhibition, watch a film explaining the events and walk on an outside circuit. You can take a stroll around the battle trail (open all year) with information boards at various points.

a: Ambion Lane, Sutton Cheney, Market Bosworth, Leicestershire, CV13 0AD
www.leics.gov.uk

DERBYSHIRE

Crich Tramway Village

Take a tram ride through time - an ideal destination for all ages. Visitors can ride our world renowned vintage trams through our unique period street and out into the open countryside for spectacular views. Explore fascinating exhibitions and watch as trams are restored from our Workshop Viewing Gallery. This captivating journey into history is made complete with a stroll on our fascinating Woodland Walk & Sculpture Trail and a trip to Red Lion Pubs.

a: Crich, Matlock, Derbyshire, DE4 5DP
t: 01773 854321 | **www.tramway.co.uk**

⚑ Food & Wine Festivals
East Midlands

DERBYSHIRE

Derbyshire Food & Drink Festival | 21st May 2011 - 22nd May 2011
www.derbyshirefoodfestival.co.uk
Address: Hardwick Hall, North East Derbyshire | **Tel:** 01629 538464 | **email:** stephanie.walsh@derbyshire.gov.uk

LINCOLNSHIRE

South Holland Food Festival | July - August
www.food-festival.net
Address: South Holland, Lincolnshire | **Tel:** 01775 764598 | **email:** info@food-festival.net

NORTHAMPTONSHIRE

Braunston Festival | August
www.braunstonfestival.org.uk
Address: Braunston, Northamptonshire | **Tel:** 01785 816955 | **email:** info@braunstonfestival.org.uk

NOTTINGHAMSHIRE

Nottingham Food & Drink Festival | September
www.wearenottingham.co.uk
Address: Old Market Square, Nottingham | **Tel:** 01159 585287

Notes:

Yorkshire & the Humber

✚ England

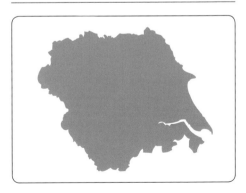

Northern Lincolnshire, Yorkshire

Yorkshire & the Humber

The second smallest wine region, with just 9 wine estates covering the area of Yorkshire and North Lincolnshire, is your door to so many different experiences.

t's big and boundless with magnetic landscapes, seductive seascapes and vibrant cities. Unwind amongst the timeless green vales and dales dotted with traditional villages. Enjoy the fast-moving city scenes, feel sea breezes in your face and sand between your toes or take a trip back in time to castles, abbeys and historic houses.

Yorkshire is a unique mix of influences and inspirational places. It's restful and zestful, forward looking yet founded on a bedrock of traditional values. They're a friendly, straight-talking lot in those parts and they take great pride and pleasure in introducing visitors to Yorkshire's many and varied faces.

Plain speaking may be part of Yorkshire's character, but there's nothing plain about this captivating part of Britain. Country or city, trendy or traditional, ancient history or cutting-edge contemporary - Yorkshire has it all.

Selected Wineries
Holmfirth Vineyard (West Yorkshire)
Leventhorpe Vineyard (West Yorkshire)
Ryedale Vineyards (North Yorkshire)

Holmfirth Vineyard

Holmfirth Vineyard is situated at Woodhouse Farm covering seven acres and planted with 7000 vines. The farm was originally a sheep rearing business until August 2007. The vineyard sits in the beautiful location of Holmfirth, in the Holme Valley, West Yorkshire and is surrounded by panoramic views of the Peak District National Park home to 'the Last of the Summer Wine' TV series. The tour & tasting takes about 1½ -2 hours and includes a walk around the vineyard, showing how it was planted and why particular varieties were chosen; answering any questions you may have.

Leventhorpe Vineyard

Leventhorpe Vineyard, situated within the boundaries of the City of Leeds, is within easy reach of the M1 motorway and rail network. The vineyard revives the tradition of wine making in Yorkshire established by the Cistercian monks of Kirkstall Abbey, Leeds and the Benedictines of York.

The five-acre vineyard was established in 1985. It employs traditional methods together with modern equipment and techniques to produce a range of

wines – white, red and sparking (made in the traditional method). The main wines are Seyval and Madeleine Angevine, both early ripening white varieties and Triomphe, a red grape. Other white varieties are available in smaller quantities.

Ryedale Vineyards
Head to North Yorkshire, to Ryedale Vineyards and stay the weekend. The two-room B&B at Ryedale Vineyards allows you to experience the 7-acre wine estate for a weekend of relaxation, wine-tasting, a tour of the vineyards and a full Yorkshire breakfast just 12 miles from the historic city of York. Planted in 2006 Ryedale Vineyards produced their first wines in 2008. They manage both the Vineyard and Bed and Breakfast in an environmentally friendly way.

> 'Yorkshire is a unique mix of influences and inspirational places. It's restful and zestful, forward looking yet founded on a bedrock of traditional values.'

Selected Destinations

Halifax: A town that grew to prominence during the Industrial Revolution when the textile industry boomed. One of the town's most notable buildings is the Piece Hall, dating from 1779. In this quadrangled hall, boasting 315 rooms, merchants displayed pieces of cloth on market days. The Piece Hall holds a general market every Friday and Saturday.

Other attractions include the Wainhouse Tower, an elaborate chimney built in 1871 for a dye house but never used, and the Halifax Gibbet, where 50 people were executed for stealing cloth between 1550 and 1650. There are also plenty of parks and open spaces and a spectacular section of the Rochdale Canal running through the Calder Valley.

Leeds
The second largest metropolitan district in the UK. Green Belt countryside and excellent parks make Leeds one of the greenest cities.

The famous Marks and Spencer department store started with Michael Marks' Penny Bazaar in Leeds Market; Waddington's of Monopoly fame was founded in Leeds, and the largest clothing factory in Europe spread the Burtons name far and wide.

Whitby: Dominated by the cliff-top ruins of the beautiful 13th century Whitby Abbey. 199 steps lead down from the Abbey to the old town where you find yourself in a shoppers' paradise. Whitby is set among fine stretches of coast with spectacular cliffs, beaches and bays.

York: The History of York is the History of England. There is 2000 years worth of history in this beautiful North Yorkshire city. Renowned for its exquisite architecture, tangle of quaint cobbled streets and the iconic York Minster, York is well worth a stop. Take time out to enjoy some of the country's most talented street entertainers or simply watch the world go by while sipping a drink by the river.

Harrogate: Famous for its healing waters, this Victorian spa town oozes cosmopolitan charm, smart streets and quaint mews. Enjoy shopping in the stylish Montpellier Quarter, relax in atmospheric cafés, enjoy fine restaurants or stroll through an abundance of green open spaces.

Yorkshire & the Humber

Map	Wine estate	Tel number	Opening times
E3	Acomb Grange Vineyard	08712 884763	Open to the public
B2	Bolton Castle Vineyard	01969 623981	Apr-Oct Tue-Sun 10.00-17.00
E2	Helmsley Walled Garden Vineyard	01439 771427	Apr-Oct Mon-Sun 10.30-17.00, Closed weekend Nov, Jan-Feb
C4	Holmfirth Vineyard	01138 155588	By appointment only
D3	Leventhorpe Vineyard	01132 889088	Mon-Sat 11.00-16.30, Sun 12.00-16.00
E2	Ryedale Vineyards	01653 658507	Open to the public
D4	Summerhouse Vineyard	01302 721688	Open to the public
C3	Womack's Vineyard	07802 358737	Not open to the public
D3	Yorkshire Heart Vineyard	01423 330716	By appointment only

North Yorkshire
Acomb Grange Vineyard
Acomb Grange is ideally suited to viticulture, even though it is much further north than many vineyards. Historically, it is known that good wines were made from grapes grown on vineyards in the vicinity.

a: Grange Lane, York, North Yorkshire, YO23 3QZ
t: 08712 884763
www.acombgrange.co.uk

North Yorkshire
Bolton Castle Vineyard
Stocked with a modern hybrid, frost hardy and early ripening variety of red grape, Vitis Vinifera x Vitis Amurensis. In time, this small vineyard should produce up to 1000 bottles of wine a year.

a: Bolton Castle, Leyburn, North Yorkshire, DL8 4ET
t: 01969 623981
www.boltoncastle.co.uk

North Yorkshire
Helmsley Walled Garden Vineyard
We have an outdoor vineyard of six white varieties and one red. They are trained along wires in the double guyer method. They are modern varieties that we are trialling to see how they do in the north.

a: Cleveland Way, Helmsley, North Yorkshire, YO62 5AH
t: 01439 771427
www.helmsleywalledgarden.org.uk

North Yorkshire
Holmfirth Vineyard
A seven acre vineyard, planted with 7000 vines, surrounded by panoramic views of the Peak District National Park which is home to 'The last of the summer wine' TV series. 3 red varieties and 2 white.

a: Woodhouse Farm, Woodhouse Lane, Holmbridge, Holmfirth, HD9 2QR | t: 01138 155588
www.holmfirthvineyard.com

North Yorkshire
Leventhorpe Vineyard
The five-acre vineyard was established in 1985. It employs traditional methods together with modern equipment and techniques to produce a range of red, white, sparkling (made in the traditional method).

a: Bullerthorpe Lane, Woodlesford, Leeds, West Yorkshire, LS26 8AF | t: 01132 889088
www.ukvines.co.uk/vineyards/levens.htm

North Yorkshire
Ryedale Vineyards
Set in rolling countryside to the north east of the City of York. We produce red, white, rosé and sparkling wines, many of which will be made from organically grown grapes on a total of ten acres.

a: Farfeld Farm, Westow, York, North Yorkshire, YO60 7LS
t: 01653 658507
www.ryedalevineyards.co.uk

North Yorkshire
Summerhouse Vineyard
The first vines were planted in 2005 in the limestone soils on a one-hectare parcel of land selected for its gently sloping southerly aspect. We have 5 grape varieties producing red, white, rose and sparkling.

a: New Close Lane, Skelbrooke, Doncaster, South Yorkshire, DN6 8NB | t: 01302 721688
www.summerhousevineyard.co.uk

North Yorkshire
Womack's Vineyard
Grape varieties: Bacchus

a: 25 Eastville Terrace, Harrogate, North Yorkshire, HG1 3HJ
t: 07802 358737

North Yorkshire
Yorkshire Heart Vineyard
A new venture in the Vale of York. The vines were planted in 2006/07 and included several varieties of red grape, including the classic Cabernet Franc, which has never been grown this far north before.

a: The Firs, Kirk Hammerton Lane, Green Hammerton, York, YO26 8BS | t: 01423 330716
www.ukvines.co.uk/vineyards/yorks.htm

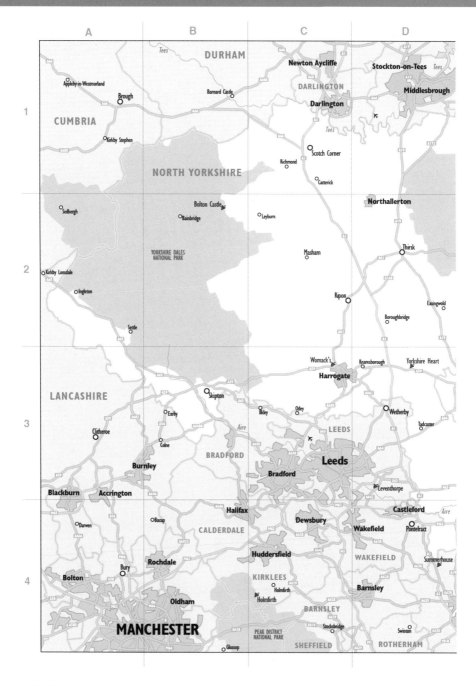

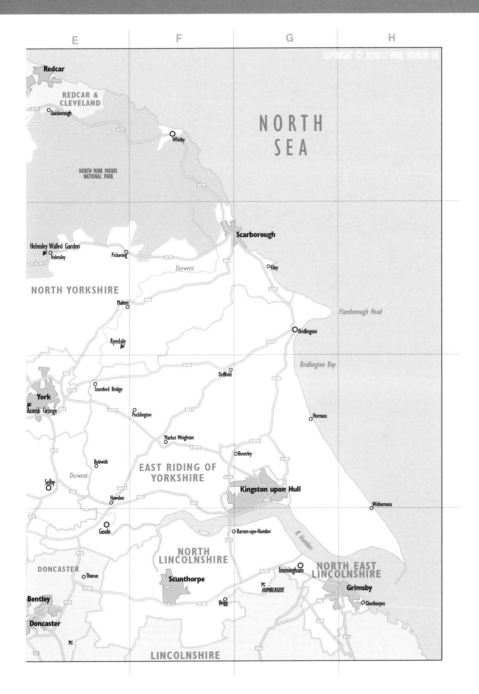

YORKSHIRE

Bempton Cliffs RSPB reserve

A family favourite, and easily the best place in England to see, hear and smell seabirds! More than 200,000 birds (from April to August) make the cliffs seem alive – with adults bringing food to their nests, or young chicks making their first faltering flights. The easily recognisable puffins (here between April and July) are always a delight. From March to October, the visitor centre is open daily 10 am to 5 pm. From November to February, 10 am to 4 pm.

a: The reserve is on the cliff road from the village of Bempton, which is on the B1229 road from Flamborough to Filey | t: 01262 851179 | **www.rspb.org.uk**

YORKSHIRE

Betty's Café Harrogate

One of Harrogate's most famous assets which opened in 1919 and boasts 400 different lines of mouth-watering cakes. A traditional family business based in the heart of Yorkshire.

a: 1 Parliament Street, Harrogate, HG1 2QU
t: 01423 814070 | **www.bettysandtaylors.co.uk**

YORKSHIRE

Burton Constable Hall

A large Elizabethan mansion set in a 300 acre park with nearly 30 rooms open to the public. The interiors of faded splendour are filled with fine furniture, paintings and sculpture, a library of 5,000 books and a remarkable 18th century 'cabinet of curiosities' which contains fossils, natural history specimens and a collection of scientific instruments. Occupied by the Constable family for over 400 years, the house still maintains the atmosphere of a home.

a: The Burton Constable Foundation, Burton Constable, Skirlaugh, East Yorkshire, HU11 4LN
t: 01964 562400 | **www.burtonconstable.com**

YORKSHIRE

Flamingo Land Theme Park and Zoo

One price family adventure park with over 100 rides and attractions including the UK's only motorbike launch rollercoaster, the free falling cliff hanger and Kamali, the suspended looping rollercoaster. There is also 5 family shows plus the UK's largest privately owned zoo, home to many exotic species including giraffes, lions, rhinoceros and tigers. There is an en-suite Holiday Village, with brand new log cabins, luxury holiday homes and campsite for tents and caravans.

a: Kirby Misperton, Malton, North Yorkshire, YO17 6UX
t: 0871 911 8000 | **www.flamingoland.co.uk**

YORKSHIRE

Jorvik Viking Centre

Standing on the site of one of the most famous and astounding discoveries of modern archaeology. Thirty years ago the archaeologists from York Archaeological Trust revealed the houses, workshops and backyards of the Viking-Age city of Jorvik, as it stood 1,000 years ago. Over 800 extraordinary finds discovered on site can be seen. Meet the famous JORVIK Vikings in our three exciting exhibitions that delve further into life 1000 years ago.

a: Coppergate, York, YO1 9WT
t: 01904 615505 | **www.jorvik-viking-centre.co.uk**

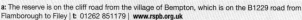

YORKSHIRE

Magna Science Adventure Centre

The UK's 1st science adventure centre is set in the Templeborough steelworks in Rotherham. Set in this cavernous space are 4 pavilions where you can explore the elements, earth, air, fire and water. Here you can have fun firing a giant water cannon, launch rockets, board an airship and spin in a gyroscopic chair. See lightning bolts, fiery tornadoes, explode rock faces and work real JCBs!

a: Sheffield Road, Templeborough, Rotherham, South Yorkshire, S60 1DX
t: 01709 720002 | **www.visitmagna.co.uk**

YORKSHIRE

National Railway Museum

Re-live a golden era and witness history brought to life by the story of the railways. A touch of nostalgia awaits you as you stroll past the treasures in the Warehouse or down the red carpets of Station Hall, towards the famous Royal Carriages. Step on to the futuristic, Japanese Bullet Train, gaze up at our stunning replica of Stephenson's Rocket, delve in to our Workshops and watch live demonstrations of the turntable and Winding Engine in action!

a: Leeman Road, York, North Yorkshire, YO26 4XJ
t: 0844 815 3139 | **www.nrm.org.uk**

YORKSHIRE

Royal Armouries Museum

Over 8,000 objects displayed in five galleries - War, Tournament, Oriental, Self Defence and Hunting. Among the treasures are Henry VIII's tournament armour and the world record breaking elephant armour. Regular jousting and horse shows. Experience the excitement of reliving some of the most important moments in our history with costumed performances, jousting tournaments and falconry displays - visit the Menagerie and get to know the Armouries' animals.

a: Armouries Drive, Leeds, West Yorkshire, LS10 1LT
t: 08700 344344 | **www.royalarmouries.org**

YORKSHIRE

Salts Mill, Saltaire

An impressive art gallery, home to one of the largest collections of David Hockney's work.

a: Shipley, Saltaire, West Yorkshire, BD18 3LA, UK
t: 01274 531163 | **www.saltsmill.org.uk**

YORKSHIRE

The Baroque Wing, Wentworth Castle

Wentworth Castle Gardens & Stainborough Park is the only Grade One Listed landscape in South Yorkshire, and contains a fascinating collection of 26 listed buildings and monuments. Over 500 acres of historic parkland can be explored from the Parkland Trail, which links several restored follies and native woods, through the beautiful countryside of Stainborough. There is an exciting children's adventure playground, with zip slide, swings and a castle.

a: Wentworth Castle Gardens, Lowe Lane, Stainborough, Barnsley, S75 3ET
t: 01226 776040 | **www.wentworthcastle.org**

YORKSHIRE

The Deep

The Deep is Hull's £53million Millennium Commission Lottery Project. Full with over 3500 fish and more than 40 sharks, it tells the story of the world's oceans using live animals and the latest hands on interactive. Experience the dramatic story of the world's oceans, from the dawn of time and into the future at 'submarium', home to 40 sharks and 3500 fish! Highlights include Europe's deepest viewing tunnel and a glass lift ride through the 10m deep tank.

a: Tower Street, Hull, HU1 4DP
t: 01482 381000 | **www.thedeep.co.uk**

YORKSHIRE

The National Coal Mining Museum

The National Coal Mining Museum for England provides a great day out with a unique opportunity to travel 140 metres underground down one of Britain's oldest working mines. Situated in a rural setting, it offers an unusual combination of exciting experiences, whilst providing a genuine insight into the hard working lives of miners through the ages. As the museum is a real coal mine, warm clothes and sensible flat shoes are recommended.

a: Caphouse Colliery, New Road, Wakefield, West Yorkshire, WF4 4RH
t: 01924 848806 | **www.ncm.org.uk**

YORKSHIRE

The National Media Museum

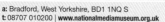

A fabulous free museum in Bradford, devoted to film, photography, TV, radio and the web. Journey through popular photography, visit IMAX, the world's most powerful giant screen experience, discover the past, present and future of television in Experience TV, watch your favourite TV moments in TV Heaven, play with light, lenses and colour in the Magic Factory and explore the world of animation. We also host children's parties, sleepovers and festivals.

a: Bradford, West Yorkshire, BD1 1NQ S
t: 08707 010200 | **www.nationalmediamuseum.org.uk**

YORKSHIRE

Xscape

Xscape is an amazing leisure complex complete with a multi-plex cinema, restaurants, bars, coffee houses and a wealth of sporting activities that you won't find anywhere else in Yorkshire. Real snow indoor ski slope, Indoor skate park, Rock climbing, Aerial assault course, Laser quest, Tobogganing, Cosmic golf, Cineworld, Bowling, Amusements, Dodgems. Also a fantastic range of stores, featuring big names such as Quicksilver, Animal and Billabong.

a: Colorado Way, Glasshoughton, Castleford, West Yorkshire, WF10 4TA
t: 08712 003221 | **www.xscape.co.uk**

YORKSHIRE

York Minster

York Minster is one of the great cathedrals of the world. We invite you to enjoy its vast spaces, filled with music and revealing the human imagination at work on glass, stone, and other fabrics. Whatever your faith and culture, you are welcome here, to see for yourself the life of a centre of Christian belief. Explore the history beneath your feet in the Undercroft and enjoy magnificent views from the tower top. Open daily subject to services.

a: Deangate, York, North Yorkshire, YO1 7HH
t: 08449 390016 | **www.yorkminster.org**

North West

+ England

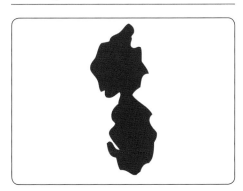

**Cumbria, Lancashire, Greater Manchester,
Merseyside, Cheshire**

North West

The smallest of our wine regions with only 3 wine producers, reflecting the harsher climate as you travel north.

C overing Cumbria, including the breathtaking Lake District, Lancashire, Greater Manchester, Merseyside and Cheshire, this area is packed with things to do.

This is a region for city breaks, exploring famously-fashionable haunts, historic streets and buildings and a region to walk, cycle and discover the landscapes and wildlife of unspoilt villages.

There is always a feast of sporting entertainment including international cricket, championship golf courses and Premiership football. There are great places to stay in chic city centre hotels, rural retreats, country houses and cosy pubs.

Selected vineyard:
Carden Park Hotel Vineyard (Cheshire)

Carden Park Hotel Vineyard
Carden Park is extremely proud of the rebirth of its very own sparkling wine after an absence of five years. In collaboration with Halfpenny Green Winemakers of South Staffordshire, Carden Park is now growing, harvesting and producing a very special selection

of two classic British Sparkling Wines using grapes grown on the estate. Although the vast majority of their vineyard was planted in 1988, considerable work has been undertaken over the last two years to bring this completely unique Cheshire Vineyard back into production.

Their current grape variety Seyval Blanc, well suited to the British climate, produces a light, nutty and crisp sparkling wine and is made using the ultra-classic "methode champagnois."

Selected Destinations:
Cumbria & the Lake District: With 16 magnificent lakes, England's highest mountains, sheltered valleys, heather moorlands and salty seascapes, Cumbria and the Lake District has been a joy to millions of visitors but there's more to see than just scenery. The area has a rich heritage to discover, a vibrant and contemporary cultural scene, and a growing reputation for fine food and drink.

Chester: Encircled by a 2-mile ring of Roman and medieval walls, Chester is a blend of the ancient and traditional with modern cosmopolitan chic.

Situated on the River Dee, Chester is home to 2,000 years of history and is one of Britain's Heritage Cities. It has fantastic Georgian and Victorian architecture alongside its ancient and dynamic past, Chester is one of Britain's best breaks.

Manchester: Situated in England's North Country, Manchester has emerged as one of Britain's coolest cities with great bars and world-class hospitality. This once industrial city has become a truly contemporary metropolis, with modern buildings such as the Lowry Centre, and a thriving art and culture scene.

'This is the region for city breaks, exploring famously-fashionable haunts, historic streets and buildings. It's a region to walk, cycle and discover the landscapes and wildlife of unspoilt villages.'

Liverpool: known around the world for its architecture, football, literature and music this city was awarded European Capital of Culture in 2008. Liverpool is fast becoming one of Europe's most popular city break destinations. It boasts more theatres, museums and galleries than any other UK city outside London.

Elements of Manchester's industrial past can be found as you travel around; it's that mix of old and new which gives Manchester its unique character.

Blackpool: A loud and proud traditional English seaside resort, its famous pleasure beach is packed with wall to wall attractions and entertainment.

🐓 North West

Map	Wine estate	Tel number	Opening times
C8	Carden Park Hotel Vineyard	01829 731000	Open to the public
C4	Mount Pleasant Vineyard	01524 732038	Not open to the public
D7	Plot 19 Vineyard	01617 499348	Not open to the public

Cheshire

Carden Park Hotel Vineyard

We are extremely proud to announce the rebirth of our very own sparkling wine after an absence of five years. We now grow, harvest and produce a very special selection of two classic British Sparkling Wines.

a: Carden, Chester, Cheshire, CH3 9DQ
t: 01829 731000
http://www.cardenpark.co.uk/the-vineyard.html

Lancashire

Mount Pleasant Vineyard

We are a small vineyard established in 1996 on a 0.5 acre (about 500 vines) SSE facing site. This is currently the only vineyard in Lancashire and the most northerly in Britain. The soil is alkaline, with loam over gravel.

a: Mount Pleasant Lane, Bolton-le-Sands, Carnforth, Lancashire, LA5 8AD | t: 015247 32038
www.ukvines.co.uk/vineyards/mount.htm

Manchester

Plot 19 Vineyard

Planted five years ago. The wine is getting better each year as I gain more experience and the vintages are also becoming bigger each year as the vines mature. There are 95 vines of white and red grapes.

a: 23 Clifton Road, Urmston, Manchester, M41 5RU
t: 01617 499348
www.plot19vineyard.co.uk

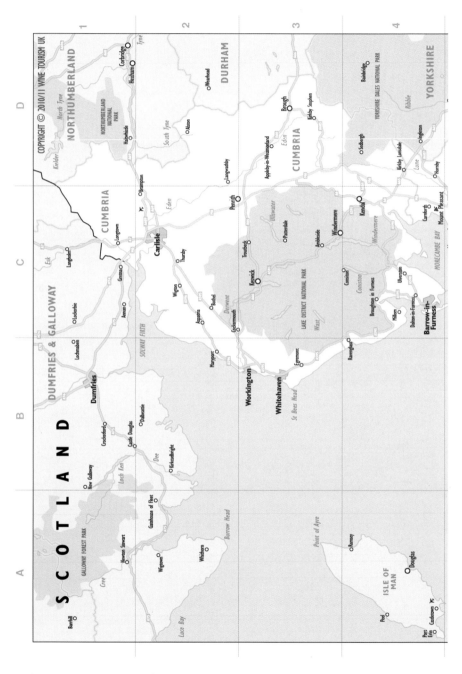

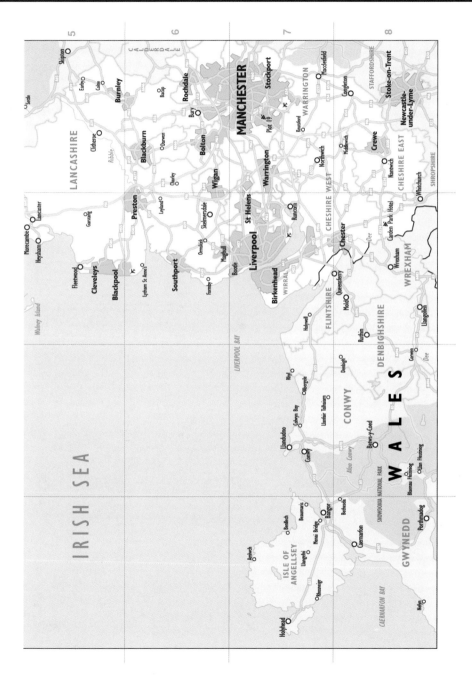

Chester Zoo

CHESHIRE

Chester Zoo is home to thousands of rare and exotic species from all over the world, ranging from our magnificent herd of elephants, two types of rhino 'crashes', lions and tigers, a mixture of monkeys both large and small including our chimps, and our exciting Realm of the Red Ape exhibit where gibbons and orang-utans live and play side by side in the largest (and possibly the noisiest!) enclosure of its kind in Europe.

a: Upton By Chester, Chester, Cheshire, CH2 1EU
t: 01244 380280 | **www.chesterzoo.org**

Jodrell Bank Visitor Centre

CHESHIRE

A fantastic day out to visit the world-famous Lovell Radio telescope. Visitors can get closer to the telescope than ever before on the observational pathway, which stretches 180 degrees around the base. During your visit you can take a trip to Mars in the 3D theatre, walk around the small exhibition and shop area or take a relaxing lunch in the café. The arboretum is a tree lovers' paradise as it offers over 2,500 species of trees and scrubs.

a: Macclesfield, Cheshire, SK11 9DL
t: 01477 571339 | **www.jodrellbank.manchester.ac.uk/visitorcentre**

Tatton Park

CHESHIRE

Tatton Park is often quoted as England's most complete historic estate, with its fine Neo-Classical mansion full of art treasures and original furnishings. The impressive Neo-Classical mansion was designed by Samuel and Lewis Wyatt. A visit includes the permanent Maurice Egerton exhibition and a number of temporary exhibitions portraying different aspects of Tatton Park throughout the year.

a: Knutsford, Cheshire, WA16 6QN
t: 01625 374400 | **www.tattonpark.org.uk**

Muncaster Experience

CUMBRIA

Historic haunted Castle home to the Pennington family for 800 years. A 70-acre garden famous for its collection of rhododendrons and azaleas set against the stunning backdrop of the Lakeland fells. World Owl Centre home to over 40 species.

a: Cumbria, Ravenglass, Cumbria, CA18 1RQ
t: 01229 717614 | **www.muncaster.co.uk**

Imperial War Museum North

GREATER MANCHESTER

The multi-award winning Imperial War Museum North (one of the top 4 Large Visitor Attractions in England 2010) is one of the most celebrated Museums in Britain today. Imperial War Museum North is about people and their stories, about how lives have been and still are shaped by war and conflict. The award-winning building by international architect Daniel Libeskind is a symbol of our world torn apart by conflict.

a: Trafford Wharf Road, The Quays, Manchester, Greater Manchester, M17 1TZ
t: 01618 364000 | **www.north.iwm.org.uk**

LANCASHIRE

Blackpool Pleasure Beach

There's something for everyone. There are over 125 rides and attractions plus spectacular shows. For the ultimate in thrills why not brave the UK's tallest, fastest rollercoaster - the Pepsi Max Big One. Hold your breath as you board Infusion, the exhilarating, five looping coaster which is the first in the world to be suspended completely over water. Brave Valhalla - the world's most spectacular dark rides, which feature amazing thrills, spills and special effects.

a: Ocean Boulevard, Promenade, Blackpool, Lancashire, FY4 1EZ
t: 08712 221234 | **www.blackpoolpleasurebeach.com**

LANCASHIRE

Lancaster Castle

Steeped in almost 1000 years of history including the trials of the Pendle Witches and the Birmingham Six, Lancaster Castle is one of the most important historic monuments in the North West. Come and visit the dungeons, Shire Hall and Crown. The Castle is also one of Europe's longest serving operational prisons. In the Shire Hall is a magnificent display of heraldic shields. Open daily for guided tours, 10am to 5pm (Court sittings permitting).

a: Castle Parade, Lancaster, Lancashire, LA1 1YJ
t: 01524 64998 | **www.lancastercastle.com**

MERSEYSIDE

Beatles story

A unique visitor attraction that transports you on an enlightening and atmospheric journey into the life, times, culture and music of the Beatles. See how four young lads from Liverpool were propelled to the dizzy heights of worldwide fame and fortune, becoming the greatest band of all time along the way! Also don't forget to head over to our second home, Beatles Story Pier Head in the Mersey Ferries Terminal.

a: Britannia Vaults, Albert Dock, Liverpool, Merseyside, L3 4AD
t: 01517 091963 | **www.beatlesstory.com**

MERSEYSIDE

The Tate, Liverpool

Tate Liverpool is the home of the National Collection of Modern Art in the north. Located on the Grade One listed Albert Dock and within easy walking distance from the City centre, Tate Liverpool has become a venue for major exhibitions of international modern art, as well as hosting large and changing displays from the national collection, making it the ideal place to either see your favourite artwork or discover something new.

a: Albert Dock, Liverpool, Merseyside, L3 4BB
t: 0151 702 7400 | **www.tate.org.uk/liverpool**

NORTHUMBERLAND

Hadrian's Wall Path National Trail

This 84 mile footpath that follows mostly the historic line of Hadrian's Wall opened to the public on May 23 2003. Visitors are advised to view www.nationaltrail.co.uk/hadrianswall for details of key publications and information. The main facilities and services are listed in the 'Essential Guide to Hadrian's Wall Path'.

a: Hadrian's Wall, Hexham, Northumberland
t: 01912 691600 | **www.nationaltrail.co.uk/hadrianswall**

⮇Food & Wine Festivals
North West

CHESHIRE

Chester Food Drink and Lifestyle | 23rd April 2011 - 25th April 2011
www.chesterfoodanddrink.com
Address: Chester Racecourse, Cheshire | **Tel:** 01244 355474 | **email:** alex@scwirrel.com, rebecca@whiteevents.co.uk

CHESHIRE

Congleton Food & Drink Festival | June
www.foodanddrinkfestival.net
Address: Congleton, Cheshire | **Tel:** 01260 291156 | **email:** jo@congletoncommunityprojects.org

CHESHIRE

Nantwich Food & Drink Festival | September
www.nantwichfoodfestival.co.uk
Address: Nantwich, Cheshire | **email:** trade@nantwichfoodfestival.co.uk

CHESHIRE

North West Food Lovers Festival at Tatton Park | 28th October 2011 - 30th October 2011
www.nwfoodloversfestival.com
Address: Tatton Park, Cheshire | **Tel:** 01244 355474 | **email:** rebecca@scwirrel.com, eve@whiteevents.co.uk

LANCASHIRE

Lancashire Food Festival, Accrinton Hall | 9th April 2011 - 10th April 2011
www.lancashirefoodfestival.co.uk
Address: Accrington, Lancashire | **Tel:** 01254 380293 | **email:** kerry.smith@leisureinhyndburn.co.uk

LANCASHIRE

Pennine Lancashire Festival of Food & Culture | August/September
www.penninelancashirefestivals.com
Address: Blackburn Visitor Centre, Church Street, Blackburn, Lancashire, BB1 5AL | **Tel:** 01254 688040

MANCHESTER

Manchester Food & Drink Festival | October
www.foodanddrinkfestival.com
Address: Manchester. There is no single location! | **Tel:** 01618 393461 | **email:** hello@foodanddrinkfestival.com

MERSEYSIDE

Liverpool Food & Drink Festival | September
www.liverpoolfoodanddrinkfestival.co.uk
Address: Sefton Park, Merseyside, Liverpool | **Tel:** 01515 229362

☐ Notes:

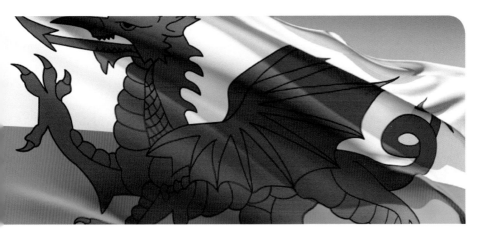

Wales

 Wales

Blaenau Gwent, Bridgend, Caerphilly, Cardiff, Carmarthenshire, Ceredigion, Conwy, Denbighshire, Flintshire, Gwynedd, Isle of Anglesey, Merthyr Tydfil, Monmouthshire, Newport, Neath Port Talbot, Pembrokeshire, Powys, Rhondda Cynon Taff, Swansea, Torfaen, Vale of Glamorgan, Wrexham

Wales

A proud and independent nation where the Welsh language is the first language of many, particularly in the north and west.

Wales, a land of 600 castles but only 18 wine estates. There is a strong tradition of choral singing and the Welsh love of music in all its forms. Literature and poetry also abound in the large number of eisteddfods, a tradition going back at least eight centuries. The decline in the mining industry has resulted in tourism now being the most important industry.

Selected wineries
Ancre Hill Vineyard (Monmouthshire)
Llanerch Vineyard (Vale of Glamorgan)
Penarth Vineyard (Powys)

Ancre Hill Vineyard
The first phase of the vineyard was planted in April 2006, with a further plantation in April 2007. The vineyard comprises two sites at The Ancre Hill on the outskirts of Monmouth town. The Folly View site of 6 acres is principally planted with Chardonnay and Seyval Blanc, but also has some Pinot Noir and Triomphe. The newer Town site of 3 acres is totally dedicated to Pinot Noir. Both sites are south facing on good draining, limestone soil and the long hours of sunshine and comparatively low rainfall all combine to

make it an ideal location for vines. Set in the middle of the Wye Valley, the vineyard is blessed with its own unique meso-climate, surrounded by tree topped hills on all sides, with the famous Brecon Beacons to the north. Visit their Cellar Door, browse around their shop and taste some of their wines. Or why not enjoy the cheese platter lunch using only Welsh cheeses, washed down by a glass of Estate wine. Or take advantage of one of the guided vineyard tours and enjoy the ambience of the vineyard.

Llanerch Vineyard
Llanerch Vineyard is the largest and oldest premier vineyard in Wales. Standing in more than 20 acres of beautiful Glamorganshire countryside yet only 15 minutes from Cardiff, it offers a range of superb accommodation and an opportunity to participate in gourmet activities by learning about and sampling great wine and food.

Llanerch Vineyard nestles among meadows and grazing pastures, woodlands and gardens and has two tranquil lakes brimming with ornamental carp, all of which are open to residents and visitors alike. Take a tour of the vineyard to see the six different varieties of vines, taste any one (or more!) of the seven labels from the award winning Cariad range, which you can enjoy with a sumptuous lunch or teatime picnic.

Whether you are looking for a comfortable and elegant place to stay during your trip to Wales, want to learn how to appreciate good wine and cook fantastic food by visiting the Llanerch Cookery School, or just feel like taking time out to visit the grounds and wander among the vines, Llanerch Vineyard is the perfect place.

Penarth Vineyard
Penarth Vineyard is situated on a unique riverside location in the Montgomeryshire region of Powys in mid-Wales.

Penarth Estate sparkling wines have been produced in the traditional method. Two years in stainless steel tanks on lees and a 12 month bottle maturation creates a wine that compares favourably to French counterparts.

Penarth Estate wines are made from the produce of the vineyards in Montgomeryshire in Mid Wales, whilst the wines are made at Three Choirs Vineyard. Their Welsh wine is unique as they grow varieties which are believed to be unsuitable for the local climate, yet their grapes are grown outside and face the elements giving them a richness of flavours and depth of character.

Selected destinations:
Millennium Stadium: Built in 1999 in readiness for the Rugby World Cup, the stadium has hosted countless major rugby and football matches as well as other top class sporting events including the FA Cup final during the years of the re-construction of the new Wembley Stadium. The stadium is also a fabulous music venue hosting concerts for many of the world's superstars. A visit to the Millennium Stadium, whether for an event or behind the scenes tour, should not be missed.

Mount Snowdon
Snowdon rates amongst the most beautiful mountains in the world. with grandeur and size to impress.

'A land of 600 castles but only 18 wine estates.'

It radiates six magnificent ridges each with their own special and individual characters. The deep glaciated valleys range from the easily accessible to hanging valleys only reached by the more experienced. This mountain has rare flowers and insects, old mines, fascinating volcanic rock formations to fossils on the summit. Whatever your interests, the mountains have something for everyone.

Portmeirion:
Located on its own private peninsula on the coast of Snowdonia. This fascinating fantasy village was the setting for the cult viewing 1960s TV series 'The Prisoner'.

Cardiff
The City centre is a mix of old and new. The part Roman, part Norman, part Victorian Castle stands next to the modern Millennium Stadium and modern high street shops and malls are interlaced with old Victorian and Edwardian arcades.

Wales

Map	Wine estate	Tel number	Opening times
D7	Ancre Hill Vineyard	01600 714152	Apr-Sep Wed-Sun 10.30-16.30, other times by appointment
D8	Bryn Ceilog Vineyard	02920 711017	Not open to the public
A7	Cwm Deri Vineyard	01834 891274	Open to the public
D8	Gelynis Vineyard	02920 844440	Open to the public
C8	Glyndwr Vineyard	01446 774564	By appointment only
B7	Jabajak Vineyard	01994 448786	Open to the public
B5	Llaethliw Vineyard	01545 571879	Not open to public
B1	Llanbadrig Vineyard	01407 710416	Open to the public
C8	Llanerch Vineyard	01443 225877	Open to the public
D7	Monnow Valley Vineyard	01600 716209	By appointment only
B3	Pant Du Vineyard	01286 880806	By appointment only
D7	Parva Farm Vineyard	01291 689636	Everyday except Weds 11.30-17.30, until dusk during winter
D4	Penarth Vineyard	01686 610383	By appointment only
D7	Sugar Loaf Vineyard	01873 853066	Easter-Oct Tue-Sat 10.30-17, Sun 12.00-17.00
B2	Ty Croes Vineyard	01248 440358	Open to the public
D7	Wernddu Vineyard	01600 740104	By appointment only
D7	White Castle Vineyard	01783 821443	By appointment only
D3	Worthenbury Vineyard	01948 770257	By appointment only

Monmouthshire

Ancre Hill Vineyard

Planted in April 2006/07. Principally planted with Chardonnay and Seyval Blanc, but also has Pinot Noir and Triomphe. Come and visit our Cellar Door, browse our shop and taste some of our wines.

a: Ancre Hill Estates, Monmouth, Monmouthshire, NP25 5HS | t: 01600 714152
www.ancrehillestates.co.uk

Vale of Glamorgan

Bryn Ceilog Vineyard

Red and White wines from grapes hand-picked in Leckwith

a: Fairfield, 14 Clinton Road, Penarth, Vale of Glamorgan, CF64 3JB. Location of vineyard: Beggan Farm, Leckwith, Vale of Glamorgan, CF11 8AS | t: 02920 711017

Pembrokeshire

Cwm Deri Vineyard

First opened to the public in 1992 and the vineyard is now one of Wales' foremost visitor attractions. Enjoy a tasting of our wines and liqueurs, either in our shop or on our patio and terrace.

a: Martletwy, Narberth, Pembrokeshire, SA67 8AP
t: 01834 891274
www.cwm-deri.co.uk

Cardiff

Gelynis Vineyard

Producing from the vines at the farm, both medium dry and fume. The guest house was built in 1574. Dressed stone windows and doors have been restored to accommodate our 21st Century guests.

a: Gelynis Fruit Farm, Morganstown, Cardiff, CF15 8LB
t: 02920 844440
www.gelynisfarm.co.uk

Vale of Glamorgan

Glyndwr Vineyard

The oldest established and family run vineyard in Wales. Planted in 1982, the estate comprises some 6,000 vines grown on gently south-east facing slopes in the heart of the beautiful Vale of Glamorgan.

a: Llanblethian, Cowbridge, Vale of Glamorgan, CF71 7JF
t: 01446 774564
www.glyndwrvineyard.co.uk

Carmarthenshire

Jabajak Vineyard

Our Vineyard, planted in 2006, is about to mature. You can stroll amongst the 2000 vines (of 5 varietals) and observe the abundance of wildlife. We offer 5 star accommodation and have a restaurant.

a: Banc-Y-Llain, Llanboidy, Whitland, Carmarthenshire, SA34 0ED | t: 01994 448786
www.jabajak.co.uk

Ceredigion

Llaethliw Vineyard

Organic vineyard.
Grape varieties: Solaris, Rondo, Regent, Orion.

a: Neuaddlwyd, Aberaeron, Ceredigion, SA48 7RF
t: 01545 571879

Isle of Anglesey

Llanbadrig Vineyard

Winery tours, vineyard tours, wine sales, vines for sale. The camp site is now open for tents, motor homes, touring caravans are permitted. The site is a little exposed with views across the sea.

a: Gwinllan Padrig, Cae Owain, Cemaes Bay, Anglesey, LL67 0LN | t: 01407 710416
www.llanbadrigvineyard.com

Vale of Glamorgan

Llanerch Vineyard

The largest and oldest premier vineyard in Wales in more than 20 acres of beautiful countryside. Offering a range of accommodation and an opportunity to learn about and sample great wine and food.

a: Hensol, Pendoylan, Vale of Glamorgan, CF72 8GG
t: 01443 225877
www.llanerch-vineyard.co.uk

Monmouthshire

Monnow Valley Vineyard

A one acre vineyard planted in 1979 extended to four acres in 1988. Grown on the steep slopes of the River Monnow. The grapes produce a dry to medium-dry wine that is fruity and full of character.

a: Great Osbaston Farm, Monmouth, Monmouthshire, NP25 5DL
t: 01600 716209

Gwynedd

Pant Du Vineyard

Owned by Richard Wyn and Iola Huws and their family. It is hoped that they can make white, red, rosé and sparkling wine. They estimate that it will produce 11 thousand bottles of wine a year!

a: Y Wern, Pant Du, Hen Lon, Penygroes, Gwynedd, LL54 6PY
t: 01286 880806

Montgomeryshire

Penarth Vineyard

Our sparkling wines have been produced in the traditional method. Two years in stainless steel tanks on lees and a 12 month bottle maturation created a wine comparable to that of our French counterparts.

a: Pool Road, Newtown, Montgomeryshire, SY16 3AN
t: 01686 610383
www.welshwine.co.uk

Isle of Anglesey

Ty Croes Vineyard

Established vineyard covering two and a half acres of vines that have now been turned into delicious Welsh wines ready for you to sample. Come and join us for a vineyard tour and tasting tour.

a: Ty Croes Farm, Dwyran, Llanfairpwll, Anglesey, LL61 6RP
t: 01248 440358
www.tycroesvineyard.co.uk

Monmouthshire

White Castle Vineyard

Grape varieties: Pinot Noir, Regent, Rondo, Phoenix, Seyval Blanc. Open at the weekends.

a: Crodt Farm, Llanvetherine, Abergavenny, Monmouthshire, NP7 8RA
t: 01783 821443

Monmouthshire

Parva Farm Vineyard

A privately owned and run vineyard in the village of Tintern, South Wales. Producing award-winning wines, meads and sparkling wines for all occasions. Open year-round for visiting.

a: Tintern, Chepstown, Monmouthshire, NP16 6SQ
t: 01291 689636
www.parvafarm.com

Monmouthshire

Sugar Loaf Vineyard

We have 7 varieties of grapes planted on 5 acres of south facing slopes. Our wines have achieved "Quality Status" from the European Wine Standards Board and won awards in national competitions.

a: Dunman Farm, Pentre Lane, Abergavenny, Monmouthshire, NP7 7LA | t: 01873 853066
www.sugarloafvineyard.co.uk

Monmouthshire

Wernddu Vineyard

A family-run business who plant, grow, harvest and bottle all our wine, cider and perry here at the farm as well as harvesting local fruit. We'd love you to come and visit. Winery, tasting room.

a: Wernddu Farm, Pen-Y-Clawdd, Monmouth, Monmouthshire, NP25 4BW | t: 01600 740104
www.wernddu.com

Wrexham

Worthenbury Vineyard

The wine is made at the Three Choirs Vineyard by award winning Winemaker, Martin Fowke. Chardonnay and Pinot Noir produces the sparkling wine. White wine is Sauvignon Blanc, red Pinot Noir.

a: The Old Rectory, Worthenbury, Wrexham, LL13 0AW
t: 01948 770257
www.worthenburywines.co.uk

Chapter five
The UK wine regions | Wales

Rocky welsh cove

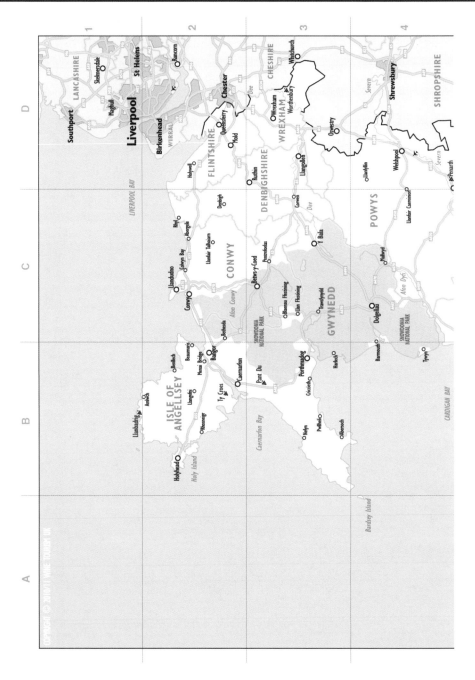

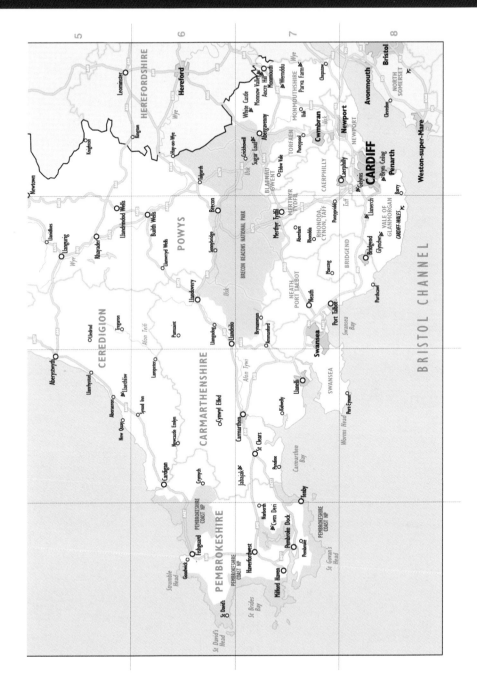

CARDIFF

Techniquest

The UK's most family friendly science centre with more than 150 hands-on exhibits and puzzles, Science Theatre, Planetarium, Discovery Room, Laboratory and The Hub.

a: Stuart Street, Cardiff Bay, Cardiff, Cardiff Area, CF10 5BW
t: 02920 475475 | **www.techniquest.org**

DENBIGHSHIRE

Llangollen Wharf

From Llangollen Wharf you can embark on either a horse drawn boat trip or a motorised aqueduct cruise. The horse drawn trip lasts about 45 minutes and runs every hour taking you through some of the most beautiful canals in Britain. The aqueduct cruise takes you across the famous Pontcysylite Aqueduct, built by Thomas Telford, the biggest navigable aqueduct, 126 feet above the River Dee.

a: Wharf Hill, Llangollen, Denbighshire, LL20 8TA
t: 01978 860702 | **www.horsedrawnboats.co.uk**

GWYNEDD

Bala Lake Railway

Steam narrow gauge railway, Bala Lake Railway offers a 9 mile return journey through the beautiful Snowdonia National Park. The 2ft narrow gauge steam trains gives excellent views of the lake amid its surrounding pastoral and woodland scenery, and of the nearby mountains, Arenig Fawr, Aran Benllyn and Aran Fawddwy.

a: Railway, The Station, Llanuwchllyn, Bala, Gwynedd, LL23 7DD
t: 01678 540666 | **www.bala-lake-railway.co.uk**

GWYNEDD

Greenwood Forest Park

Ride the world's first people-powered rollercoaster and zoom down our 70m sledge slide. Explore TreeTop Towers, find the Crocodile hidden in the Maze and get happy feet at Wales's first Barefoot Trail. Take the Jungle Boats challenge before bouncing along to the Giant Jumper! Adventure playgrounds, Mini-tractors and Longbows and inside the Medieval-style Great Hall you'll find the 'World of Trees' Exhibition, Gift Shops and the Conservatory Café.

a: Y Felinheli, Caernarfon, Gwynedd, LL56 4QN
t: 01248 671493 | **www.greenwoodforestpark.co.uk**

GWYNEDD

Snowdonia National Park

Snowdonia National Park is a living working area, home to over 26,000 people. As well as being the largest National Park in Wales, Snowdonia boasts the highest mountain in Wales, and the largest natural lake in Wales, as well as a wealth of picturesque villages like Betws y Coed and Beddgelert. Snowdonia is an area steeped in culture, and local history, where more than half its population speak Welsh.

a: Penrhyndeudraeth, Gwynedd
www.snowdonia-npa.gov.uk

Oakwood Theme Park

Oakwood Park is one of Wales's largest tourist attractions with over 60 rides and 400,000 visitors each year. Whatever the weather, there is something for everyone from white knuckle rides including Megafobia or The Bounce to family favourites including The Pirate Ship and Treetops coaster. Try your hand at the grazy golf or the pedalos on the boating lake. For the smaller kids there is plenty of fun to be had in KidzWorld.

a: Canaston Bridge, Narberth, Pembrokeshire, SA67 8DE
t: 01834 861889 | **www.oakwoodthemepark.co.uk**

The Dinosaur Park

The Dinosaur Park is home to twenty two life size, animated dinosaurs, in a woodland setting. Other attractions include a mini theatre with daily programmes, an adventure playground and Dino's Play Den for younger children, a unique dinosaur-themed restaurant and a sun terrace cafe and snack bar.

a: Great Wedlock, Gumfreston, Tenby, Pembrokeshire, SA70 8RB
t: 01834 845272 | **www.thedinosaurpark.co.uk**

Brecon Beacons National Park Authority

This is a beautiful part of Wales, with traditional market towns, stunning landscape, canal paths, castles and plenty of family attractions. The scenery here is both beautiful and diverse - rolling countryside and valleys, wide open spaces to the wild beauty of the waterfalls and caves. There is also an excellent programme of Guided Walks, Children's activities and Family Events

a: Plas y Ffynnon, Cambrian Way, Brecon, Powys, LD3 7HP
t: 01874 624437 | **www.breconbeacons.org**

Centre for Alternative Technology

Reclaiming the site of an old slate quarry in southern Snowdonia. Seven acres of interactive displays in a park setting on green building, waste and recycling, energy and power and a free information service. Spend a day there picking up hints and tips on saving energy and saving money. There are free kids' activities in the school holidays and an adventure playground, cafe and shop. Leave the car at home and travel by train and get in for half price.

a: Machynlleth, Powys, SY20 9AZ
t: 01654 705950 | **www.cat.org.uk**

King Arthur's Labyrinth

An Underground Storytelling Adventure. Travel by boat deep inside the vast caverns of the Labyrinth and far back in time. Enjoy tales of King Arthur, and other ancient Welsh legends as you explore the spectacular underground setting. Dramatic scenes, light shows and sound effects create a real adventure for all ages. Back above ground, take on the challenge of the Bards' Quest and search for legends and stories lost along the paths of time.

a: Corris, Machynlleth, Powys, SY20 9RF
t: 01654 761584 | **www.kingarthurslabyrinth.co.uk**

Food & Wine Festivals
Wales

CARDIFF

Cardiff Festival | July-September
www.cardiff-festival.com
Address: Cardiff | **Tel:** 02920 872087 | **email:** events@cardiff.gov.uk

CARDIFF

Great British Cheese Festival | September 2011
www.greatbritishcheesefestival.co.uk
Address: Cardiff Castle, Cardiff | **Tel:** 02920 230130 | **email:** h.a.brown@cardiff.gov.uk

MONMOUTHSHIRE

Abergavenny Food Festival | September
www.abergavennyfoodfestival.com
Address: Abergavenny, Gwent, Monmouthshire | **Tel:** 01873 851643 | **email:** affinfo@abergavennyfoodfestival.com

POWYS

Llanwrtyd Wells Gourmet Festival of Fine Food & Drink | April
www.llanwrtydfoodfestival.webs.com
Address: Bromsgrove Hall and Fields, Llanwrtyd Wells, Powys | **Tel:** 01591 610264 | **email:** foodfoodfood@lycos.com

POWYS

Welsh Food Festival | 3rd September 2011 - 4th September 2011
www.welshfoodfestival.co.uk
Address: Welshpool, Powys, SY21 8AH | **Tel:** 01686 640916 | **email:** welshfoodfestival@hotmail.com

GLAMORGAN

Cowbridge Food & Drink Festival | October
www.cowbridgefoodanddrink.org
Address: Arthur John Car Park, North Road, Cowbridge, Vale of Glamorgan

GLAMORGAN

The Big Cheese Festival | 29th July 2011 - 31st July 2011
www.caerphilly.gov.uk/bigcheese/english/index
Address: Crescent Road Caerphilly, Vale of Glamorgan CF83 1JL | **Tel:** 02920 880011 | **email:** tourism@caerphilly.gov.uk

wine
Tourism UK

Conwy suspension bridge viewed from the castle, Conwy, Wales

❧ Chapter six

Events and festivals

194.....Introduction
196.....Festival dates

Introduction

A great deal of wine tourism revolves around the events and festivals held around England and Wales throughout the year.

From English Wine Week to the Taste Festivals in London, Edinburgh and Birmingham to the myriad of Food and Drink festivals in most major towns and cities in England and Wales; there really is something for everyone to experience and enjoy.

• You can visit vineyards and see first-hand how the grapes are grown and turned into wine.

• You can attend special local events with activities ranging from art exhibitions to gourmet dinners to walks in beautiful gardens.

• You can attend tours and tastings of wines, chocolates and cheeses and immerse yourself in speciality food promotions with top celebrity chefs, local chefs sampling local and international food and much, much more.

There is no shortage of things to see and do around England & Wales, and all the family can get involved and have fun.

So, if you are reading this from the comfort of your home in the UK or abroad, why not make a journey of discovery to the events and festivals in England & Wales.

2011

January
S	M	T	W	T	F	S
						1
2	3	4	5	6	7	8
9	10	11	12	13	14	15
16	17	18	19	20	21	22
23	24	25	26	27	28	29
30	31					

February
S	M	T	W	T	F	S
		1	2	3	4	5
6	7	8	9	10	11	12
13	14	15	16	17	18	19
20	21	22	23	24	25	26
27	28					

March
S	M	T	W	T	F	S
		1	2	3	4	5
6	7	8	9	10	11	12
13	14	15	16	17	18	19
20	21	22	23	24	25	26
27	28	29	30	31		

April
S	M	T	W	T	F	S
					1	2
3	4	5	6	7	8	9
10	11	12	13	14	15	16
17	18	19	20	21	22	23
24	25	26	27	28	29	30

May
S	M	T	W	T	F	S
1	2	3	4	5	6	7
8	9	10	11	12	13	14
15	16	17	18	19	20	21
22	23	24	25	26	27	28
29	30	31				

June
S	M	T	W	T	F	S
			1	2	3	4
5	6	7	8	9	10	11
12	13	14	15	16	17	18
19	20	21	22	23	24	25
26	27	28	29	30		

July
S	M	T	W	T	F	S
					1	2
3	4	5	6	7	8	9
10	11	12	13	14	15	16
17	18	19	20	21	22	23
24	25	26	27	28	29	30
31						

August
S	M	T	W	T	F	S
1	2	3	4	5	6
7	8	9	10	11	12	13
14	15	16	17	18	19	20
21	22	23	24	25	26	27
28	29	30	31			

September
S	M	T	W	T	F	S
				1	2	3
4	5	6	7	8	9	10
11	12	13	14	15	16	17
18	19	20	21	22	23	24
25	26	27	28	29	30	

October
S	M	T	W	T	F	S
						1
2	3	4	5	6	7	8
9	10	11	12	13	14	15
16	17	18	19	20	21	22
23	24	25	26	27	28	29
30	31					

November
S	M	T	W	T	F	S
		1	2	3	4	5
6	7	8	9	10	11	12
13	14	15	16	17	18	19
20	21	22	23	24	25	26
27	28	29	30			

December
S	M	T	W	T	F	S
				1	2	3
4	5	6	7	8	9	10
11	12	13	14	15	16	17
18	19	20	21	22	23	24
25	26	27	28	29	30	31

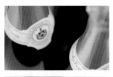

Festival dates

March

▷4th March 2011 - 6th March 2011
Feast East
www.feasteast.co.uk
Address: Chilford Hall, Linton, Cambridgeshire,
CB21 4LE | **Tel:** 01473 785883
email: enquiries@tastesofanglia.com

April

▷April
Llanwrtyd Wells Gourmet Festival
of Fine Food & Drink
www.llanwrtydfoodfestival.webs.com
Address: Bromsgrove Hall and Fields,
Llanwrtyd Wells, Powys, Wales | **Tel:** 01591 610264
email: foodfoodfood@lycos.com

▷9th April 2011 - 10th April 2011
Lancashire Food Festival, Accrinton Hall
www.lancashirefoodfestival.co.uk
Address: Accrington, Lancashire | **Tel:** 01254 380293
email: kerry.smith@leisureinhyndburn.co.uk

▷23rd April 2011 - 25th April 2011
Chester Food Drink and Lifestyle
www.chesterfoodanddrink.com
Address: Chester Racecourse, Cheshire
Tel: 01244 355474 | **email:** alex@scwirrel.com,
rebecca@whiteevents.co.uk

▷29th April 2011 - 1st May 2011
Exeter Food and Drink Festival
www.exeterfoodanddrinkfestival.co.uk

Address: Regal courtyard of Exeter Castle and the
surrounding Northernhay Gardens, Devon
Tel: 01392 278801

▷30th April 2011 - 2nd May 2011
The Dales Festival of Food & Drink
www.dalesfestivaloffood.org
Address: Leyburn, Middleham, Wensleydale, Yorkshire
Tel: 01748 828747
email: leyburn.tic@richmondshire.gov.uk

May

▷5th May 2011 - 8th May 2011
Real Food Festival
www.realfoodfestival.co.uk
Address: Earls Court, London, SW5 9TA

▷6th May 2011 - 13 May 2011
Christchurch Food Fest
www.christchurchfoodfest.co.uk
Address: Christchurch, Dorset | **Tel:** 01202 471780
email: enquiries@christchurchtourism.info

▷14th May 2011 - 15th May 2011
The Essex Food Show (Spring)
www.theessexfoodshow.co.uk
Address: On B1018 between Braintree and Witham,
Essex, CM77 8PD | **Tel:** 01621 773403
email: contact@theessexfoodshow.co.uk

▷14th May 2011
Plumpton College Open Day
www.plumpton.ac.uk

Address: Plumpton College, Ditchling Road, Nr Lewes, East Sussex, BN7 3AE | **Tel:** 01273 890454

▷ **21st May 2011 - 22nd May 2011**
Derbyshire Food & Drink Festival
www.derbyshirefoodfestival.co.uk
Address: Hardwick Hall, North East Derbyshire
Tel: 01629 538464
email: stephanie.walsh@derbyshire.gov.uk

▷ **17th May 2011 - 19th May 2011**
The London International Wine Fair
www.2011.londonwinefair.com
Address: ExCel, London | **Tel:** 02079 736401
email: wine@hgluk.com

▷ **21st May 2011 - 22nd May 2011**
Malton Food Lovers Festival
**www.worldwideshoppingmall.co.uk/malton/
food-lovers-festival.asp**
Address: Market Square, Malton, Yorkshire
Tel: 01943 603133 | **email:** jeni@jenicropper.co.uk

▷ **End of May and mid September 2011**
Alfresco Parkland Spring Food Festival
www.swintonpark.com/events/alfresco-food-festival.html
Address: Swinton Park, North Yorkshire
Tel: 01765 680900
email: enquiries@swintonpark.com

June
▷ **June**
Congleton Food & Drink Festival
www.foodanddrinkfestival.net
Address: Congleton, Cheshire | **Tel:** 01260 291156
email: jo@congletoncommunityprojects.org

▷ **June**
Hove Champagne Festival
www.hovechampagnefestival.co.uk
Address: Hove Lawns, Brighton and Hove, E.Sussex
Tel: 01273 778811 | **email:** info@goaheadevents.com

▷ **June**
Taste of Birmingham Cannon Hill Park
www.taste.visitbirmingham.com
Address: Cannon Hill Park, Birmingham, Warwickshire
Tel: 01212 025024
email: info@marketingbirmingham.com

▷ **9th June 2011 - 11th June 2011**
South of England Agricultural Show
www.seas.org.uk
Address: Ardingly, West Sussex, RH17 6TL
Tel: 01444 892700 | **email:** seas@btclick.com

▷ **10th June 2011 - 12th June 2011**
Toast Festival
www.toastfestivals.co.uk
Address: London | **Tel:** 08712 30559
email: info@goaheadevents.com

▷ **15th June 2011 - 19th June 2011**
BBC Summer Good Food Show
www.bbcgoodfoodshowsummer.com
Address: NEC Birmingham, Warwickshire
Tel: 08445 811341
email: bbcgoodfoodshow@haymarket.com

▷ **16th June 2011 - 19th June 2011**
Taste of London Festival
www.tastefestivals.com/london
Address: Regents Park, London | **Tel:** 02074 711080

▷ **18th June 2011 - 19th June 2011**
St Ives Food and Drink Festival
www.stivesfoodanddrinkfestival.co.uk
Address: St Ives Town Centre, Cornwall
Tel: 08456 038456 | **email:** info@mercury-pr.co.uk

▷ **25th June 2011 - 26th June 2011**
Colchester Food & Drink Festival
www.colchesterfoodanddrinkfestival.co.uk
Address: Castle Park, Colchester, Essex, CO1 1UD
Tel: 01206 525527 | **email:** don.quinn@ntlworld.com

July
▷ **July** | Bristol Wine and Food Fair
www.bristolwineandfood.co.uk
Address: Lloyds Amphitheatre & Waterfront Square, Bristol, BS1 5LL | **Tel:** 01173 169736

▷ **July-September**
Cardiff Festival
www.cardiff-festival.com
Address: Cardiff, Wales | **Tel:** 02920 872087
email: events@cardiff.gov.uk

▷ **July**
Oswestry Food & Drink Festival
www.oswestryfoodfestival.co.uk
Address: Oswestry Town Centre, Oswestry, Shropshire
Tel: 08453 300232

▷ **July - August**
South Holland Food Festival
www.food-festival.net
Address: South Holland, Lincolnshire
Tel: 01775 764598 | **email:** info@food-festival.net

▷ **1st July 2011 - 31 July 2011**
The Hampshire Food Festival
www.hampshirefare.co.uk
Address: Hampshire | **Tel:** 01962 847098
email: sophie.boxall@hants.gov.uk

▷ **16th July 2011 - 17th July 2011**
The Glynde Food & English Wine Festival
www.glynde.co.uk
Address: Glynde Place, Gynde, East Sussex, BN8 6SX
Tel: 01273 858224 | **email:** subscribe@glynde.co.uk

▷ **23rd July 2011 - 24th July 2011**
The Melford Hall Food & Drink Festival

www.colchesterfoodanddrinkfestival.co.uk
Address: Melford Hall, Braintree, Suffolk, CO10 9AA
Tel: 01206 525527 | **email:** don.quinn@ntlworld.com

▷**29th July 2011 - 31st July 2011**
The Big Cheese Festival
www.caerphilly.gov.uk/bigcheese/english/index
Address: Crescent Road Caerphilly, Vale of Glamorgan
CF83 1JL | **Tel:** 02920 880011
email: tourism@caerphilly.gov.uk

August
▷**August**
Braunston Festival
www.braunstonfestival.org.uk
Address: Braunston, Northamptonshire
Tel: 01785 816955
email: info@braunstonfestival.org.uk

▷**August**
Newlyn Fish Festival
www.newlynfishfestival.org.uk
Address: North Pier, Newlyn, Cornwall, TR18 5JB
Tel: 07518 603955
email: info@newlynfishfestival.org.uk

▷**August/September**
Pennine Lancashire Festival of Food & Culture
www.penninelancashirefestivals.com
Address: Blackburn Visitor Centre, Church Street,
Blackburn, Lancashire, BB1 5AL | **Tel:** 01254 688040

▷**6th August 2011 - 7th August 2011**
Helmingham Hall Food & Drink Festival
www.colchesterfoodanddrinkfestival.co.uk
Address: Helmingham Hall, Helmingham, Suffolk
Tel: 01206 525527 | **email:** don.quinn@ntlworld.com

▷**11th August 2011 - 14th August 2011**
Huddersfield Food & Drink Festival
www.huddersfield-htcpl.co.uk/foodanddrink
festival/index.htm
Address: St George's Square, Huddersfield, Yorkshire
Tel: 01484 487933 | **email:** htcpl@kirklees.gov.uk

September
▷**September**
Abergavenny Food Festival
www.abergavennyfoodfestival.com
Address: Abergavenny, Gwent,
Monmouthshire, Wales | **Tel:** 01873 851643
email: affinfo@abergavennyfoodfestival.com

▷**September/October**
Brighton & Hove Food and Drink Festival
www.brightonfoodfestival.com
Address: Brighton & Hove, East Sussex

▷**September**
Cornwall Food & Drink Festival
www.cornwallfoodanddrinkfestival.com
Address: Centre of Truro, Cornwall

Tel: 01840 250010
email: info@cornwallfoodanddrinkfestival.com

▷**September 2011**
Great British Cheese Festival
www.greatbritishcheesefestival.co.uk
Address: Cardiff Castle, Cardiff
Tel: 02920 230130 | **email:** h.a.brown@cardiff.gov.uk

▷**September**
Hastings Seafood and Wine Festival
Address: Hastings Old Town, Rock-a-nore Road,
Hastings, East Sussex, TN34 3AR
Tel: 01424 451066 | **email:** hic@hastings.gov.uk

▷**September**
Liverpool Food & Drink Festival
www.liverpoolfoodanddrinkfestival.co.uk
Address: Sefton Park, Merseyside, Liverpool
Tel: 01515 229362

▷**September**
Ludlow Food Festival
www.foodfestival.co.uk
Address: Ludlow, Shropshire
Tel: 01584 873957
email: info@foodfestival.co.ukv

▷**September**
Nantwich Food & Drink Festival
www.nantwichfoodfestival.co.uk
Address: Nantwich, Cheshire
email: trade@nantwichfoodfestival.co.uk

▷**September/October**
Newquay Fish Festival
www.newquayfishfestival.co.uk
Address: Newquay Harbor, Cornwall

▷**September**
Norfolk food festival
www.norfolkfoodfestival.co.uk
Address: Norfolk | **email:** mail@maryruddpr.co.uk

▷**September**
Nottingham Food & Drink Festival
www.wearenottingham.co.uk
Address: Old Market Square, Nottingham
Tel: 01159 585287

▷**September**
Tetbury Food Festival
www.tetburyfooddrinkfestival.com
Address: Tetbury, Gloucestershire
Tel: 08712 30559

▷**September**
The Free Cambridge Food & Garden Festival
www.oakleighfairs.co.uk
Address: CB1 1JF, Cambridgeshire
Tel: 0800 141 2823
email: web-contact@oakleighfairs.co.uk

▷ **3rd September 2011**
Colchester Carnival Oyster Fair
www.colchesterfoodanddrinkfestival.co.uk
Address: Castle Park, Colchester, Essex, CO1 1UD
Tel: 01206 525527
email: don.quinn@ntlworld.com

▷ **3rd September 2011 - 4th September 2011**
Welsh Food Festival
www.welshfoodfestival.co.uk
Address: Welshpool, Powys SY21 8AH, Wales
Tel: 01686 640916
email: welshfoodfestival@hotmail.com

▷ **10th September 2011 - 11th September 2011**
Royal Leamington Spa Food & Drink Festival
www.leamingtonfoodfestival.co.uk
Address: Royal Pump Room and Gardens,
Leamington Spa, Warwickshire | **Tel:** 01926 470634

▷ **2nd/3rd weekend in September 2011**
Salisbury Food and Drink Festival
www.salisburyfestival.co.uk
Address: Salisbury city centre, Wiltshire
Tel: 01722 332241

▷ **16th September 2011 - 25th September 2011**
York Food & Drink Festival
www.yorkfoodfestival.com
Address: Parliament Street, York Guildhall, York,
Yorkshire | **Tel:** 01904 635149
email: admin@yorkfoodfestival.com

▷ **17th September 2011 - 18th September 2011**
Feast of Dorset
www.feastofdorset.com
Address: Deans Court, Wimborne, Dorset
Tel: 01202 880515 | **email:** info@feastofdorset.co.uk

October
▷ **October**
Cowbridge Food & Drink Festival
www.cowbridgefoodanddrink.org
Address: Arthur John Car Park, North Road,
Cowbridge, Vale of Glamorgan

▷ **October**
Eastbourne Beer Festival
www.eastbournebeerfestival.co.uk
Address: Held at the Winter Garden, East Sussex
Tel: 01323 412000 | **email:** info@goaheadevents.com

▷ **8th October 2011 - 9th October 2011**
The Essex Food Show (Autum)
www.theessexfoodshow.co.uk
Address: on B1018 between Braintree and Witham,
Essex, CM77 8PD | **Tel:** 01621 773403
email: contact@theessexfoodshow.co.uk

▷ **October**
Manchester Food & Drink Festival
www.foodanddrinkfestival.com

Address: Manchester
There is no single location!
Tel: 01618 393461
email: hello@foodanddrinkfestival.com

▷ **October**
Stone Food & Drink Festival
www.stonefooddrink.org.uk
Address: Stone, Staffordshire | **Tel:** 01785 816955

▷ **1st October 2011 - 2nd October 2011**
Boscastle Food, Art and Crafts Festival
www.boscastlefestival.co.uk
Address: Boscastle, Cornwall
Tel: 01840 250010
email: sales@castang-wines.co.uk

▷ **13th October 2011 - 16th October 2011**
Falmouth Oyster Festival
www.falmouthoysterfestival.co.uk
Address: Events Square, Falmouth, Cornwall
Tel: 01326 312300 | **email:** info@falmouthtic.co.uk

▷ **28th October 2011 - 30th October 2011**
North West Food Lovers Festival at Tatton Park
www.nwfoodloversfestival.com
Address: Tatton Park, Cheshire
Tel: 01244 355474 | **email:** rebecca@scwirrel.com,
eve@whiteevents.co.uk

November
▷ **November**
Good Food Show Winter
www.bbcgoodfoodshow.com
Address: NEC Birmingham, Warwickshire
Tel: 08445 811341
email: bbcgoodfoodshow@haymarket.com

▷ **11th November 2011 - 13th November 2011**
The Wine Show
www.wineshow.co.uk
Address: Olympia, London | **Tel:** 02082 678358

▷ **26th November 2011 - 27th November 2011**
Christmas Food & Craft Show
www.theessexfoodshow.co.uk
Address: on B1018 between Braintree and Witham,
Essex, CM77 8PD | **Tel:** 01621 773403
email: contact@theessexfoodshow.co.uk

December
▷ **December**
Taste of Christmas
www.tasteofchristmas.com
Address: Excel, London | **Tel:** 02072 443164
email: vickys@brandevents.co.uk

▷ **3rd December 2011 - 4the December 2011**
Festive Food & Drink Fayre
www.seas.org.uk
Address: Ardingly, West Sussex, RH17 6TL
Tel: 01444 892700 | **email:** seas@btclick.com

 # Chapter seven

Buying and storing wine

201.......Buying and storing wine

Buying and storing wine

English wines have never been more available; and there are now many ways you can obtain them...

The most popular being:

- Online merchants
- Supermarkets & Off Licences
- Specialist wine merchants & food stores
- The vineyards / winemakers - in person, online or mail order

> 'There are an increasing number of Independent Retailers around the country that now stock English wine.'

All of the major supermarket chains list English wines, although it is not always guaranteed that every branch will stock them. It is always worth asking the wine department for them, or take a look at their websites for more information. The same applies to High Street Off Licences. In both cases some companies make a policy of supplying regional products in their regional branches – i.e. Shropshire wines in branches in Shropshire. This allows some vineyards who cannot supply nationally to make their wines available in the High Street.

There are an increasing number of Independent Retailers around the country that now stock English wine. Being specialist retailers they can often carry an interesting selection of wines.

A growing method of buying wine is by Mail Order. Again, a number of merchants list English wines, and do not forget that many vineyards themselves operate a very efficient mail order service. There are even mail order companies that specialise in English wines, who deliver throughout the UK, so you need never run out of your favourite wine, even if you do not live nearby.

In short, there are plenty of opportunities to find English wines!

It is worth looking at the websites of the vineyards themselves, particularly if you are looking for a specific wine or vineyards' wines. Many of them now sell their wines on-line. The web site addresses (where available) are listed in the relevant sections in this guide.

The following list is by no means exhaustive but gives a good idea of the range of online merchants who offer English & Welsh wines:

Colchester Carnival	
Oyster Fair	123
Colchester Food & Drink Festival	123
Colchester Zoo	121
Commonwood Vineyard	128,130
Compton Green Vineyard	46,51
Congham Vineyard	110,112
Congleton Food & Drink Festival	176
Cornish Garden Nurseries	46,51
Cornwall Food & Drink Festival	66
Coton Orchard Vineyard	110,112
Cottonworth Vineyard	75,83
Court Garden Vineyard	75,83
Court Lane Vineyard	75,83
Coventry	127
Coventry Cathedral	138
Coventry Transport Museum	138
Coventry & Warwickshire Food & Drink Awards	139
Cowbridge Food & Drink Festival	190
Cowley Estate Vineyard	46,51
Coxley Vineyard	46,51
Crawthorne Vineyard	46,51
Crich Tramway Village	152
Croft Castle Vineyard	128,130
Crown Vines	110,113
Cumbria & The Lake District	168
Cwm Deri Vineyard	182,183
D	
Dales Festival of Food & Drink	165
Danebury Vineyard	75,83
Davenport Vineyard	75,83
Daws Hill Vineyard	75,83
Deans Farm Vineyard	75,83
Decanter Magazine Vineyard	75,84
Deep The	164
Denbies Wine Estate	75,84
Derby	143
Derbyshire Food & Drink Festival	153
Didcot Railway Centre	103
Dinosaur Park	189
Ditchling Vineyard	75,84
Doles Ash Farm Vineyard	46,51
Dover	71
Dover Castle	102
Dropmore Vineyard	75,84
Drusillas Zoo Park	100
Dudley Zoo	138
Dunkery Vineyard - Exmoor	46,51
Dunleavy Vineyards	46,51
Dunley Vineyard	75,84
E	
East Bridgeford Vineyard	144,145
Eastbourne Beer Festival	104
East Meon Vineyard	75,84
East Sutton Vine Garden	75,84
Eastcott Vineyard	46,51
Ebernoe Vineyard	75,84
Eden Project	62
Eglantine Vineyard	143,144,145
Elham Valley Vineyard	75,84
Elysian Fields Vineyard	110,113
English Oak Vineyard	46,52
English Wine Centre	75,84
Essex Food Show - Autum	123
Essex Food Show - Spring	123
Exeter Cathedral	63
Exeter Food & Drink Festival	66
Exton Park Estate Vineyard	75,85
F	
Falmouth Oyster Festival	66
Fawley Vineyard	75,85
Feast East	123
Feast of Dorset	66
Felsted Vineyard	110,113
Fernhurst Vineyard	75,85
Festive Food & Drink Fayre - Ardingly	105
Fitzwilliam Museum	120
Flamingo Land Theme Park and Zoo	162
Fleurfields Vineyard	143,144,145
Floreys Vineyard	75,85
Fonthill Glebe Vineyard	46,52
Forstal Farm Vineyard	75,85
Forty Hall Vineyard	75,85
Four Foxes Vineyard	128,130
Free Cambridge Food & Garden Festival	123
Friday Street Vineyard	75,85
Frithsden Vineyard	110,113
Frome Valley Vineyard	128,130
Furleigh Estate	46,52
G	
Gelynis Vineyard	182,183
Giffords Hall Vineyard	109,110,113
Glastonbury Abbey	64
Glynde Food & English Wine Festival	104
Glyndwr Vineyard	182,183
Godstone Vineyard	75,85
Gog Magog Vineyard	110,113
Golden Hind	63
Good Earth Vineyard	144,145
Good Food Show Winter	139
Goonhilly Station	62
Goose Green Vineyard	75,85
Grange Farm Vineyard	75,85
Great British Cheese Festival	190
Gravel Lane Vineyard	110,113
Greenwood Forest Park	188
Greyfriars Vineyard	75,86
Groombridge Place Vineyard	75,86
Gusbourne Estate Vineyard	75,86
H	
Habberley Vineyard	128,130
Hadrian's Wall Path National Trail	175
Hale Valley Vineyard	75,86
Halfpenny Green Vineyard	126,128,130
Halifax	157
Halnaker Vineyard	76,86
Hambledon Vineyard	76,86
Hampshire Food Festival	104
Harbourne Vineyard	76,86
Harden Vineyard	76,86
Hargrove Estate	128,130
Harlestone Allotment Vineyard	144,145
Harrogate	157
Hastings Seafood & Wine Festival	104
Hatfield House	121
Hattingley Valley Vineyard	76,86
Hazel End Vineyard	110,113
Head of the Vale Vineyard	46,52
Heart of England Vineyard	128,130
Helmingham Hall Food & Drink Festival	123
Helmsley Walled Garden Vineyard	158,159
Hendred Vineyard	76,86
Henners Vineyard	76,87
Hereford	127
Hereford Light Infantry Museum	136
Herons Ghyll Estate	76,87
Herts Oak Farm Vineyard	110,113
Heveningham Hall	110,113
Hever Castle & Gardens	102

Hidden Spring Vineyard 76,87
High Clandon Vineyard 76,87
High Cross Vineyard 144,145
Highdown Vineyard 76,87
Higher Bumsley Vineyard 46,52
Higher Sandford Vineyard 46,52
Hilders Field Vineyard 110,114
Hobdens Vineyards 76,87
Holmfirth Vineyard 156,158,159
Horsmonden Vineyard 76,87
Hove Champagne Festival 104
Huddersfield Food
& Drink Festival 165
Hunt Hall Farm Vineyard 128,130
Hush Heath Estate Vineyard 76,87
Huxbear Vineyard 46,52

I
Ickworth Vineyard 110,114
Imperial War Museum
- Cambridge 120
Imperial War Museum - North 174
Ipswich 109
Ironbridge Gorge Museums 136
Iron Railway Vineyard 76,87
Isle of Wight 71

J
Jabajak Vineyard 182,183
Jamaica Inn 62
Jane Austen Centre 64
Jays Farm Vineyard 76,87
Jenkyn Place Vineyard 76,88
Jodrell Bank Visitor Centre 174
Jorvik Viking Centre 162

K
Kempes Hall Vineyard 76,88
Kemps Vineyard
(Northants) 144,145
Kemp's Vineyard (Suffolk) 110,114
Kenton Vineyard 46,52
Kents Green Vineyard 46,52
Keyham Vineyard 144,145
Kilcott Valley Vineyard 47,52
King Arthur's Labyrinth 189
Kingfishers' Pool Vineyard 144,146
Kings College Chapel 120
Kit's Coty Vineyard 76,88
Knettishall Vineyard 110,114
Knightshayes Vineyard 47,53

L
La Mare Vineyard 42,45,47,53
Lamberhurst Vineyard 76,88
Lambourne Vineyard 47,53
Lancashire Food Festival 176

Lancaster Castle 175
Land's End 62
Laverstoke Park Vineyard 76,88
Leckford Estate Vineyard 76,88
Leeds 157
Leeds Castle and Gardens 102
Legoland 100
Leicester 143
Leigh Park Hotel Vineyard 47,53
Leventhorpe Vineyard 156,158,159
Lewes Castle & Barbican
Museum 100
Lily Farm Vineyard 47,53
Linch Hill Vineyard 76,88
Lincoln 143
Lincoln Cathedral 152
Lincoln Vineyard 144,146
Little Foxes Vineyard 47,53
Little Knoxbridge Vineyard 76,88
Little West End Farm
Vineyard 76,88
Littlebredy Vineyard 47,53
Liverpool 169
Liverpool Food & Drink
Festival 176
Llaethliw Vineyard 182,183
Llanbadrig Vineyard 182,183
Llanerch Vineyard 180,182,183
Llangollen Wharf 188
Llanwrtyd Wells Gourmet
Festival of Fine Food 190
London International
Wine Fair 105
Lopen Vineyard 47,53
Ludlow 127
Ludlow Food Festival 139
Ludlow Vineyard 127,128,130
Lulham Court Vineyard 128,131
Lurgashall Winery 76,88
Lyme Bay Winery 47,53
Lyme Regis 45
Lyveden New Bield 150

M
Magna Science
Adventure Centre 163
Magpie Lane Vineyard 76,89
Malton Food Lovers Festival 165
Manchester 169
Manchester Food & Drink
Festival 176
Manor Farm Vineyard 144,146
Manor Fields Vineyard 76,89
Manstree Vineyard 47,53

Marden Organic Vineyard 76,89
Marlings Vineyard 76,89
Master's Garden Lord
Leycester Hospital 137
Mayshaves Vineyard 76,89
Meadowgrove Vineyard 76,89
Melbury Vale Vineyard 47,54
Melford Hall Food & Drink
Festival 123
Melton Lodge Vineyard 110,114
Meopham Valley Vineyard 76,89
Mersea Island 121
Mersea Island Vineyard 110,114
Methersham Vineyard 76,89
Millennium Stadium 181
Mill Hill Village Vineyard 76,89
Mill Lane Vineyard 144,146
Mimram Valley Vineyard 110,114
Moat House Vineyard 110,114
Monnow Valley Vineyard 182,183
Morville St. Gregory
Vineyard 128,131
Mount Harry Vines 76,89
Mount Pleasant Vineyard 170
Mount Snowdon 181
Mount Vineyard 76,90
Mr Straw's House 150
Mumfords Vineyard 47,54
Muncaster Experience 174
Mystole Members Vineyard 76,90

N
Nantwich Food & Drink
Festival 176
Nash Vineyard 128,131
National Coal Mining
Museum 164
National Fruit Collection
- Brogdale 76,90
National Media Museum 164
National Railway Museum 163
National Space Centre 151
Needles Park Isle of Wight 102
Netherland Vineyard 76,90
New Forest 71
New Hall Vineyards 110,114
New House Farm Vineyard 77,90
New Lodge Vineyard 144,146
Newlyn Fish Festival 66
New Mill Vineyard 47,54
Newquay Fish Festival 66
Newstead Abbey 151
Newtown Nurseries 47,54
Norfolk Food Festival 123

Norfolk Lavender	122
Norfolk & Suffolk Broads	109
North Court Farm Vineyard	77,90
Northbrook Springs	77,90
North West Food Lovers Festival - Tatton Park	176
Nottingham Food & Drink Festival	153
Nutbourne Lane Vineyard	77,90
Nutbourne Vineyards	77,90
Nyetimber Vineyard	77,90

O

Oak Hill Vineyard	110,114
Oakford Vineyard	47,54
Oakwood Theme Park	189
Oatley Vineyard	47,54
Old Grove House Vineyard	128,131
Old Oak Vineyard	144,146
Old Rectory Vineyard	110,115
Old Walls Vineyard	44,47,54
Olding Manor Vineyard	77,91
Ollivers Farm Vineyard	110,115
Oswestry Food & Drink Festival	139
Otter Farm Vineyard	47,54
Oxford	71

P

Painshill Park Vineyard	77,91
Pant Du Vineyard	182,184
Parhams Vineyard	47,54
Paultons Family Theme Park	101
Parva Farm Vineyard	182,184
Peak District	143
Pear Tree at Purton Vineyard	47,54
Pebblebed Clyst St. George Vineyard	47,55
Pebblebed Ebford Vineyard	47,55
Pebblebed West Hill Vineyard	47,55
Penarth Vineyard	181,182,184
Penberth Valley Vineyard	47,55
Pengethley Manor Hotel Vineyard	128,131
Pennine Lancashire Festival of Food & Culture	176
Pheasants Ridge Vineyard	77,91
Plot 19 Vineyard	170
Plumpton College Open Day	104
Plumpton College Vineyard	77,91
Polgoon Vineyard	47,55
Pollaughan Vineyard	47,55

Polmassick Vineyard	47,55
Port Lympne	77,91
Portesham Vineyard	47,55
Portmeirion	181
Portsmouth Historic Dockyard	101
Potash Vineyard	110,115
Primrose Hill Vineyard	77,91
Priors Dean Vineyard	77,91
Priory Visitor Centre	138
Purbeck Vineyard	47,55

Q

Quantock Hills Vineyard	47,55
Quoins Organic Vineyard	47,55

R

Railway Vineyard	110,115
Ravensthorpe Vineyard	144,146
Real Food Festival	104
Redfold Farm Vineyard	77,91
Red House Glass Cone	137
Redyeates Wedge Vineyard	47,55
Renishaw Hall Vineyard	140,144,146
RHS Garden Wisley	103
RidgeView Wine Estate	10,77,91
River Walk Vineyard (West Sussex)	77,91
River Walk Vineyard (Notts)	144,146
Robert Fleming Wines	110,115
Rock Lodge Vineyard	77,92
Rock Moors Vineyard	47,56
Roman Baths	64
Roman Villa Vineyard	77,92
Rose Bank Vineyard	128,131
Rosemary Farm Vineyard	77,92
Rosemary Vineyard	77,92
Rossi Regatta Vineyard	77,92
Rossiters Vineyard	77,92
Rother Valley Vineyard	77,92
Royal Armouries Museum	163
Royal Leamington Spa Food & Drink Festival	139
Royal Pavilion Brighton	101
RSPB Minsmere Nature Reserve	122
Russetts Vineyard	10,115
Rutland	143
Rutland Belle	151
Ryedale Vineyards	158,158,159

S

Saffron Grange Vineyard	110,115
Sainsburys Centre for Visual Arts	122

Saint Andrew's Vineyard	77,92
Saint Anne's Vineyard	47,56
Saint Augustine's Vineyard	47,56
Saint Martin's Isles of Scilly Vineyard	47,56
Saint Mary Magdalen Vineyard	110,115
Saint Mary's Vineyard	47,56
Salisbury Food & Drink Festival	67
Salts Mill Saltaire	163
Sandhurst Vineyard	77,92
Sandridge Barton Vineyard	47,56
Sandyford Vineyard	110,115
Sculdown Vineyard	77,92
Sealwood Cottage Vineyard	144,146
Secret Valley Vineyard	48,56
Sedlescombe Organic Vineyard	72,77,93
Sea Life Centre Birmingham	137
Sea Life Centre Brighton	101
Seal Watching at Blakeney	122
Seaquarium	65
78 Derngate	150
Setley Ridge Vineyard	77,93
Shardeloes Vineyard	77,93
Sharpham Vineyard	48,56
Shawsgate Vineyard	111,115
Sheffield Park Vineyard	77,93
Sherborne Castle Vineyard	48,56
Shere Vineyard	77,93
Sherwood Forest	151
Shotley Vineyard	111,116
Shrewsbury	127
Snowdonia National Park	188
Somborne Valley Vineyard	77,93,147
Somerby Vineyards	144,147
Sour Grapes Vineyard	77,93
South Holland Food Festival	153
South of England Agricultural Show	105
South Pickenham Estate Vineyard	111,116
South Shore Vineyard	144,147
Southcote Vineyard	48,56
Southcott Vineyard	48,57
Southlands Valley Vineyard	77,93
Southwood Vineyard	48,57
Sparchall Vineyard	128,131
Spring Cottage Vineyard	128,131
Springfield Vineyard	77,93

Springfields Vineyard	77,93
Squerryes Court Vineyard	77,94
SS Great Britain	64
Stalbridge Weston Vineyard	48,57
Standen Vineyard	77,94
Stanford Bridge Vineyard	78,94
Stanlake Park Wine Estate	73,78,94
Staplecombe Vineyard	48,57
Staverton Vineyard	111,116
St Ives Food & Drink Festival	66
Stoke-on-Trent	127
Stone Food & Drin Festival	139
Stonehenge	65
Stopham Vineyard	78,94
Storrington Priory Vineyard	78,94
Stratford-upon-Avon	127
Strawberry Hill Vineyard	48,57
Struddicks Farm Vineyard	48,57
Sugar Loaf Vineyard	182,184
Summerhouse Vineyard	158,159
Summermoor Vineyard	48,57
Sunnybank Vineyard and Vine Nursery	128,131
Surrenden Vineyard	78,94
Sustead Lane Vineyard	111,116
Sutton Hoo Burial Site	122
Syndale Valley Vineyards	78,94
T	
Tarrington Court Vineyard	128,131
Taste of Birmingham Cannon Hill Park	139
Taste of Christmas	104
Tatse of London Festival	104
Tas Valley Vineyard	111,116
Tate - Liverpool	175
Tatton Park	174
Techniquest	188
Tenterden Vineyard	78,94
Terlingham Vineyard	78,94
Tern Valley Vineyard	128,132
Tetbury Food Festival	67
The Somerset Distillery	48,57
Theale Vineyard	10,78,95
Thelnetham Vineyard	111,116
Thornbury Castle Vineyard	48,57
Thorncroft Vineyard	78,95
Thorpe Park	103
Three Choirs Vineyard	44,48,57
Three Sisters Vineyard	144,147
Throwley Vineyard	78,95
Ticehurst Vineyard	78,95
Tiltridge Vineyard	128,132

Timber Lane Vineyard	48,58
Tinwood Vineyard	78,95
Titchfield Vineyard	78,95
Tixover Vineyard	144,147
Toast Festival	105
Torquay	45
Torview Wines	48,58
Townsend Farm Vineyard	128,132
Treago Vineyard	128,132
Treak Cliff Cavern	150
Trevibban Mill Vineyard	48,58
Truro	45
Tullens Vineyard	78,95
Twinlakes Park	152
Ty Croes Vineyard	182,184
Tyringham Hall Vineyard	78,95
Tytherley Vineyard	48,58
U	
Upperton Vineyard	78,95
Upperton Vineyard (Nyetimber)	78,95
V	
Valley Farm Vineyards	111,116
Vernon Lodge Vineyard	144,147
Virginia Water Vineyard	78,96
W	
Waitrose Estate	78,96
Walton Brook Vineyard	144,147
Warden Abbey Vineyard	111,116
Wardour Castle	65
Wareside Wines	111,116
Warnham Vale Vineyard	78,96
Warren Farm Vineyard	78,96
Warwick Castle	137
Watchcombe Vineyard	48,58
Wayford Vineyard	48,58
Webb Ellis Rugby Football Museum	137
Webb's Land Vineyard	78,96
Weir Quay Vineyard	48,58
Welcombe Hills Vineyard	128,132
Welland Valley Vineyard	142,144,147
Wells Cathedral	65
Welsh Food Festival	190
Wentworth Castle	163
Wernddu Vineyard	182,184
Westward House Vineyard	78,96
Westwell Wines	78,96
Whitby	157
White Castle Vineyard	182,184
White Horse Vineyard	78,96
Wickham Vineyards	78,96

Willhayne Vineyard	48,58
Willow Grange Vineyard & Winery	111,116
Winchester Cathedral	101
Winchester Vineyard	78,96
Windmill Vineyard	144,147
Windsor	71
Windsor Castle	100
Wine Show	105
Winner Hill Vineyard	48,58
Wisley Vineyard at the RHS Garden	78,97
Wiston Estate Vineyard	78,97
Wistow Maize Maze	150
Woburn Abbey	120
Wodetone Vineyard	48,58
Womack's Vineyard	158,159
Wooldings Vineyard	78,97
Wootton Park Vineyard	78,97
Wootton Vineyard	48,58
Worcester	127
Worthenbury Vineyard	182,184
Wrangling Lane Vineyard	78,97
Wraxall Vineyard	48,58
Wroxeter Roman City	136
Wroxeter Roman Vineyard	127,128,132
Wychwood House Vineyard	78,97
Wyfold Vineyard	78,97
Wyken Vineyard	111,117
Wylye Valley Vineyard	48,58
X	
Xscape	164
Y	
Yearlstone Vineyard	48,58
York	157
York Food & Drink Festival	165
Yorkshire Heart Vineyard	158,159
York Minster	164